21 世纪全国高职高专机电系列技能型规划教材

机电专业英语

戴正阳 主编

内 容 简 介

本书系高职高专机电专业英语教材，旨在满足机电一体化及相关专业技能型人才培养的需要，也是行业从业人员学习专业英语的参考书。

依据高度理论知识与较强技能相结合的培养原则，本书突显实际工程应用情况，突出工程实践中"会用、管用"为准，理论以"必需、够用"为度，并力求易懂、好学、用得上。

本书共 7 个项目，每个项目均包含与企业实际紧密结合的专业英语实例。

本书既可作为高职高专、成人高校及相关院校的专业英语教材，也可用作企业培训教材，及有关教师、学生和技术人员的参考用书。

图书在版编目(CIP)数据

机电专业英语/戴正阳主编. —北京：北京大学出版社，2011.6
(21 世纪全国高职高专机电系列技能型规划教材)
ISBN 978-7-301-18852-1

Ⅰ. ①机… Ⅱ. ①戴… Ⅲ. ①机电工程—英语—高等职业教育—教材 Ⅳ. ①H31

中国版本图书馆 CIP 数据核字(2011)第 078992 号

书　　　名：	机电专业英语
著作责任者：	戴正阳　主编
策划编辑：	赖　青　张永见
责任编辑：	李娉婷
标准书号：	ISBN 978-7-301-18852-1/TH・0239
出　版　者：	北京大学出版社
地　　　址：	北京市海淀区成府路 205 号　100871
网　　　址：	http://www.pup.cn　http://www.pup6.com
电　　　话：	邮购部 62752018　发行部 62750672　编辑部 62750667　出版部 62754962
电子邮箱：	pup_6@163.com
印　刷　者：	三河市博文印刷厂
发　行　者：	北京大学出版社
经　销　者：	新华书店
	787mm×1092mm　16 开本　14 印张　327 千字
	2011 年 6 月第 1 版　2013 年 8 月第 2 次印刷
定　　　价：	28.00 元

未经许可，不得以任何方式复制或抄袭本书之部分或全部内容。
版权所有　侵权必究　　举报电话：010-62752024
　　　　　　　　　　　电子邮箱：fd@pup.pku.edu.cn

前　言

本书全面贯彻落实"以服务为宗旨，以就业为导向，以能力为本位"的职业教育办学指导思想，采用最新的项目教学法编写而成。本书综合考虑英语就业岗位多样化等多种因素以及高职专业英语教育的实际情况，结合机电行业工作岗位对专业英语的使用要求，具有良好的通用性，又注意实践性和针对性，按照技能培养的要求，将专业英语融入到机电专业所涉及的绝大多数领域，重复过程而不重复内容，循序渐进地培养学生的专业英语阅读和翻译能力，同时兼顾增强学生的机电专业素养。

本书具有如下特色。

(1) 本书中的文章全部选自英美等以英语为母语的国家的专业文献著作。只做删节，不做改写，力求保持原著的语言风格、精神实质和原著作者对机电专业知识的理解，使学生原汁原味地接触专业英语，从而与原著作者实现思想的撞击。

(2) 本书以能力培养为本位，以训练为手段，不仅在每个项目任务后都配有练习，而且在每篇文章的旁边都配有猜词断义等练习，实现边看边练，切实提高读者阅读和理解机电类专业英语的能力。

(3) 文章中的注释标注在正文一侧，以便读者参考。

(4) 本书图文并茂，可以与实践类课程相结合进行教学，实现理论与实践相结合。

(5) 本书文章主要以现代机电技术中的主流先进技术和产品为载体，体现时代性，也兼顾未来技术发展的趋势。

(6) 本书中的文章短小精悍，便于教学。

本书可作为高职高专院校机电一体化、机械制造及自动化、数控技术应用、模具设计及制造、电气自动化等专业的专业英语教材，也可供从事机电工程领域工作的工程技术人员参考。

本书由戴正阳主编，独立完成。

由于编者水平有限，加之时间仓促，书中难免存在不足与遗漏之处，敬请读者批评指正。

编　者
2011 年

Contents

Project I Automobile 1

    1.1   The Lead-in of the Project 1
    1.2   The Contents of the Project 2
    1.3   What is Mechatronics (Task 1) 2
    1.4   Engineering Mechanics of the Automobiles (Task 2) 10
    1.5   Engineering Materials of the Automobiles (Task 3) 20
    1.6   Language Study 29
    1.7   Practical skill 31

Project II Robots 34

    2.1   The Lead-in of the Project 34
    2.2   The Contents of the Project 35
    2.3   The Mechanical Elements of the Robots (Task 1) 36
    2.4   Motor and Motion Control Systems of the Robots (Task 2) 42
    2.5   Industrial Robots (Task 3) 48
    2.6   Language Study 55
    2.7   Practical Skill 59

Project III Elevator 62

    3.1   The Lead-in of the Project 62
    3.2   The Contents of the Project 63
    3.3   PLC of the Elevator (Task 1) 63
    3.4   Sensors of the Elevators (Task 2) 70
    3.5   Hydraulic and Pneumatic Elevators (Task 3) 78
    3.6   Language Study 86
    3.7   Practical Skill 88

Project IV MP4 Player 93

    4.1   The Lead-in of the Project 93
    4.2   The Contents of the Project 94
    4.3   What is MCU (Task 1) 94
    4.4   Semiconductor Materials (Task 2) 102
    4.5   Circuit of the MP4 Player (Task 3) 109

4.6　Language Study 114

4.7　Practical Skill 117

Project V　Mechanical Design and Manufacture 119

5.1　The Lead-in of the Project 119

5.2　The Contents of the Project 119

5.3　Basic Knowledge (Task 1) 120

5.4　Material Forming Processes (Task 2) 125

5.5　Components of CIMS (Task 3) 131

5.6　Language Study 139

5.7　Practical Skill 141

Project VI　Modern and New Technology 144

6.1　The Lead-in of the Project 144

6.2　The Contents of the Project 144

6.3　Microelectromechanical Systems (MEMS) Technology (Task 1) 144

6.4　Future Robots (Task 2) 150

6.5　Opto-Mechatronic Systems (Task 3) 153

6.6　Language Study 159

6.7　Practical Skill 160

Project VII　Job Application in Mechatronic Trades 163

7.1　Job Advertisement (Task 1) 163

7.2　Letters of Application (Task 2) 164

7.3　Resume (Task 3) 166

7.4　Interview (Task 4) 167

7.5　Exercise: Translate the Following Paragraphs 168

Appendix　Translation 170

参考文献 216

Project I Automobile

1.1 The Lead-in of the Project

Automobile is a self-propelled vehicle used for travel on land. The term is commonly applied to a four-wheeled vehicle designed to carry two to six passengers and a limited amount of cargo, as contrasted with a truck, as shown in Fig.1.1, which is designed primarily for the transportation of goods and is constructed with larger and heavier parts, or a bus (or omnibus or coach), which is a large public conveyance designed to carry a large number of passengers and sometimes additionally small amounts of cargo.

Fig. 1.1 Automobile and Truck

The evolution of modern mechatronics can be illustrated with the example of the automobile. All other functions were entirely mechanical or electrical, such as the starter motor and the battery charging systems. For instance, before the introduction of sensors and microcontrollers, a mechanical distributor was used to select the specific spark plug to fire when the fuel-air mixture was compressed. But the mechanically controlled combustion process was not optimal in terms of fuel efficiency. The electronic ignition system was one of the first mechatronic systems to be introduced in the automobile in the late 1970s. The electronic ignition system consists of a crankshaft position sensor, camshaft position sensor, airflow rate, throttle position, rate of throttle position change sensors, and a dedicated microcontroller determining the timing of the spark plug firings, depicted in Fig.1.2.

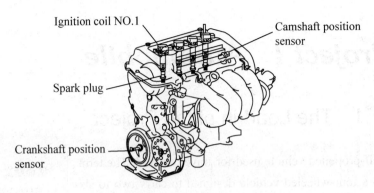

Fig. 1.2 Electronic Ignition System

ignition　n. 点火
crankshaft　n. 曲轴
camshaft　n. 凸轮轴
airflow　n. 气流
throttle　n. 控油气阀门
dedicated　a. 献身的，专注的

1.2　The Contents of the Project

Mechatronics solves technological problems using interdisciplin-ary knowledge consisting of mechanical engineering, electronics, and computer technology.

To solve these problems, traditional engineers used knowledge provided only in one of these areas (for example, a mechanical engineer uses some mechanical engineering methodologies to solve the problem at hand).

Later, due to the increase in the difficulty of the problems and the advent of more advanced products, researchers and engineers were required to find novel solutions for them in their research and development. This motivated them to search for different knowledge areas and technologies to develop a new product (for example, mechanical engineers tried to introduce electronics to solve mechanical problems).

The development of the microprocessor also contributed to encouraging the motivation. Consequently, they could consider the solution to the problems with wider views and more efficient tools; this resulted in obtaining new products based on the integration of interdisciplinary technologies.[1]

猜词断义 &
词义注释

interdisciplinary
a. 多学科的

advent
n. 出现，到来
novel:

motivate:

contribute
v. 贡献，归功于
consequently
adv. 因此，所以
obtain　v. 获得

1.3　What is Mechatronics (Task 1)

1.3.1　Introduction to the Mechatronics (Text 1)

Mechatronics, the term coined in Japan in the 1970s, has evolved over the past 25 years and has led to a special breed of intelligent products. What is mechatronics?

(1) Mechatronics is a methodology used for the optimal design of electromechanical products. The word, mechatronics, is composed of

猜词断义 &
词义注释

coin:

"mecha" from mechanism and the "tronics" from electronics. In other words, technologies and developed products will be incorporating electronics more and more into mechanisms, intimately and organically, and making it impossible to tell where one ends and the other begins.[2] A mechatronic system is not just a marriage of electrical and mechanical systems and is more than just a control system; it is a complete integration of all of them, depicted in Fig.1.3.

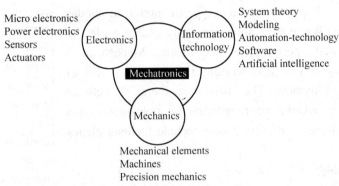

Fig. 1.3 Main Components Of A Mechatronic System

(2) Mechatronics is the application of complex decision making to the operation of physical systems.

Today, mechatronic systems are commonly found in homes, offices, schools, shops, and of course, in industrial applications.

Common mechatronic systems include:
- Domestic appliances, such as fridges and freezers, microwave ovens, washing machines, vacuum cleaners, dishwashers, cookers, timers, mixers, blenders, stereos, televisions, telephones, lawn mowers, digital cameras, videos and CD players, camcorders, and many other similar modern devices;
- Domestic systems, such as air conditioning units, security systems, automatic gate control systems;
- Office equipment, such as laser printers, hard drive, liquid crystal displays, tape drives, scanners, photocopiers, fax machines, as well as other computer peripherals;
- Retail equipment, such as automatic labeling systems, bar-coding machines, and tills found in supermarkets;
- Banking systems, such as cash registers, and automatic teller machines;
- Manufacturing equipment, such as numerically controlled (NC) tools, pick-and-place robots, welding robots, automated guided vehicles (AGVs), and other industrial robots;

evolve
v. 演变，进化
breed
n. 种类，品种
intelligent
a. 聪明的，职能的
compose
v. 组成，构成
incorporate
v. 包含，加入
intimate
a. 亲密的，密切的
organic
a. 有机的
marriage:

integrate
v. 结合成为整体
Integration:

artificial
a. 人造的，人工的
complex
a. 复杂的
application
n. 申请，应用
decision:

domestic
a. 本国的，家用的
appliance:

retail:

- Aviation systems, such as cockpit controls and instrumentation, flight control actuators, landing gear systems, and other aircraft subsystems.

1.3.2　Introduction to the Basic Mechanisms (Text 2)

Complex machines are made up of moving parts such as inclined planes, levers, gears, cams, cranks, spring, belts, and wheels. Machines deliver a certain type of movement to a desired location from an input force applied somewhere. Some machines simply convert one type of motion to another type, such as rotary to linear. While there are a seemingly endless variety of machines, they are all based upon simple mechanisms. Mechanism, a composition of links (or a system of parts working together in a machine), can accomplish determined motion. The difference therefore between mechanism and machine is whether it transforms or transmits energy outward. The common mechanisms discussed here include inclined planes, levers, wheel and axles.

Inclined Plane——Wedge

Under the condition of the same work, an inclined plane, depicted in Fig.1.4, decreases the force required to raise an object a given height by increasing the distance over which a force must be applied. You can imagine lifting something twice your weight to a 4 feet high shelf, or rolling the same mass up a gently sloping surface. The latter would be much easier.

猜词断义 & 词义注释

desired:

incline　v. 倾斜
plane　n. 平面
lever　n. 杠杆
gear　n. 齿轮
cam　n. 凸轮
crank　n. 曲轴
spring　n. 弹簧
rotary　a. 旋转的，转动的
linear　a. 沿直线的，线性的
mechanism　n. 机构
composition　n. 组合，构成
accomplish　v. 完成，实现
determined:

wedge　n. 楔
height　n. 高度
shelf　n. 架子，棚子
roll　v. 滚动，卷起
mass:

sloping　a. 倾斜的，有坡度的
perpendicular　a. 垂直的

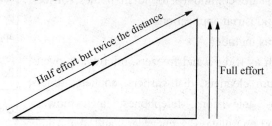

Fig. 1.4　Inclined Plane

Inclined planes are commonly put to use in cutting devices (e.g. an axe) and often two inclined planes are put back-to-back to form a wedge, as shown in Fig.1.5, forward movement is converted into a parting movement acting perpendicularly to the face of the blade. A zipper is simply a combination of two lower wedges for closing and an upper wedge for opening.

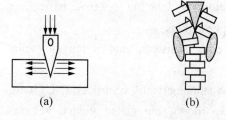

Fig. 1.5　The Inclined Plane at Work

Lever

The simplest machine, and perhaps the one with which you are most familiar, is the lever. A seesaw is a familiar example of a lever in which one weight balances the other. As shown in Fig.1.6 to Fig.1.8, there are three different classes of levers defined by the relative position of the fulcrum, effort, and load.

(1) Examples of first class levers are a balance, a crow bar, and scissors, etc.

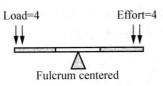

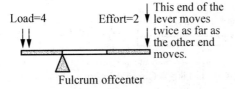

Fig. 1.6 Lever(1)

(2) In the second class lever the load is placed between the fulcrum and the effort. Examples of second class levers are a wheelbarrow, a bottle opener, and a nutcracker, etc.

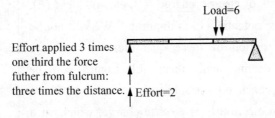

Fig. 1.7 Lever(2)

(3) The third class levers place the effort between the fulcrum and the load. Examples of third class levers are a hammer, a fishing rod, and tweezers, etc.

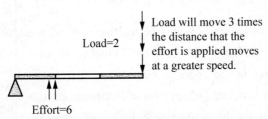

Fig. 1.8 Lever(3)

Most machines that employ levers use a combination of several levers or often of different classes.

Wheel and Axle

Both the inclined plane and levers could lower the force required for a task at the price of having to apply that force over a longer distance. With wheels and axles the same is true: a force and movement of the axle is converted to a greater movement, but less force, at the circumference of the wheel. As a matter of fact, the wheel and axle can be thought of as simply a circular lever, depicted in Fig.1.9. Many common items rely on the wheel and axle such as the screwdriver, the steering wheel, the wrench, and faucet, etc..

employ:

convert
v. 转换，转变
circumference
n. 圆周
screwdriver
n. 螺丝刀
steering wheel
n. 方向盘
wrench   *n.* 扳手
faucet   *n.* 水龙头

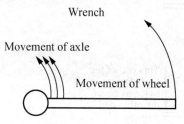

Fig. 1.9   The Wheel and Axle Is Like A Circular Lever

1.3.3   Introduction to the Basic Electronics (Text 3)

Current and Voltage

Most mechatronic systems contain electrical components and circuits, hence a knowledge of the concepts of electric charge (Q), electric field (E), and magnetic field (B), as well as, potential (V) is important. We will not be concerned with a detailed description of these quantities but will use approximation methods when dealing with them. Electronics can be considered as a more practical approach to these subjects.

The fundamental quantity in electronics is electric charge, which, at a basic level, is due to the charge properties of the fundamental particles of matter. For all intents and purposes it is the electrons (or lack of electrons) that matter. The role of the proton charge is negligible.

The aggregate motion of charge, the current (I), is given as $I(t) = \dfrac{dQ}{dt}$, where dQ is the amount of positive charge crossing a specified surface in a time dt. It is accepted that the charges in motion are actually negative electrons.[3] Thus the electrons move in the opposite direction to the current flow. The SI unit for current is the ampere (A). For most electronic circuits the ampere is a rather large unit so the milliampere (mA), or even the microampere (μA), unit is more common.

猜词断义 &
词义注释

charge:

field:

magnetic
a. 有磁性的，磁的
approximation
n. 接近，近似值
approach
n. 接近，方法
fundamental
a. 基本的，基础的
particle   *n.* 粒子
quantity
n. 数目，大小
proton   *n.* 质子
negligible
a. 可忽略的
current   *n.* 电流

Current flowing in a conductor is due to a potential difference between its ends. Electrons move from a point of less positive potential to more positive potential and the current flows in the opposite direction.

It is often more convenient to consider the electrostatic potential (V) rather than the electric field (E) as the motivating influence for the flow of electric charge. The generalized vector properties of E are usually not important. The change in potential dV across a distance dx in an electric field is $dV = -E \times dx$.

A positive charge will move from a higher to a lower potential. The potential is also referred to as the potential difference, or incorrectly as just voltage: $V = V_{21} = V_2 - V_1 = \int_{V_1}^{V_2} dV$.

The SI unit of potential difference is the volt (V). Direct current (DC) circuit analysis deals with constant currents and voltages, while alternating current (AC) circuit analysis deals with time-varying voltage and current signals whose time average values are zero.

External Energy Sources

Charge can flow in a material under the influence of an external electric field. Eventually the internal field due to the repositioned charge cancels the external electric field resulting in zero current flow. To maintain a potential drop (and flow of charge) requires an electromagnetic force (EMF), that is, an external energy source (battery, power supply, signal generator, etc.).

There are basically two types of EMFs that are of interest.

- The ideal voltage source, which is able to maintain a constant voltage regardless of the current that must be put out ($I \to \infty$ is possible).
- the ideal current source, which is able to maintain a constant current regardless of the voltage that is needed ($V \to \infty$ is possible).

Because a battery cannot produce an infinite amount of current, a suitable model for the behavior of a battery is an internal resistance in series with an ideal voltage source (zero resistance). Real-life EMFs can always be approximated with ideal EMFs and appropriate combinations of other circuit elements.

So long as the battery continues to produce voltage and the continuity of the electrical path isn't broken, electrons will continue to flow in the circuit. Following the metaphor of water moving through a pipe, this continuous, uniform flow of electrons through the circuit is called a current. So long as the voltage sources keep "pushing" in the same direction, the current will continue to move in the same direction in the circuit. This single-direction flow of electrons is called a Direct Current, or DC.

---

aggregate
n. 总计，总和
opposite
a. 对面的，相反的
flow *n. v.* 流动
SI: 国际单位制 System International
circuit *n.* 电路
conductor
n. 导体
potential difference:

vector
n, 矢量，向量
property
n. 属性，特性

对比记忆

positive
a. 积极的，正的
negative:

猜词断义 & 词义注释

eventually
adv. 最后，最终
constant:

regardless of
adv. 不管，不顾
infinite
a. 无限的
resistance
n. 阻抗，电阻值
in series with
prep. 与……串联
approximate
v. 接近，近似
appropriate
a. 恰当的，适当的
metaphor
n. 比喻，暗喻
uniform
a. 完全一样的，不变的

Ground

A voltage must always be measured relative to some reference point. We should always refer to a voltage (or potential difference) being "across" something, and simply referring to voltage at a point assumes that the voltage point is stated with respect to ground.[4] Similarly current flows through something, by convention, from a higher potential to a lower (do not refer to the current "in" something). Under a strict definition, ground is the body of the Earth (it is sometimes referred to as earth). It is an infinite electrical sink. It can accept or supply any reasonable amount of charge without changing its electrical characteristics.

猜词断义 & 词义注释
measure *v.* 测量
assume *v.* 假设，猜想
with respect to 关于
by convention 通常
definition *n.* 定义
infinite *a.* 无限的，无穷的
sink:

1.3.4 Exercises to the Task

I. Brief answer to the question according to the text.

1. Compared with trucks and buses, what does characterize the automobile?

2. Please illustrate some types of vehicles.

3. How does an engine work?

4. When and where did mechatronics originate?

5. What are the purposes of mechatronics?

6. How do these basic mechanisms lighten people's intensity of labor?

7. What's the difference between the electrical charge and current?

8. What is the Direct Current?

9. Is the earth a conductor, why?

II. Translate the following sentences into Chinese.

[1] Consequently, they could consider the solution to the problems with wider views and more efficient tools; this resulted in obtaining new products based on the integration of interdisciplinary technologies.

[2] In other words, technologies and developed products will be incorporating electronics more and more into mechanisms, intimately and organically, and making it impossible to tell where one ends and the other begins.

[3] It is accepted that the charges in motion are actually negative electrons.

[4] We should always refer to a voltage (or potential difference) being "across" something, and simply referring to voltage at a point assumes that the voltage point is stated with respect to ground.

1.3.5 Knowledge Widening: Reading Material

Millimeter wave radar technology has recently found applications in automobiles. The millimeter wave radar detects the location of objects (other vehicles) in the scenery and the distance to the obstacle and the velocity in real-time. A detailed description of a working system is given by Suzuki. Fig. 1.10 shows an illustration of the vehicle-sensing capability with millimeter-waver radar. This technology provides the capability to control the distance between the vehicle and an obstacle (or another vehicle) by integrating the sensor with the cruise control and ABS systems. The driver is able to set the speed and the desired distance between the cars ahead of him. The ABS system and the cruise control system are coupled together to safely achieve this remarkable capability. One logical extension of the obstacle avoidance capability is

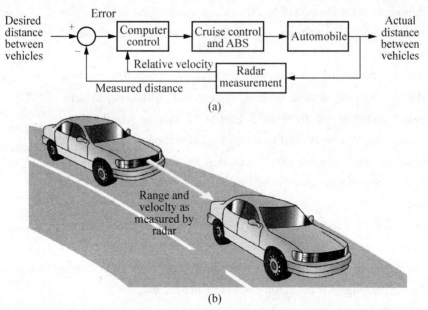

Fig. 1.10 Using Radar to Measure Distances

slow speed semi-autonomous driving where the vehicle maintains a constant distance from the vehicle ahead in traffic jam conditions. Fully autonomous vehicles are well within the scope of mechatronics development within the next 20 years. Supporting investigations are underway in many research centers on development of semi-autonomous cars with reactive path planning using GPS based, continuous traffic model updates and stop-and-go automation. A proposed sensing and control system for such a vehicle, involves differential global positioning systems (DGPS), real-time image processing, and dynamic path planning.

1.4 Engineering Mechanics of the Automobiles (Task 2)

Nearly all of today's cars are made up of engine, chassis, body and electrical equipments, depicted in Fig.1.11.

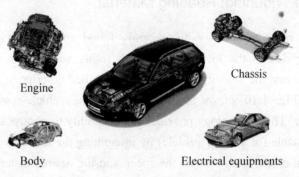

Fig. 1.11 Structure of Automobile

The engine provides the power to drive the wheels of the vehicle. The engine must be built strong enough to hold the pressure and temperatures caused by combustion.

The chassis consists of the drivetrain and running gear. The running gear includes the steering system, braking system and suspension system. The drivetrain transfers power from the engine to the driving wheels of the vehicle. The steering system is used to control the direction of the car. The braking system is used to slow down and stop the car. The suspension system is used to absorb road shocks and help the driver maintain control on bumpy roads.

The parts of these major systems are mounted on steel frames and the frame is covered with body panels. These panels shape the car and protect the parts inside from the damage outside. And they also offer some protection to the passengers if the automobile is in an accident.

Electrical equipment contains battery, generator, meter, light, wire, radio and air conditioner. Automobile have many circuits that carry electrical current from the battery to individual components. So the electrical

猜词断义 & 词义注释

chassis:

pressure *n.* 压力
combustion *n.* 燃烧
drivetrain *n.* 传动系统
gear:

steer *v.* 驾驶，掌舵
brake *v.* 刹车
suspension *n.* 悬挂
absorb *v.* 吸收
shock *n.* 振动
bumpy *a.* 崎岖的

equipment can work.

As a mechatronic product, there is always a risk that the working stress to which an automobile is subjected will exceed the strength of its material.[1] The purpose of a material mechanics is to analyze and minimize this risk.

近形记忆
bump
dump
lump
hump
pump
stress *n.* 应力
subject:

exceed *v.* 超过

1.4.1 Axial Tension and Compression (Text 4)

Review of Statics

statics
n. 静力学
axial
a. 轴向的

- The structure is designed to support a 30kN load.
- Perform a static analysis to determine the internal force in each structural member and the reaction forces at the supports.
- The structure consists of a boom and rod joined by pins (zero moment connections) at the junctions and supports.

Structure Free-Body Diagram

Structure is detached from supports and the loads and reaction forces are indicated.

a boom and rod
n. 杆件

pin *n.* 销子
junction
n. 连接点

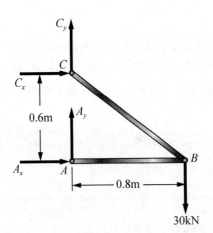

detach
v. 拆卸，使分开
indicate
v. 标示，指出
equilibrium
n. 平衡，均衡

Conditions for static equilibrium:

$\sum M_C = 0 = A_x(0.6) - (30\text{kN})(0.8)$, $A_x = 40\text{kN}$;

$\sum F_x = 0 = A_x + C_x$, $C_x = -A_x = -40\text{kN}$;

$\sum F_y = 0 = A_y + C_y - 30\text{kN} = 0$, $A_y + C_y = 30\text{kN}$.

A_y and C_y can not be determined from these equations.

equation:

Component Free-Body Diagram

In addition to the complete structure, each component must satisfy the conditions for static equilibrium.

Consider a free-body diagram for the boom:

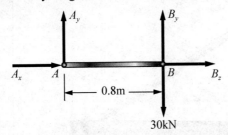

substitute
v. 代替

$\sum M_B = 0 = -A_y(0.8\text{m})$, $A_y = 0$

substitute into the structure equilibrium equation:

$$C_y = 30\text{kN}$$

joint
n. 接合点

Results:

$A = 40\text{kN} \rightarrow$ $C_x = 40\text{kN} \leftarrow$ $C_y = 30\text{kN} \uparrow$

Reaction forces are directed along boom and rod.

Method of Joints

The boom and rod are 2-force members, i.e., the members are subjected to only two forces which are applied at member ends.

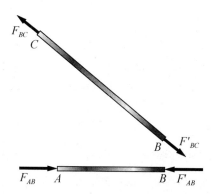

For equilibrium, the forces must be parallel to an axis between the force application points, equal in magnitude, and in opposite directions.[2]

Joints must satisfy the conditions for static equilibrium which may be expressed in the form of a force triangle.

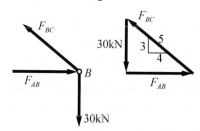

$\sum F_B = 0$, $\dfrac{F_{AB}}{4} = \dfrac{F_{BC}}{5} = \dfrac{30\text{kN}}{3}$, $F_{AB} = 40\text{kN}$, $F_{BC} = 50\text{kN}$.

Stress Analysis

Can the structure safely support the 30kN load?

From a statics analysis:

$F_{AB} = 40\text{kN}$ (compression)

$F_{BC} = 50\text{kN}$ (tension)

At any section through member BC, the internal force is 50kN with a force intensity or stress of $\sigma_{BC} = \dfrac{P}{A} = \dfrac{50 \times 10^3 \text{N}}{314 \times 10^{-6} \text{m}^2} = 159\text{MPa}$.

$d_{BC} = 20\text{mm}$

From the material properties for steel, the allowable stress is $\sigma_{all} = 165\text{MPa}$.

Conclusion: the strength of member BC is adequate.

parallel	
a. 平行的	
axis	
n. 轴	
magnitude	
n. 大小	
express	
v. 表达	
triangle	
n. 三角	
compression	
n. 压，压力	
tension	
n. 拉，拉力	
section	
n. 部分	
property	
n. 性能，特性	
adequate	
a. 充分的，适当的	

Design

Design of new structures requires selection of appropriate materials and component dimensions to meet performance requirements.

For reasons based on cost, weight, availability, etc., the choice is made to construct the rod from aluminum ($\sigma_{all} = 100\text{MPa}$). What is an appropriate choice for the rod diameter?

$$\sigma_{all} = \frac{P}{A}, \quad A = \frac{P}{\sigma_{all}} = \frac{50 \times 10^3 \text{N}}{100 \times 10^6 \text{Pa}} = 500 \times 10^{-6} \text{m}^2, \quad A = \pi \frac{d^2}{4}$$

$$d = \sqrt{\frac{4A}{\pi}} = \sqrt{\frac{4(500 \times 10^{-6} \text{m}^2)}{\pi}} = 2.52 \times 10^{-2} \text{m} = 25.2 \text{mm}$$

An aluminum rod 26mm or more in diameter is adequate.

1.4.2 Torsion and Shearing (Text 5)

Torsionally loaded shafts are among the most commonly used structures in engineering. For instance, the drive shaft of a standard rear-wheel drive automobile, depicted in Fig.1.12, serves primarily to transmit torsion. These shafts are almost always hollow and circular in cross section, transmitting power from the transmission to the differential joint at which the rotation is diverted to the drive wheels. We study them here because they illustrate the role of shearing stresses and strains.

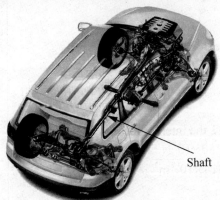

Fig. 1.12 In The Automotive Power Train Shown The Shaft Transmits Power From The Engine To The Rear Wheels

The model of Torsions is shown in Fig.1.13.

From observation, the angle of twist of the shaft is proportional to the applied torque and to the shaft length.

$$\phi \propto T, \quad \phi \propto L$$

When subjected to torsion, every cross-section of a circular shaft remains plane and undistorted.

dimension
n. 尺寸，规模
availability:
aluminum
n. 铝
diameter
n. 直径

猜词断义 & 词义注释
torsionally
adv. 扭转地
shaft *n.* 轴
drive shaft:
depict
v. 描述，表达
circular
a. 圆的，循环的
cross section:
shear *v.* 剪
twist
v.n. 扭，拧
proportional
a. 成比例的
torque
n. 扭转力

Cross-sections for hollow and solid circular shafts remain plain and undistorted because a circular shaft is axisymmetric.

distort
v. 扭曲，歪曲
solid
a. 固体的，实心的，结实的
axisymmetric
a. 轴对称的

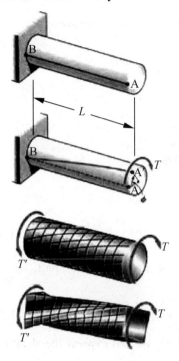

Fig. 1.13 The Model Of Torsions

Cross-sections of noncircular (nonaxisymmetric) shafts are distorted when subjected to torsion.

Considering a shaft AB subjected at A and B to equal and opposite torques T and T', we pass a section perpendicular to the axis of the shaft through some arbitrary point C. The free-body diagram of the portion BC of the shaft must include the elementary shearing forces dF, perpendicular to the radius of the shaft, that portion AC exerts on BC as the shaft is twisted, and we write

perpendicular
a. 垂直的
arbitrary
a. 随意的，主观的
radius
n. 半径
portion
n. 一部分

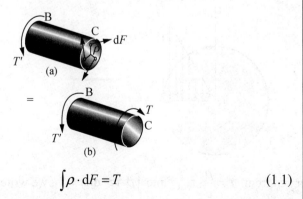

$$\int \rho \cdot \mathrm{d}F = T \qquad (1.1)$$

or, since $\mathrm{d}F = \tau \cdot \mathrm{d}A$, where τ is the shearing stress on the element of area dA, we also write.

$$\int \rho \cdot (\tau \cdot \mathrm{d}A) = T \qquad (1.2)$$

Recalling Hooke's law for shearing stress and strain, we write

$$\tau = G\gamma \qquad (1.3)$$

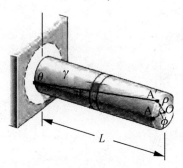

$$\gamma = \frac{\rho \phi}{L} \qquad (1.4)$$

The shearing strain is maximum on the surface of the shaft, where $\rho = c$. We have

$$\gamma_{max} = \frac{c\phi}{L} \qquad (1.5)$$

Eliminating ϕ from Eqs.(1.4) and (1.5), we can express the shearing strain γ at a distance ρ from the axis of the shaft as

$$\gamma = \frac{\rho}{c} \gamma_{max} \qquad (1.6)$$

where G is the modulus of rigidity or shear modulus of the material. Multiplying both members of Eqs.(1.6) by G, we write

$$G \cdot \gamma = G \cdot \frac{\rho}{c} \cdot \gamma_{max} \qquad (1.7)$$

or

$$\tau = \frac{\rho}{c} \cdot \tau_{max} \qquad (1.8)$$

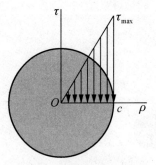

Substituting for τ from $\tau = \frac{\rho}{c} \cdot \tau_{max}$ into $\int \rho \cdot (\tau \cdot \mathrm{d}A) = T$, we write

---

recall
v. 回忆，回想

strain
n. 应变

eliminate :

modulus
n. 系数，模数
rigidity
n. 刚性，硬度
multiply
v. 乘，(使)相乘

$$T = \int \rho \cdot \tau \cdot dA = \frac{\tau_{max}}{c} \int \rho^2 dA \qquad (1.9)$$

But the integral in the last member represents the polar moment of inertia J of the cross section with respect to its center O. We have therefore

$$T = \frac{\tau_{max} J}{c} \qquad (1.10)$$

or, solving for τ_{max}

$$\tau_{max} = \frac{T \cdot c}{J} \qquad (1.11)$$

Substituting for τ_{max} from $\tau_{max} = \frac{T \cdot c}{J}$ into $\tau = \frac{\rho}{c} \cdot \tau_{max}$, we express the shearing stress at any distance ρ from the axis of the shaft as

$$\tau = \frac{T \cdot \rho}{J} \qquad (1.12)$$

Sample Problem

The preliminary design of a large shaft connecting a motor to a generator calls for the use of a hollow shaft with inner and outer diameter of 4 in. and 6 in., respectively. Knowing that the allowable shearing stress is 12 ksi, determine the maximum torque that can be transmitted (1) by the shaft as designed, (2) by a solid shaft of the same weight, (3) by a hollow shaft of the same weight and of 8-in. outer diameter.

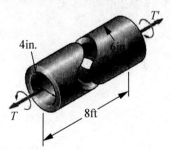

Solution

(1) Hollow Shaft as Designed.

For the hollow shaft we have

$$J = \frac{\pi}{2}(c_2^4 - c_1^4) = \frac{\pi}{2}[(3\text{in.})^4 - (2\text{in.})^4] = 102.1 \text{in}^4$$

$$\tau_{max} = \frac{Tc_2}{J} \qquad 12\text{ksi} = \frac{T(3\text{in.})}{102.1\text{in}^4} \qquad T = 408\text{kip} \cdot \text{in.}$$

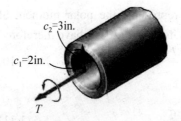

(2) Solid Shaft of Equal Weight.

For the shaft as designed and this solid shaft to have the same weight and length, their cross-sectional areas must be equal.

$$A_{(1)} = B_{(2)}$$
$$\pi[(3\text{in.})^2 - (3\text{in.})^2] = \pi c_3^2 \qquad c_3 = 2.24\text{in.}$$

Since $\tau_{all} = 12\text{ksi}$, we write

$$\tau_{max} = \frac{Tc_3}{J} \qquad 12\text{ksi} = \frac{T(2.24\text{in.})}{\frac{\pi}{2}(2.24\text{in.})^4} \qquad T = 211\text{kip} \cdot \text{in.}$$

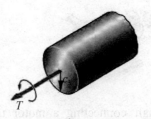

(3) Hollow Shaft of 8-in. Outer Diameter.

$$A_{(1)} = B_{(3)}$$
$$\pi[(3\text{in.})^2 - (2\text{in.})^2] = \pi[(4\text{in.})^2 - c_5^2] \qquad c_5 = 3.317\text{in.}$$

For $c_5 = 3.317\text{in.}$ and $c_4 = 4\text{in.}$

$$J = \frac{\pi}{2}[(4\text{in.})^4 - (3.317\text{in.})^4] = 212\text{in}^4$$

With $\tau_{all} = 12\text{ksi}$ and $c_4 = 4\text{in.}$,

$$\tau_{max} = \frac{Tc_4}{J} \qquad 12\text{ksi} = \frac{T(4\text{in.})}{212\text{in}^4} \qquad T = 636\text{kip} \cdot \text{in.}$$

1.4.3 Exercises to the Task

I. Brief answer to the question according to the text.

1. Today, which main components make up a car?

2. What purpose of mechanics analysis?

3. What are the 2-force members?

4. How to compute the tension and compression stress of a rod?

5. Which stress commonly exits in a drive shaft?

6. Why the drive shaft is hollow and circular?

II. Translate the following sentences into Chinese.

[1] As a mechatronic product, there is always a risk that the working stress to which an automobile is subjected will exceed the strength of its material.

[2] For equilibrium, the forces must be parallel to an axis between the force application points, equal in magnitude, and in opposite directions.

1.4.4 Knowledge Widening: Reading Material

The Mechanics of Materials aims to find relations between the four main physical entities defined above (external and internal forces, displacements and deformations). Schematically, we may state that, in a solid body which is deformed as a consequence of the action of external forces, or in a flowing liquid under the action gravity, inertia, or other external forces, the following relations may be established.

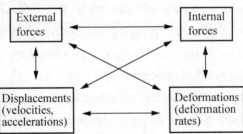

When the validity of the hypothesis of continuity is accepted, these relations may be grouped into three distinct sets.

$$\text{force} \xleftrightarrow{①} \text{stress} \xleftrightarrow{③} \text{strain} \xleftrightarrow{②} \text{displacement}$$

① *Force-stress relations*—Group of relations based on force equilibrium conditions. Defines the mathematical entity which describes the stress—the stress sensor—and relates its components with the external forces. This set of relations defines the theory of stresses. This theory is completely independent of the properties of the material the body is made of, except that the continuity hypothesis must be acceptable (otherwise stress could not be defined).

② *Displacement-strain relations*—Group of relations based on kinematic compatibility conditions. Defines the strain sensor and relates its components to the functions describing the displacement of the points of the body. This set of relations defines the theory of strain. It is also independent of the rheological behavior of material.

③ *Constitutive law*—Defines the rheological behavior of the material, that is, it establishes the relations between the stress and strain sensors. As mentioned above, the material rheology is determined by the complex physical phenomena that occurs in the internal structure of the material, at the level of atom, molecule, crystal, etc.. Since, as a consequence of this complexity, the material behavior still cannot be quantified by deductive means, a phenomenological approach, based on experimental observation, must used in the definition of the constitutive law. To this end, given forces are applied to a specimen of the material and the corresponding deformations are measured, or vice versa. These experimentally obtained force-displacement relations are then used to characterize the rheological behavior of the material.

1.5 Engineering Materials of the Automobiles (Task 3)

In everyday life we encounter a remarkable range of engineering materials: metals, plastics and ceramics are some of the generic terms that we use to describe them. The size of the artefact may be extremely small, as in the silicon microchip, or large, as in the welded steel plate construction of a suspension bridge. We acknowledge that these diverse materials are quite literally the stuff of our civilization and have a determining effect upon its character, just as cast iron did during the Industrial Revolution.[1] The ways in which we use, or misuse, materials will obviously also influence its future. We should recognize that the pressing and interrelated global problems of energy utilization and environmental control each has a substantial and inescapable "materials dimension".[2]

So far as the main classes of available materials are concerned, it is initially useful to refer to the type of diagram shown in Fig. 1.14. The principal sectors represent metals, ceramics and polymers. All these materials can now be produced in non-crystalline forms, hence a glassy "core" is shown in the diagram. Combining two or more materials of very different properties, a centuries-old device, produces important composite materials: carbon-fiber-reinforced polymers (CFRP) and metal-matrix composites (MMC) are modern examples.

猜词断义 & 词义注释

encounter
v. 遇到，遭遇
plastic *n.* 塑料
ceramic *n.* 陶瓷
artefact
n. 人工制品
generic
a. 属的，类的
silicon *n.* 硅
chip *n.* 片，芯片
weld *v.* 焊接
bridge:

diverse
a. 不同的，多种多样的
literally:

stuff
n. 材料，东西
cast iron *n.* 铸铁
revolution *n.* 革命

Project I Automobile

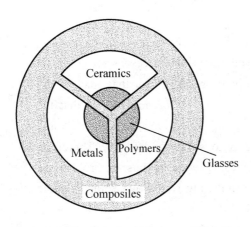

Fig. 1.14 The Principal Classes of Materials

misuse:

pressing:

interrelated:

substantial
a. 坚固的，客观的，实质的
inescapable:

polymer
n. 聚合物
crystalline
a. 水晶的，结晶的
composite
a. 混合成的，综合成的
carbon *n.* 碳
fiber *n.* 纤维
reinforce
v. 强化，加强
metal-matrix composite
金属基复合材料

1.5.1 Metallic Material (Text 6)

Metallics, or metallic materials, include metal alloys. In a strict definition, metal refers only to an element such as iron, gold, aluminum, and lead. The definition used for a metal will differ depending on the field of study.[3] Chemists might use a different definition for metals than that used by physicists.

Metals are elements that can be defined by their properties, such as ductility, toughness, malleability, electrical and heat conductivity, and thermal expansion.

Metals are also large aggregations. Metals usually have fewer than four valence electrons, as opposed to nonmetals, which generally have four to seven. The metal atom is generally much larger than the atom of the nonmetal.

Alloys consist of metal elements combined with other elements. Steel is an iron alloy made by combining iron, carbon, and some other elements. Aluminum-lithium alloys provide a 10% saving in weight over

猜词断义 &
词义注释

alloy *n.* 合金
lead *n.* 铅
ductility
n. 延展性
toughness
n. 刚性
malleability
n. 柔韧性
conductivity
n. 传导性
thermal
a. 热的，热量的

conventional aluminum alloy.

While metals comprise about three-fourths of the elements that we use, few find service in their pure form. There are several reasons for not using pure metals. Pure metals may be too hard or too soft, or they may be too costly because of their scarcity, but the key factor normally is that the desired property sought in engineering requires a blending of metals and elements. Thus, the combination forms (alloys) find greatest use. Therefore, metals and metallic become interchangeable terms. Metals are broken into subgroups of ferrous and nonferrous metals. Fig.1.15 shows some valuable metals.

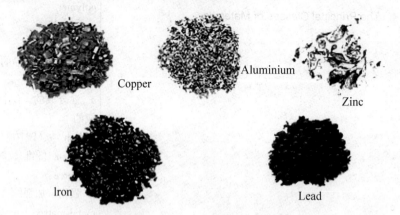

Fig. 1.15 Valuable Metals

Cast Iron

The cast iron is obtained by re-melting pig iron with coke and limestone in a furnace known as cupola. It is primarily an alloy of iron and carbon. The carbon contents in cast iron vary from 1.7 percent to 4.5 percent. It also contains small amounts of silicon, manganese, phosphorous and sulphur.

Ores consist of non-metallic elements like oxygen or sulphur combined with the wanted metal. Iron is separated from the oxygen in its ore heating it with carbon monoxide derived from coke (a form of carbon made from coal). Limestone is added to keep impurities liquid so that the iron can separate from them, as shown in Fig.1.16.

Steel

It is an alloy of iron and carbon, with carbon content up to a maximum of 1.5%. The carbon occurs in the form of iron carbide, because of its ability to increase the hardness and strength of the steel. Other elements e.g. silicon, sulphur, phosphorus and manganese are also present to greater or lesser amount to impart certain desired properties to it. Most of the steel produced now-a-days is plain carbon steel. A carbon steel is defined as a steel which has its properties mainly due to its carbon content and does not contain more than 0.5% of silicon and 1.5% of manganese. The plain carbon steels varying from 0.06% carbon to 1.5% carbon are divided into the following types depending upon the carbon content.

(1) Dead mild steel   up to 0.15% carbon.
(2) Low carbon or mild steel   0.15% to 0.45% carbon.
(3) Medium carbon steel   0.45% to 0.8% carbon.
(4) High carbon steel   0.8% to 1.5% carbon.

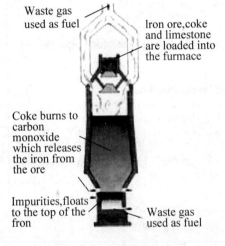

Fig. 1.16   Smelting

1.5.2 Non-metallic Material (Text 7)

A Closer Look at Plastics

There are many types of plastic in use. Plastic must be sorted by type for recycling, since each type melts at a different temperature and has different properties. The plastics industry has developed an identification system to label different types of plastic. The system divides plastic into seven distinct groups and uses a number code generally found on the bottom of containers. The following table explains the seven code systems.

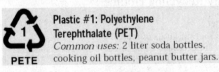

This is the most widely recycled plastic and the only one with a redemption value under the California "Bottle Bill". Recycling programs and centers request that you remove caps and flatten the bottles.

Plastic #2: High Density Polyethylene (HDPE)
Common uses: detergent bottles, milk jugs, grocery bags.

Most curbside recycling programs accept rigid narrow neck containers. Check the curbside recycling matrix or contact your curbside recycling service provider about whether it accepts plastic #2 and if containers need to be sorted by color.

Plastic #3: Polyvinyl Chloride (PVC)
Common uses: plastic pipes, outdoor furniture, shrink wrap, water bottles, salad dressing and liquid detergent containers.

Recycling centers rarely take #3 plastic. Look for alternatives whenever possible.

Plastic #4: Low Density Polyethylene (LDPE) *Common uses:* dry cleaning bags, produce bags, trash can liners, food storage containers.

Recycling centers rarely take #4 plastic. Look for alternatives whenever possible.

Plastic #5: Polypropylene (PP)
Common uses: aerosol caps, drinking straws.

Recycling centers rarely take #5 plastic. Look for alternatives whenever possible.

Plastic #6: Polystyrene (PS)
Common uses: packaging pellets or "Styrofoam peanuts", cups, plastic tableware, meat trays, to-go "clam shells".

Many shipping or packaging stores will accept polystyrene peanuts and other packaging materials for reuse. Cups, meat trays, and other containers that have come in contact with food are difficult to recycle. If you have large quantities, call the Alameda County Recycling Hotline.

Plastic #7: Other
Common uses: certain kinds of food containers and Tupperware.

This plastic category, as its name of "other" implies, is any plastic other than the named #1～#6 plastic types. These containers can be any of the many different types of plastic polymers. Recycling centers rarely take

redemption
n. 赎回
flatten:

HDPE 高密度聚乙烯
detergent
n. 洗涤剂
jug *n.* 罐，壶
grocery
n. 食品杂货店
curbside
n. 路边
rigid *a.* 坚硬的，不变的
PVC
聚氯乙烯
furniture
n. 家具
shrink wrap
热塑性塑料袋
salad dressing:

LDPE
低密度聚乙烯
trash can
垃圾桶
liner *n.* 衬里
PP 聚丙烯
aerosol
n. 喷雾剂
straw *n.* 稻草

PS 聚苯乙烯
pellet
n. 颗粒状物
styrofoam
n. 聚苯乙烯泡沫塑料
tableware
n. 餐具
tray *n.* 浅盘
clam shell
瓦楞子

plastic #7. Look for alternatives.

The low-density and high-density forms of polyethylene, LDPE and HDPE, were developed in the 1940s and 1950s. Respectively, extruded LDPE is widely used as thin films and coatings (e.g. packaging).

Polyvinyl chloride (PVC) is the dominant plastic in the building and construction industries and has effectively replaced many traditional materials such as steel, cast iron, copper, lead and ceramics. For example, the unplasticized version (UPVC) is used for window frames and external cladding panels because of its stiffness, hardness, low thermal conductivity and weather resistance. PVC is the standard material for piping in underground distribution systems for potable water (blue) and natural gas (yellow), being corrosion resistant and offering small resistance to fluid flow.[4] Although sizes of PVC pipes tend to be restricted, PVC linings are used to protect the bore of large-diameter pipes (e.g. concrete). The relatively low softening temperature of PVC has stimulated interest in alternative piping materials for under floor heating systems.

Polyamides (nylon). There are several different types of nylon (e.g. nylon 6, nylon 11), but as a family their characteristics of strength, stiffness and toughness have earned them a reputation as engineering plastics. Typical applications for nylon include small gears, bearings, bushes, sprockets, terminal blocks and slide rollers. An important design consideration is that nylon absorbs moisture which can affect its properties and dimension stability. The glass reinforcement reduces this problem and produces an extremely strong, impact resistant material. Another major application of nylon is in fibers which are notoriously strong. The density of nylon is about 1100 kg/m^3.

ABS materials have superior strength, stiffness and toughness properties to many plastics and so they are often considered in the category of engineering plastics. They compare favorably with nylon in many applications and are generally less expensive. However, they are susceptible to chemical attack by acids and alkalis. Typical applications are housings for TV sets, telephones, fascia panels, hair brush handles, luggage, helmets and linings for refrigerators.

Ceramic Brake

When driving an automobile, few performance attributes are taken more for granted than the vehicle's braking capabilities.[5] Simply put, drivers expect their vehicles' brakes to work every time, without exception. In North America, however, customer satisfaction rests on more than just pure stopping power. Brake noise, vibration and harshness (NVH), as well as brake dusting characteristics, are major considerations among virtually all motorists.

Fig. 1.17 Ceramic Brakes

Today's advanced ceramic brake pad technology, as shown in Fig.1.17, was derived from extensive industry-wide R&D activities beginning in the early 1980s to develop asbestos-free brake friction materials. At the time, a number of developed countries around the world had announced plans to ban the use of asbestos due to a myriad of legitimate health issues. Akebono, Nisshinbo (NBK) and Sumitomo led an effort to develop asbestos-free friction products, focusing first on development of low metallic steel fiber brake pad technologies.

In the 1980s, Akebono introduced the industry's first ceramic brake pad technology for mass production. That year, contracts were signed to supply the product for the hugely popular Honda Accord and Toyota Camry passenger cars, many of which were sold in North America. Not surprisingly, imitation products from competitors appeared about one year later, the result of aggressive reverse-engineering by a number of manufacturers who recognized Akebono's technological breakthrough.[6] Therefore, Akebono is a pioneer in ceramic friction technology, as shown in Fig.1.18.

Fig.1.18 A Pioneer in Ceramic Friction Technology, Akebono Can Test Brake System Noise And Vibration Performance On Complete Vehicles

acids   *n.* 酸
alkalis   *n.* 碱
fascia   *n.* 仪表板
helmet   *n.* 头盔
housing
n. 外壳，外罩
轴承盖，轴承座

attribute   *n.* 属性，特性，品质
simply put
简单地说

harshness
n. 尖叫，刺耳音

asbestos
n. 石棉
ban
v. 禁止
issue:

myriad
n. 无数，极大数量

hugely   *adv.* 非常
imitation
n. 仿制品
contract
n. 合同
competitor
n. 竞争对手

Refined during the past 25 years, Akebono's ceramic brake pad technology offers a number of performance advantages over traditional semi-metallic and other NAO products. Akebono's advanced friction technology is carefully formulated to provide optimal NVH performance under a variety of driving conditions (See Table 1.1).

aggressive
a. 好斗的，积极进取的
reverse-engineering
n. 逆向工程
refine
v. 提炼，精炼，精制
formulate
v. 制定，阐述

Table 1.1　Ceramics vs. Semi-metallics: Performance Comparison

Friction Material	Cold Friction	Fade Low Temp	Wear			Noise			Corrosion	Friction Stability
			Low Temp	High Temp	Roughness	Vibration	Squeal	Groan		
Akebono Ceramics	●	◆	●	●◆	●	●◆	●	●	●	●
Semi-Metallics	■	◆	■	●	■	■	◆	■	■	■

Excellent ●　Good ◆　Fair ■

1.5.3　Exercises to the Task

I. Brief answer to the question according to the text.

1. Please illustrate some ceramic stuff in our common life.

2. Why there is a glassy "core" is shown in the diagram?

3. Do the chemists care about the ductility, toughness, malleability, electrical and heat conductivity of metal, why?

4. Why pure metal doesn't meet the engineering requirement?

5. What's the difference between the steel and iron?

6. What's the defect of PVC used for floor heating systems?

7. Why do many countries restrict the use of asbestos?

8. Why did the competitors of Akebono imitate ceramic brakes, and how about the result?

II. Translate the following sentences into Chinese.

[1] We acknowledge that these diverse materials are quite literally the stuff of our civilization and have a determining effect upon its character, just as cast iron did during the Industrial Revolution.

[2] We should recognize that the pressing and interrelated global problems of energy utilization and environmental control each has a substantial and inescapable "materials dimension".

[3] The definition used for a metal will differ depending on the field of study.

[4] PVC is the standard material for piping in underground distribution systems for potable water (blue) and natural gas (yellow), being corrosion resistant and offering small resistance to fluid flow.

[5] When driving an automobile, few performance attributes are taken more for granted than the vehicle's braking capabilities.

[6] Not surprisingly, imitation products from competitors appeared about one year later, the result of aggressive reverse-engineering by a number of manufacturers who recognized Akebono's technological breakthrough.

1.5.4 Knowledge Widening: Reading Material

Nanocrystalline Metals and Alloys—Methods for Improvement and Space Applications

The thermomechanical characteristics of metals and alloys can also be improved by controlling the nanostructure or microstructure of the materials. Melting points and sintering temperatures can be reduced up to 30%, if the material is made of nanopowders. Another advantage is the easy formability of the materials through superplasticity. In a SBIR project of NASA, nano-crystalline aluminum alloys were developed for space applications by the company, DWA (DreamWorks Animation) company Aluminum Composites, in co-operation with different US-American aerospace companies. Such materials are investigated as alternatives for titanium in components of liquid rocket engines (e.g. lines and turbopumps), since they are lighter and less susceptible to embrittlement by hydrogen.

For space application, nanostructured ceramic composites will play a role, in particular, as thermal and oxidative protection for fibre-reinforced construction materials (e.g. coating of carbon fiber materials with boron nitride). Further application could arise in sensor technology, optoelectronics and for space structures. An interesting development is the production of high-strength transparent bulk ceramics. The Fraunhofer Institute, IKTS, for example, has developed a procedure for manufacturing submicron structured corundum ceramics (Al_2O_3), which possess high firmness (600~900MPa), scratch resistance and transparency. A controlled grain growth during the sintering process makes it possible to avoid porosity to a large extent, which guarantees a dense texture and thus a high firmness. Applications in space may be seen within the range of transparent exterior surfaces and skins of spacecrafts or sensor windows.

1.6　Language Study

1.6.1　有关数学表达式的英语

1. 四则运算的表达

动词：add, subtract, multiply, divide

介词：plus, minus, times, over

结果：sum, difference, product, quotient

例如：
Four plus eight equals twelve.
Nine minus two equals seven.
Six multiplied by seven is forty-two.
Thirty divided by two is fifteen.
$(a+b-c \times d) \div e = f$：
a plus b minus c multiplied by d, all divided by e equals f.

2. 等式与不等式

$x > y$	x is greater than y
$x \geq y$	x is greater than or equal to y
$x < y$	x is less than y
$x \leq y$	x is less than or equal to y

3. 指数与对数

x^2	x squared / x to the power 2
x^3	x cubed / x to the power 3
x^4	x to the fourth / x to the power 4
x^n	x to the nth / x to the power n
x^{-n}	x to the minus n
$\sqrt{x}$	square root x / the square root of x
$\sqrt[3]{x}$	cube root x
$\sqrt[4]{x}$	fourth root x
$\sqrt[n]{x}$	nth root x
$(x+y)^2$	x plus y all squared
$\left(\dfrac{x}{y}\right)^2$	x over y all squared

$\log_n^x$		log x to the base n
$\log_{10}^x$		common logarithm of x
$\log_e^x$		natural logarithm of x

4. 函数

$f(x)$		fx / f of x
$f'(x) / \dfrac{dy}{dx}$		f prime x / the (first) derivative of y with respect to x
$f''(x) / \dfrac{d^2y}{dx^2}$		f double prime x / the second derivative of y with respect to x
$\dfrac{\partial y}{\partial x}$		the partial (derivative) of y with respect to x
$\dfrac{\partial^2 y}{\partial x^2}$		the second partial (derivative) of y with respect to x
$\int_a^b x dx$		the integral of xdx from a to b

5. 特殊值

$\lvert a \rvert$		the absolute value of a
$\bar{a}$		the mean value of a
$\lim\limits_{x \to 0}$		the limit as x approaches zero
$\lim\limits_{x \to +0}$		the limit as x approaches zero from above
$\lim\limits_{x \to -0}$		the limit as x approaches zero from below

1.6.2　专业英语词汇的特点及猜词断义的技巧

1. 给普通英语单词赋予新的词义

如：Work is the transfer of energy expressed as the product of a force and the distance through which its point of application moves in the direction of the force.

在这句话中，work，energy，product，force 都是从普通词汇中借来的物理学术语。work 的意思不是"工作"，而是"功"；energy 的意思不是"活力"，而是"能"；product 的意思不是"产品"，而是"乘积"；force 的意思不是"力量"，而是"力"。

2. 当新的技术出现时构造新的英语词汇

(1) 合成：由两个独立的词合成一个词。如：

air + craft → aircraft 飞机

metal + work → metalwork 金属制品

power + plant → powerplant 发电厂

有时加连字符。如：

cast-iron 铸铁

conveyer-belt 传送带

machine-made 机制的

有时甚至用两个或两个以上的词组成复合术语，构成一个完整的概念。如：

liquid crystal 液晶
computer language 计算机语言
linear measure 长度单位
civil engineering 土木工程

(2) 派生：由词根加上前缀或后缀构成新词。加前缀只改变词义，不改变词性；而加后缀只改变词性，不改变词义。如：

ultrasonic (*a*. 超声的) —— ultra + sonic
subsystem (*n*. 分系统) —— sub + system
discharge (*v*. 放电) —— dis + charge
non-metal (*n*. 非金属) —— non + metal
electricity (*n*. 电) —— electric + ity
conductor (*n*. 导体) —— conduct + or
maintenance (*n*. 维修) —— maintain + ance
avoidable (*a*. 可以避免的) —— avoid + able
fundamental (*a*. 基本的) —— fundament + al

3. 猜词断义的技巧

在阅读专业英语文章时，常常会遇到一些生词；还可能遇上一些熟词，但是这些词常用的词义不能恰当地表达文章的含义；同时一本字典也不一定适用于每一个专业领域等，这时就特别需要通过词汇本身、文章本身或者专业背景知识来猜词断义。

(1) 前面所述的 1、2 两点就是猜词断义的方法，即完全可以通过词汇本身的特点来加以判断。

(2) 根据上下文的逻辑关系猜词断义。如：

He is a resolute man. Once he sets up a goal, he won't give it up halfway.

句中的 resolute 是生词，但是完全可以通过后面的 won't give it up 判断出 resolute 的含义和 won't give it up 相同，故为 "坚决的，刚毅的"。

Andrew is one of the most supercilious men I know. His brother, in contrast, is quite humble and modest.

句中 supercilious 是生词，但是由 in contrast 可知，supercilious 是 humble and modest 的反义词，故为 "目空一切的，傲慢的"。

练习：Unlike his sister, who is a warm, interested person, John is <u>apathetic</u> to everyone and everything.

1.7 Practical skill

1.7.1 定语从句的译法

1. 限制性定语从句的译法

(1) 用 "的" 字结构译成前置定语。

一般来说，限制性定语从句与主句关系密切，特别是对那些不太长或不太复杂的定语从句而言更是如此。如：

The unit we use to measure voltage is the volt.
计量电压的单位是伏特。

The rate at which work is done is called power.
做功的比率是功率。

One of the jobs of the control engineer of a power station is to deal promptly with anything that goes wrong.
发电厂的技术人员的一项工作就是及时处理所发生的任何故障。

A coil of wire that moves in a magnetic field will have some induction phenomena.
在磁场中运动的线圈会产生感应现象。

(2) 长句切分开，将译句按意群断开。

有些长句层次复杂，关系冗长，应将译句按意群断开，按汉语习惯写成短句，或者后续性分句。如：

Some metals are better conductors of electricity than others, which means that the former have atoms that contain more free electrons than the latter.
某些金属比别的金属有更好的导电性，这表明前者的原子所含的自由电子数比后者要多。

The energy obtained from uranium atoms in nuclear-power stations may be used to heat boilers and produce steam for the turbines that drive the alternators.
从原子能发电厂中的铀元素中获得的能量可以用来加热锅炉、产生蒸汽、驱动汽轮机，以带动交流发电机。

(3) 练习。

There is another reason why AC is preferred to DC for long distance transmission.

Effects of processing a surfaces which alter mechanical properties are being studied.

Many electron guns include an electro-magnetic coil at the base of the gun which can be energized to cause a pre-determined deflection.

2. 非限制性定语从句的译法

(1) 非限制性定语从句与主句之间的关系较疏远，当某些从句较短时，可以按照汉语的习惯，仍把它当做限制性定语从句来翻译。如：

The electricity, which we use for electric lamp and fans, is produced by generators.
电灯、电风扇用的电是发电机发出来的。

The states of process can be separated into two categories, which change at different rates.
该处理过程的状态可分为以不同速率变化的两类。

(2) 按照句子结构在引导词前将其切断，保留原句结构来翻译。如：

More often, it consisted of several different units, such as analyzer, averager, display, etc., which had to be interconnected prior to use.
在多数情况下，它包括一些不同的部件，如解调器、均衡器和显示器等，必须在使用前将其都连接好。

Electromotive force results in electrical pressure, <u>which may be compared to water pressure</u>.
电动势可以产生电压，电压好比水压。

(3) 练习。

Semi-conductor is a new kind of material, <u>which has found a wide use in electronic industry</u>.

This type of meter is called multimeter, <u>which is used to measure electricity</u>.

1.7.2　it 充当形式主语的译法

专业英语文章主要陈述客观事实、客观真理、定理等，为了体现客观性，使文章中的观点更具说服力，往往把真正的主语(主要从句)放在后面，而用 it 充当形式主语。

1. it + be +形容词

如：It is apparent that …	显然/很明显……
It is certain that …	无疑……/……是肯定的
It is true that …	的确/确实……

2. it + be + 名词

如：It is a common knowledge that …	众所周知，……
It is a fact that …	事实是……
It is a pity that …	可惜，……

3. it + be + 过去分词

如：It is accepted that …	可接受的是/公认的是，……
It is announce that …	据称/有人宣称，……
It is considered that …	人们认为……
It is estimated that …	据估计……

Project II Robots

2.1 The Lead-in of the Project

Robots produce mechanical motion that, in most cases, results in manipulation or locomotion. For example, industrial robots (Fig.2.1) manipulate parts or tools to perform manufacturing tasks such as material handling, welding, spray painting, or assembly; automated guided vehicles are used for transporting materials in factories and warehouses. Telerobots provide astronauts with large manipulators for remotely performing spacecraft maintenance.

Fig. 2.1 Robot Assembly Line

Robots perform repetitive, high-precision operations 24 hours a day without fatigue. Robots on this automobile assembly line weld body parts together. The General Motors Corporation uses about 16,000 robots to weld, assemble, and paint automobiles.

Walking robots explore active volcanoes. Mechanical characteristics for robots include degrees of freedom of movement, size and shape of the operating space, stiffness and strength of the structure, lifting capacity, velocity, and acceleration under load. Performance measures include repeatability and accuracy of positioning, speed, and freedom from vibration. Microrobot is shown in Fig.2.2. Robots in aerospace are shown in Fig.2.3.

Project II Robots

Fig. 2.2 Microrobot

vibration *n.* 振动

联想记忆

velocity
acceleration

Fig. 2.3 Robots in Aerospace

2.2 The Contents of the Project

A robot is made up of sensors, actuators, and computational elements (a microprocessor). Actuators for moving joints of a robot are usually electric servomotors, depicted in Fig.2.4. In the past, larger robots were built with hydraulic actuation due to their high payload capacity and ability to work in explosion-prone environments. In the 1990s, there was a trend by the major manufacturers to use electric actuators in most of their industrial robots.

猜词断义 &
词义注释

sensor
n. 传感器
actuator
n. 执行机构
joint
n. 关节
servomotor
n. 伺服电机
hydraulic
a. 液压的
actuation
n. 驱动，执行
explosion-prone
a. 易暴露的

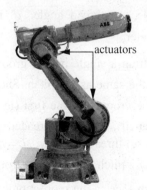

Fig. 2.4 Actuators of Robot

2.3　The Mechanical Elements of the Robots (Task 1)

2.3.1　Screws (Text 1)

Threads may be external on the screw or bolt and internal on the nut or threaded hole. The thread causes a screw to proceed into the nut when rotated. The basic arrangement of a helical thread cut around a cylinder or a hole, used as screw-type fasteners, power screws, and worms, as shown in Fig.2.5. Note that the length of unthreaded and threaded portions of shank is called the shank or bolt length. Also observe the washer face, the fillet under the bolt head, and the start of the threads. Referring to the figure, some terms from geometry that relate to screw threads are defined as follows.

Pitch p is the axial distance measured from a point on one thread to the corresponding point on the adjacent thread. Lead L represents the axial distance that a nut moves, or advances, for one revolution of the screw. Helix angle, λ, also called the lead angle, may be cut either right-handed (as shown in Fig.2.5) or left-handed. All threads are assumed to be right-handed, unless otherwise stated.

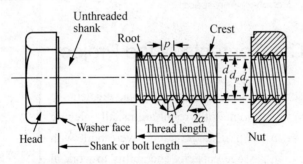

Fig .2.5　Hexagonal Bolt and Nut Illustrated the Terminology of Threaded Fasteners

Note: p =Pitch, λ =helix or lead angle, α =thread angle, d =major diameter, d_p =pitch diameter, d_r =root diameter

A single-threaded screw is made by cutting a single helical groove on the cylinder. For a single thread, the lead is the same as the pitch. Should a second thread be cut is the space between the grooves of the first (imagine two strings wound side by side around a pencil), a double-threaded screw would be formed.[1] For a multiple (two or more)-threaded screw, $L = np$ in which L =lead, n =number of threads, and p =pitch. We observe from this relationship that a multiple-threaded screw advances a nut more rapidly than a single-threaded screw of the same pitch. Most bolts and screws have a single thread, but worms and power screws sometimes have multiple threads. Some automotive power-steering screws occasionally use quintuple threads.

As noted previously, a power screw, sometimes called the linear actuator or translation screw, is in widespread usage in machinery to change angular motion into linear motion, to exert force, and to transmit power. Applications include the screws for vises, presses, micrometers, jacks (Fig.2.6), and the lead screws for lathes and other equipment. In the usual configuration, the nut rotates in place, and the screw moves axially. In some designs, the screw rotates in place, and the nut moves axially. Forces may be large, but motion is usually slow and power is small. In all the foregoing cases, power screws operate on the same principle.

thread angle
n. 牙型角
occasionally
adv. 有时候，偶尔
quintuple
a. 五的，五倍的
linear
a. 线性的
vise
n. 虎钳
press
n. 压榨机
lathe   *n.* 车床
micrometer
n. 千分尺
jack
n. 千斤顶
in place:

forego
v. 居先，走在……之前

Fig. 2.6 Worm-Gear Screw Jack

2.3.2 Gears (Text 2)

Helical gears are cut from a cylindrical gear blank and have involute teeth. These gears are used for transmitting power between parallel or nonparallel shafts. The former case is shown in Fig.2.7(a). The helix can slope in either the upward or downward direction. The terms right-hand (R.H.) and left-hand (L.H.) helical gears are used to distinguish between the two types, as indicated in the figure. Note that the rule for determining whether a helical gear is right-handed or left-handed is the same as that used for determining right-handed and left-handed screws.

猜词断义 &
词义注释

helical gear
斜齿轮
blank
n. 坯件，坯料
involute
n. 渐开线
helix
n. 螺旋，螺旋状物
slop
v. 倾斜 *n.* 斜坡
distinguish
v. 辨别，区分

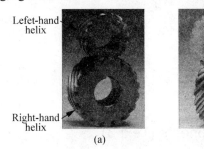

Fig. 2.7 Helical Gears
(a) Opposite-hand pair meshed on parallel axes (most common type);
(b) Same-hand pair meshed on crossed axes

Herringbone gear refers to a helical gear having half its face cut with teeth of one hand and the other half with the teeth of opposite hand (Fig.2.8). In nonparallel, nonintersecting shaft applications, gears with helical teeth are known as crossed helical gears, as shown in Fig.2.7(b). Such gears have point contact, rather than the line contact of regular helical gears. This severely reduces their load carrying capacity. Nevertheless, crossed helical gears are frequently used for the transmission of relatively small loads, such as distributor and speedometer drives of automobiles. We consider only helical gears on parallel shafts.

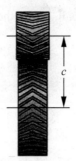

Fig. 2.8 A Typical Herringbone Gearset

Fig.2.9 illustrates the thrust, rotation, and hand relations for some helical gearsets with parallel shafts. Note that the direction in which the thrust load acts is determined by applying the right-hand or left-hand rule to the driver. That is, for the right-hand driver, if the fingers of the right hand are pointed in the direction of rotation of the gears, the thumb points in the direction of the thrust.[2] The driven gear then has a thrust load acting in the direction opposite to that of the driver, as shown in the figure.

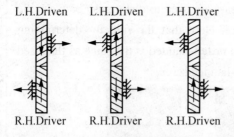

Fig. 2.9 Direction of Rotation and Thrust Load for Three Helical Gearsets with Parallel Shafts

2.3.3 Flexible Transmission Components (Text 3)

In contrast with bearings, friction is a useful and essential agent in belts, clutches, and brakes. Frictional forces are commonly developed on flat or cylindrical surfaces in contact with shorter pads or linkages or longer bands or belts. A number of these combinations are employed for brakes and clutches, and the band (chain) and wheel pair is used in belt (chain) drives as well. A robot with linkages and belts is shown in Fig.2.10.

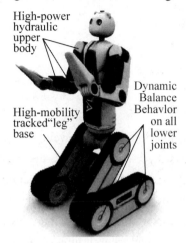

Fig. 2.10 A Robot with Linkages and Belts

V-belts are the most common means of transmitting power between electric motors and driven machinery. They are also used in other household, automotive, and industrial applications. Usually, V-belt speed should be in the range of about 4000 fpm. These belts are produced in two series: the standard V-belt, as shown in Fig.2.11, and the high-capacity V-belt. V-belts are slightly less efficient than flat belts.

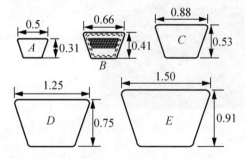

Fig. 2.11 Standard Cross Sections of V-belts (All dimensions are in inches)

Crowned pulleys and sheaves are also employed for V-belts. The "wedging action" of the belt in the groove leads to a large increase in the tractive force produced by the belt. These pulleys are employed to change the input to output speed ratio of a V-belt drive. As for the number of V-belts, as many as 12 or more can be used on a single sheave, making it a multiple drive. All belts in such a drive should <u>stretch</u> at the same rate to keep the load equally divided among them. A multiple V-belt drive (Fig.2.12) is used to satisfy high-power transmission requirements.

Fig. 2.12　Multiple V-belt Drive

There are various types of power transmission chains; however, roller chains are the most widely employed. Of its diverse applications, the most familiar is the roller chain drive on a bicycle. A roller chain is generally made of hardened steel and sprockets of steel or cast iron. The geometry of a roller chain is shown in Fig.2.13. The roller rotate in bushings that are press fitted to the inner like plates. The pins are prevented from turning by the out links' press-fit assembly. Roller chains have been standardized according to size by the American National Standards Institute.

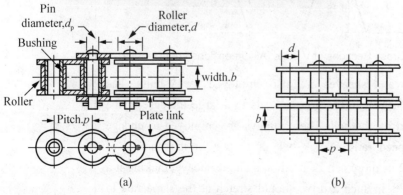

Fig. 2.13　Portion Of A Roller Chain
(a) single strand; (b) double strand

These chains are manufactured in single (Fig.2.13(a)), double (Fig.2.13(b)), triple, and quadruple strands. Clearly, the use of multi-strands increases the load capacity of a chain and sprocket system.

2.3.4 Exercises to the Task

I. Brief answer to the question according to the text.

1. What jobs the robots can do for the people?

2. In the past, what actuate the larger robots?

3. A double-threaded screw advances a nut more rapidly than a single-threaded screw of the same pitch, doesn't it?

4. Which gears make the point contact?

5. Are the common pulleys crowned? Why?

II. Translate the following sentences into Chinese.

[1] Should a second thread be cut is the space between the grooves of the first (imagine two strings wound side by side around a pencil), a double-threaded screw would be formed.

[2] That is, for the right-hand driver, if the fingers of the right hand are pointed in the direction of rotation of the gears, the thumb points in the direction of the thrust.

2.3.5 Knowledge Widening: Reading Material

A gear having tooth elements that are straight and parallel to its axis is known as a spur gear. A spur pair can be used to connect parallel shafts only. Parallel shafts, however, can also be connected by gears of another type, and a spur gear can be mated with a gear of a different type.

Helical gears have certain advantages; for example, when connecting parallel shafts they have a higher load-carrying capacity than spur gears with the same tooth numbers and cut with the same cutter. Helical gears can also be used to connect nonparallel, non-intersecting shafts at any angle to one another. Ninety degrees is the most common angle at which such gears are used.

Worm gears provide the simplest means of obtaining large ratios in a single pair. They are usually less efficient than parallel shaft gears, however, because of an additional sliding movement along the teeth. Because of their similarity, the efficiency of a worm and gear depends on the same factors as the efficiency of a screw.

2.4 Motor and Motion Control Systems of the Robots (Task 2)

2.4.1 The Role of Controls in Mechatronics (Text 4)

A mechatronic system consists by definition of a mechanical part that has to perform certain motions and an electronic part (in many cases an embedded computer system) that adds intelligence to the system. In the mechanical part of the system power plays a major role. This in contrast to the electronic part of the system where information processing is the main issue.[1] Sensors convert the mechanical motions into electrical signals where only the information content is important or even into pure information in the form of numbers (if necessary, through an AD converter).[2] Power amplifiers convert signals into modulated power. In most cases the power supply is electrical, but other sources such as hydraulic and pneumatic power supplies are possible as well. A controlled mechanical motion system thus typically consists of a mechanical construction, one or more actuators to generate the desired motions, and a controller that steers the actuators based on feed-forward and sensor-based feedback control (Fig.2.14).

猜词断义 & 词义注释

perform
v. 执行，表演
motion
n. 运动
embed
v. 嵌入，埋入
intelligence
n. 智力，职能
issue:

converter:

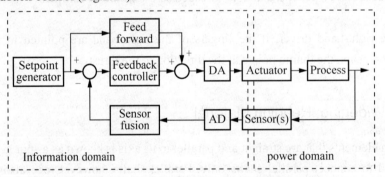

Fig. 2.14 Mechatronic System

amplifier
n. 放大器
modulate
v. 调节，调制
pneumatic
a. 气动的
supply:

steer:

Motion Control Classification

Motion control systems can be classified as open-loop or closed-loop. An open-loop system does not require that measurements of any output variables be made to produce error-correcting signals; by contrast, a closed-loop system requires one or more feedback sensors that measure and respond to errors in output variables.

Closed-Loop Motion Control System

A closed-loop motion control system, as shown in block diagram Fig.2.15, has one or more feedback loops that continuously compare the

feed-forward
a. 前馈的
feedback
a. 反馈的

system's response with input commands or settings to correct errors in motor such as load speed, load position, or motor torque. Feedback sensors provide the electronic signals for correcting deviations from the desired input commands. Closed-loop systems are also called servosystems. Each motor in a servosystem requires its own feedback sensors, typically encoders, resolvers, or tachometers that close loops around the motor and load. Variations in velocity, position, and torque are typically caused by variations in load conditions, but changes in surrounding temperature and humidity can also affect load conditions.

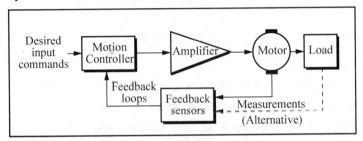

Fig. 2.15 Block Diagram of A Basic Closed-loop Motion Control System

A velocity control loop, as shown in block diagram Fig.2.16, typically contains a tachometer that is able to detect changes in motor speed. This sensor produces error signals that are proportional to the positive or negative deviations of motor speed from its preset value. These signals are sent to the motion controller so that it can compute a corrective signal for the amplifier to keep motor speed within those preset limits despite load changes.[3]

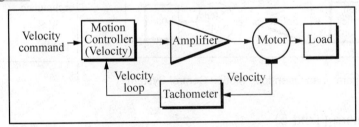

Fig. 2.16 Block Diagram of A Velocity-loop Control System

A positioncontrol loop, as shown in block diagram Fig.2.17, typically contains either an encoder or resolver capable of direct or indirect measurements of load position. These sensors generate error signals that are sent to the motion controller, which produces a corrective signal for amplifier. The output of the amplifier causes the motor to speed up or slow down to correct the position of the load. Most position control closed-loop systems also include a velocitycontrol loop.

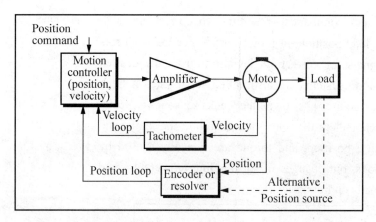

Fig. 2.17 Block Diagram of A Position-loop Control System

Open-Loop Motion Control System

A typical open-loop motion control system includes a stepper motor with a programmable indexer or pulse generator and motor driver, as shown in Fig.2.18. This system does not need feedback sensors because load position and velocity are controlled by the predetermined number and direction of input digital pulses sent to the motor driver from the controller. Because load position is not continuously sampled by a feedback sensor (as in a closed-loop servosystem), load positioning accuracy is lower and position errors (commonly called step errors) accumulate over time. For these reasons open-loop systems are most often specified in applications where the load remains constant, load motion is simple, and low positioning speed is acceptable.

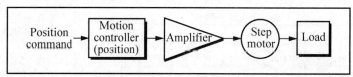

Fig. 2.18 Block Diagram of an Open-loop Motion Control System

2.4.2 Servo Mechanism (Text 5)

The most popular servomotors are permanent magnet (PM) rotary DC servomotors that have been adapted from conventional PM DC motors. These servomotors are typically classified as brush-type and brushless. The brush-type PM DC servomotors include those with wound rotors and those with lighter weight, lower inertia cup and disk coil-type armatures. Exploded view of a permanent-magnet DC senomotor with a disk-type armature is shown in Fig.2.19. Cutaway view of a permanent-magnet DC servomotor with a cup-type armature is shown in Fig.2.20. Brushless servomotors have PM rotors and wound stators. Cutaway view of a brushless DC motor is shown is Fig.2.21.

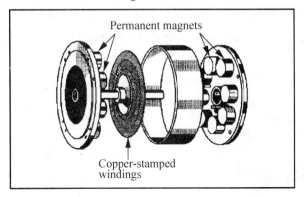

Fig. 2.19 Exploded View of A Permanent-magnet DC Servomotor with A Disk-type Armature

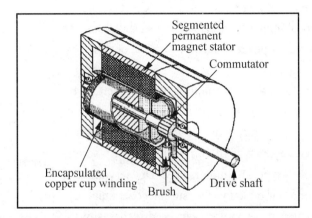

Fig. 2.20 Cutaway View of A Permanent-magnet DC Servomotor with A Cup-type Armature

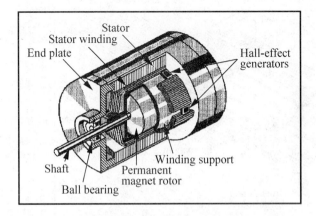

Fig. 2.21 Cutaway View of A Brushless DC Motor

Some motion control systems are driven by two-part linear servomotors that move along tracks or ways. They are popular in applications where errors introduced by mechanical coupling between the rotary motors and the load which can introduce unwanted errors in positioning. Linear motors require closed-loops for their operation, and provision must be made to accommodate the back-and-forth movement of the attached data and power cable. Linear actuator with linear servo motor is shown in Fig.2.22.

Fig. 2.22　Linear Actuator with Linear Servo Motor

Stepper or stepping motors are generally used in less demanding motion control systems, where positioning the load by stepper motors is not critical for the application.[4] Increased position accuracy can be obtained by enclosing the motors in control loops.

Permanent-magnet (PM) field DC rotary motors have proven to be reliable drives for motion control applications where high efficiency, high starting torque, and linear speed-torque curves are desirable characteristics. While they share many of the characteristics of conventional rotary series, shunt, and compound-wound brush-type DC motors, PM DC servomotors increased in popularity with the introduction of stronger ceramic and rare-earth magnets and the fact that these motors can be driven easily by microprocessor-based controllers. Cutaway view of a fractional horsepower permanent-magnet DC servomotor is shown in Fig.2.23.

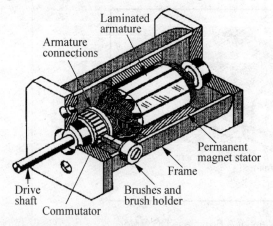

Fig. 2.23　Cutaway View of A Fractional Horsepower Permanent-magnet DC Servomotor

The increased field strength of the ceramic and rare-earth magnets permitted the construction of DC motors that are both smaller and lighter than earlier generation comparably rated DC motors with alnico (aluminum-nickel-cobalt or AlNiCo) magnets. Moreover, integrated circuitry and microprocessors have increased the reliability and cost effectiveness of digital motion controllers and motor drivers or amplifiers while permitting them to be packaged in smaller and lighter cases, thus reducing the size and weight of complete, integrated motion control systems.

A magnetic sensor as a rotor position indicator is shown is Fig.2.24.

permit:

rated
a. 额定的

cost:

while:

package:

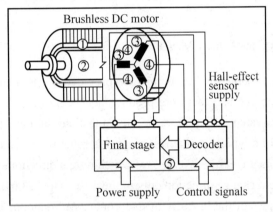

Fig. 2.24 A Magnetic Sensor as A Rotor Position Indicator

1-stationary brushless motor winding; 2-permanent-magnet motor rotor; 3-three-phase electronically commutated field; 4-magnetic sensor; 5-the electronic circuit board

2.4.3 Exercises to the Task

I. Brief answer to the question according to the text.

1. In the mechantronic system, what plays a major role?

2. What's the difference between the closed-loop control system and open-loop control system?

3. Compared the stepping motor with the servomotor, which one can reach the higher position accuracy?

II. Translate the following sentences into Chinese.

[1] This in contrast to the electronic part of the system where information processing is the main issue.

[2] Sensors convert the mechanical motions into electrical signals where only the information content is important or even into pure information in the form of numbers (if necessary, through an AD converter).

[3] These signals are sent to the motion controller so that it can compute a corrective signal for the amplifier to keep motor speed within those preset limits despite load changes.

[4] Stepper or stepping motors are generally used in less demanding motion control systems, where positioning the load by stepper motors is not critical for the application.

2.4.4 Knowledge Widening: Reading Material

The stator fields in permanent magnet (PM) motors are provided by permanent magnets, which require no external power source and therefore produce no I^2R heating. A PM motor is lighter and smaller than other equivalent DC motors because the field strength of permanent magnets is high. The radial width of a typical permanent magnet is roughly one-fourth that of an equivalent field winding. PM motors are easily reversed by switching the direction of the applied voltage, because the current and field change direction only in the rotor. The PM motor is ideal in computer control applications because of the linearity of its torque-speed relation. The design of a controller is always easier when the actuator is linear since the system analysis is greatly simplified. When a motor is used in a position or speed control application with sensor feedback to a controller, it is referred to servomotor.

2.5 Industrial Robots (Task 3)

The industrial robot is a very special type of production tool, as a result, the applications in which robots are used are quite broad. These applications can be grouped into three categories: material processing, material handling and assembly.

In material processing, robots use tools to process the raw material. For example, the robot tools could include a drill and the robot would be able to perform drilling operations on raw material.

Material handling consists of the loading, unloading, and transferring of workpieces in manufacturing facilities. These operations can be performed reliably and repeatedly with robots, thereby improving quality and reducing scrap losses.

Assembly is another large application area for using robotics. An automatic assembly system can incorporate automatic testing, robot automation and mechanical handling for reducing labor costs, increasing output and eliminating manual handling concerns. Fig.2.25 is Robot for automatic assembly.

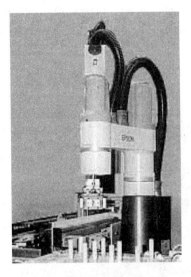

Fig. 2.25　Robot for Automatic Assembly

2.5.1　Benefits of Industrial Robotics (Text 6)

Fig.2.26 shows the benefits of industrial robotics.

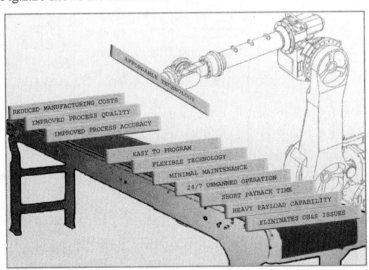

Fig. 2.26　Benefits of Industrial Robotics

猜词断义 & 词义注释

specialize
v. 专门化，专业化
underpay:

overwork:

enhance
v. 提高，加强
take over
接管，接替
aspect
n. 方面，模样
loom
n. 织布机

Ever since the advent of factories during the industrial revolution, specialized machines have had an important role in creating the products of civilization. The most common machine was the underpaid, overworked citizen—men, women, and children. Early factory conditions were dangerous, but the wages were good and nobody could argue with the efficiency factories brought.

Water and steam power, and later gas and electric power, replaced and enhanced human power, allowing us to make our products even faster and cheaper. Complex machines were created to take over many aspects of manufacture. The automatic loom is well known, as shown in Fig.2.27, but even today there are specific machines for many tasks.

Fig. 2.27　Automatic Loom

You don't normally think about it, but there is a complex machine whose only purpose is to bend wire into paperclips. There is another machine, perhaps in the same factory, which makes nails. Other machines perform other tasks. These machines, invaluable as they are for industry, are still forms of automata.

Factory automata start to become robots when they gain the ability to be programmed. But there is still a large gray area. Take that nail-making machine and add a bunch of controls to it so it can make nails from different sizes of wires, with different types of points, and different types of heads.[1] Is it an automaton or a robot? Does it make a difference if the controls are mechanical levers and knobs or electronic circuits?

In the early factories, working alongside a machine made your job more dangerous even if it made it less arduous. These early machines were large assemblies of spinning, whirring, moving parts that continued to spin, whir, and move even if a finger, foot, or other body part intruded into it. Even today, people working with machines in factories and food-processing plants face special risks. Machines are designed to be as safe as possible, but there are limits to what can be done to a metal sheer or punch press, for example, and have it remain useful.[2]

As machines improved into robots, they made some aspects of factory work safer. A robotic painter, spot welder, or assembly machine can operate in an empty space without any help at all. A supervisor stands safely outside its range of motion while the robot does the dirty and dangerous work (Fig.2.28).

plant:

supervisor:

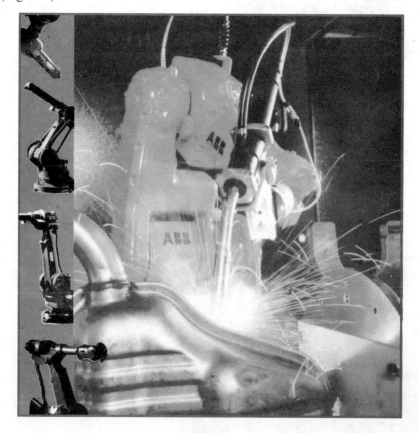

Fig. 2.28 Welding Robot

The most visible type of factory robot is the robot arm (Fig.2.29). These can be given any type of specialized "hand" needed for their job (Fig.2.30) and programmed to perform complex activities. One arm, with a set of different hands, can be programmed to perform any number of tasks. These are the robots that we recognize as "smart" machines, beginning to realize the dream promised to us.

Fig.2.29 shows an arm with welding attachment. Fig.2.30 shows an arm with cutting attachment.

visible
a. 看得见的

exploration
n. 探险，考察
hazardous
a. 冒险的，有危险的
nuclear
a. 核的，原子核的
Mars   *n.* 火星
crawl   *v.* 爬
debris
n. 碎片，残骸
survivor   *n.* 幸存者

Fig. 2.29   Arm with Welding Attachment

Fig. 2.30   Arm with Cutting Attachment

Robots make some exploration jobs not only safer but possible. Most humans would not be able to walk into the mouth of an active volcano, perform hazardous-waste cleanup at the site of a nuclear accident, explore the surface of Mars for months on end, or crawl through the debris of a fallen building looking for survivors.

2.5.2 Graspers of Robots (Text 7)

The grasper of robot is shown in Fig.2.31. There are various types of gripper mechanisms available; these include linkage actuation, gear and rack, cam, screw, rope and pulley, etc. The following describes some grippers actuated using pneumatic/hydraulic cylinders; these can be replaced with other mechanical arrangements other than cylinders.

猜词断义 & 词义注释

gripper
n. 钳子，夹子
available:

gear and rack
齿轮和齿条
cam n. 凸轮
cylinder:

arrangement:

Fig. 2.31 The Grasper of Robot

Two Finger Grippers

A non-parallel two finger gripper is shown in Fig.2.32 (a). As the pneumatic cylinder is actuated, the fingers move together and apart. A parallel finger gripper is shown in Fig.2.32 (b). Fig.2.32 (c) shows a mechanism that increases the holding force.

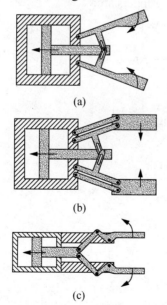

Fig. 2.32 Two Finger Grippers
(a) Non-parallel; (b) Parallel; (c) Parallel with increased grip

In the two finger gripper shown in Fig.2.33, when the pneumatic cylinder is actuated, the fingers move outward for internal gripping.

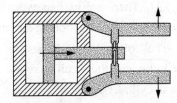

Fig. 2.33 Internal Two Finger Gripper

Magnetic Grippers

Obviously, magnetic grippers can be used only with ferrous materials. Electromagnets and permanent magnets are used. Electromagnets require a power supply and a controller. Polarity can be <u>reversed</u> on the magnet when it is put down to reverse residual magnetism. A mechanism is required to separate parts from a permanent magnet. They are good for environments that are <u>sensitive</u> to sparks.

Some of the advantages of magnetic grippers are:
- variation in part size can be tolerated;
- ability to handle metal parts with holes;
- pick up times are fast;
- requires only one surface for gripping;
- can pick up the top sheet from a stack.

Some of the disadvantages of magnetic grippers are:
- residual magnetism remains in the work piece;
- possible side slippage.

2.5.3 Exercises to the Task

I. Brief answer to the question according to the text.

1. Why there is still a large gray area?

2. Is the nail-making machine a robot?

3. What on earth is a robot?

4. What's the gripper?

5. What's the kind of the grippers?

---

polarity
n. 极性，磁场方向

reverse
v. 颠倒，反转

近形记忆

reverse
reserve
converse
conserve
sensitive
sensible

residual
a. 剩余的，残留的
variation
n. 变化
stack
n. 堆，一大堆
slippage
n. 滑动，下跌

II. Translate the following sentences into Chinese.

[1] Take that nail-making machine and add a bunch of controls to it so it can make nails from different sizes of wires, with different types of points, and different types of heads.

[2] Machines are designed to be as safe as possible, but there are limits to what can be done to a metal sheer or punch press, for example, and have it remain useful.

2.5.4 Knowledge Widening: Reading Material

Although the robot has always been a fantastic subject and produces scenes in such movies as "Star War", and even more fantastic kinds are described in science fiction books, we have found that our modern robots even seem to surpass these in reality, capacity, and development.

Humanized robots are possible if a demand for them exists. The only reason we do not have more advanced robots is not that they cannot be developed, but there has not been a need specified for them. As that need becomes obvious, they will appear in large number.

The future development of robotics depends mostly on the young and young-at heart scientists who are less conservative, who have active and imaginative brains and who have not learned to think in terms of "not practical" or "not possible". What robots can do around the home, office, factory and other places remains to be "seem" in their brains. These minds will create more wonderful inventions and adaptations than we have ever dreamed of. So let it be that the future of robotics belongs to the young and the young-at heart.

2.6 Language Study

2.6.1 有关数字的表达

1. 在英语中，除了个、十、百之外，数字常用 10^3 为单位进行分割

如：千：thousand　　　　　　　　　　10^3
　　百万：million　　　　　　　　　　10^6
　　十亿：billion　　　　　　　　　　10^9
　　万亿：trillion　　　　　　　　　　10^{12}
　　(毫)千分之一：milli-　　　　　　10^{-3}
　　(微)百万分之一：micro-　　　　　10^{-6}
　　(纳)十亿分之一：nano-　　　　　　10^{-9}
　　(皮)万亿分之一：pico-　　　　　　10^{-12}
　　(飞)千万亿分之一：femto-　　　　10^{-15}
　　(阿)百万万亿分之一：atto-　　　　10^{-18}
　　千：kilo-　　　　　　　　　　　　10^3
　　兆：mega-　　　　　　　　　　　　10^6

吉：giga-　　　　　　　　　　　　10^9

2. 成倍地增加或减少的数字用法

如：(1) The profit of wind power industry has been increased to three times as against last year.

　　　风力发电业与去年相比，利润增加到去年的 3 倍。

(2) The production of electric vehicles has reduced 3 times as much as last year.

　　电动汽车的产量与去年相比减少到原来的 1/3。

　　在描述成倍的增加或减少的数量时：

increase *N* times

increase *N* fold

increase by *N* times

increase to *N* times

increase by a factor of *N*

讲的都是同一个意思，指"增加到 *N* 倍"或"增加了 *N*-1 倍"。而

reduce *N* times

reduce *N* fold

reduce by *N* times

reduce to *N* times

reduce by a factor of *N*

讲的都是同一个意思，指"减少了 *(N*-1)/*N*"或"减少到 1/*N*"。

3. 成分数或百分数增加或减少的数字用法

与倍数不同，分数或百分数的增加、减少与动词词组中的介词有密切关系，如：

The bandwidth was increased by 120%.

带宽增加了 120% (增加到 220%)。

The bandwidth was increased to 120% of the previous.

带宽增加到原来的 120%。

The temperature was reduced to one-third.

温度降低到原来数值的 $\frac{1}{3}$。

The temperature was reduced by one-third.

温度降低了 $\frac{1}{3}$。

4. 练习

频率增加到 3 倍。

成本减少了 $\frac{1}{5}$。

2.6.2 专业英语词汇记忆技巧

语言的学习和使用遵循熟能生巧的规律，词汇的记忆有多种方法，不提倡死记硬背，要提倡坚持不懈、积累拓广。

1. 联想记忆(归类记忆)

这种记忆方式是由某一方面有联系的词汇牵引出另外一大片词汇，虽然这些词汇的含义不同，但由于处于同一个应用领域，或者经常在一起使用，或者它们有类似的含义，或者含义正好相反，所以通过归类的方法进行记忆。如：

(1) 可以由电阻联想出在电路中常用的词汇。

resistance 电阻	inductive reactance 感抗
conductance 电导	capacitance 电容
impedance 阻抗	capacitive reactance 容抗
inductance 电感	capacitive susceptance 容纳

(2) 在计算机运算中可联想到各种运算操作和运算部件。

addend 加数	divider 除数	product 乘积
subtrahend 减数	sum 和	quotient 商
multiple 倍数	difference 差	

(3) 不同专业领域中类似的词汇含义。

union 并	intersection 交	complement 补
or "或"操作	and "与"操作	not "非"操作
conjunction 合并	negation 否定	

2. 近形记忆

英语词汇中有很多词汇的拼写和字母组成非常类似，时常被错认为另一个词汇，但是只要经常分辨这些词汇间的微小差异，就能牢牢记住它们。如：

adapt 适合	institute 学院
adept 熟练的	destitute 缺乏
adopt 采纳	constitute 组成
	substitute 代替

3. 同义记忆

如同汉语一样，英语词汇中同样存在一词多义和一义多词的现象，对于一义多词，每个单词的含义有时完全相同，有时又有所区别，记住它们之间微小的区别。如：

环境：surround, circumstance, environment

促进，激励：promote, stimulate, prompt, motivate, prod, activate

4. 反义记忆

在词汇记忆中，注意利用词义互为正反的特征，相互结合进行记忆可以收到较好的效果。如：

little	a little
few	a few
enable	disable

mount　　　　　　unmount
charge　　　　　　discharge

5. 词根记忆

词根(root)即英语中的基本词，它是那些看来不可再分的词，实际上这是一个相对的概念，因为这些所谓的不可再分的词往往是过去的人们利用某些词根借用其他构词方法构成的新词。从英语发展的历史中可以知道，现代英语的祖先是日耳曼语言持有者盎格鲁-撒克逊人的语言，他们于公元449年从北方欧洲大陆登陆不列颠，占据了本属于凯尔特人的土地，吸收了少量的凯尔特人的语言。以后随着希腊罗马文化在罗马帝国统治期间以及文艺复兴时期的两次大规模传播，英语吸收了大量的希腊语、拉丁语的一些词汇，其中很多以词根的形式保留下来。即英语单词大多数的基本结构为：前缀 + 词根 + 后缀。如：

duc, duct = lead 引导

educate = e 出 + duc 引导 + ate 动词后缀 → (把……从无知状态中引导出来)教育
introduce = intro 入 + duc 引导 → (引入) 引进，介绍
conduct = con 加强语气 + duct 引导，领导 → 引导，指导，管理，指挥
conductor = conduct + or 人，工具 → 指导者，乐队指挥，管理者，导体
semiconductor = semi 半 + conductor → 半导体
product = pro 向前 + duc 引导 → (引导事物向前发展)生产，产生，引起
induce = in 入 + duc 引导 → (引导……进入……状态) 引诱，诱使
abduct = ab 离开 + duct 引导 → (引导……离开) 诱拐，劫持

fer = bring, carry 带，拿

confer = con 共同 + fer 拿 → (把意见拿到一起来)协商，商量，交换意见
differ = dif 分开 + fer 拿 → (各持己见，互异)不同，区别，相异
offer = of 向前 + fer 拿 → (拿到前面来)提出，提供，奉献，贡献
prefer = pre 先 + fer 拿 → (先拿，先取，先选，先要)宁愿，宁可，更喜欢
transfer = trans 越过，转过 + fer 拿 → (拿过去)转移，传递，传输，转让

fus = pour 灌，流，倾泻

refuse = re 回 + fus 流 → (流回，退回)拒绝，拒受
confuse = con 共同 + fus 流 → (流到一处，混在一起)使混杂，混乱，混淆
transfuse = trans 越过，转移 + fus 流 → (转流过去，移注过去)移注，灌输
infuse = in 入 + fus 流 → (流入)向……注入，灌输
diffuse = dif 分开，散开 + fus 流 → (分开流，散开流，到处流)散开，传播，扩散，散布
interfuse = inter 互相 + fus 流 → (互相流动)混合，融合，渗透

pel = push, drive 推，驱，逐

propel = pro 向前 + pel 推 → 推进，推动
propeller = propel + er → 推进器，推动者，螺旋桨

expel = ex 出，外 + pel 驱逐 → 逐出，赶出，驱逐，开除
repel = re 回 + pel 逐 → (逐回)击退，反击，抵抗
dispel = dis 分散 + pel 驱 → 驱散
compel = com 加强语气 + pel 驱逐，驱使 → (驱之使做某事)强迫，迫使
impel = im 加强语气 + pel 驱逐，驱使 → 推动，激励

6. 通过应用记忆

词汇记忆的目的是应用，只有多用才不会忘记，才能使词汇"活"起来，同时也要注意几个类似词之间在用法上的区别，对英语翻译同样有极大的帮助。如：

代替 (以 A 代替 B)
to substitute A for B
to substitute B with A
to substitute B by A
A substitute B
B be replaced by A
to replace B with A
to replace B by A
A replace B

2.7 Practical Skill

2.7.1 代词的阅读与译法

(1) 英语倾向于多用代词，其凭借代词的指代关系来交代信息的逻辑关系；而汉语则倾向于重复名词或名称，其凭借复述来传递逻辑信息。因此，汉译代词时，应注意摆脱英语原文的影响，适当减少代词或者省略，特别是人称代词的使用。如：

As soon as a positive charge approaches an electron, <u>it</u> combines with the latter.
正电荷一接触到电子，便马上与其相结合。

A battery has within <u>it</u> some resistance called internal resistance.
电池内的电阻称为内电阻。

Insulators can also conduct electricity to some extent, though <u>they</u> give a high resistance to an electric current.
虽然绝缘体对电流呈很大电阻，但还是具有一点导电性的。

(2) 顺应汉语使用代词的习惯，尽量消除不易弄清的指示代词，必要时还可还原为其所指代的名词或名称。如：

The conductor has <u>its</u> properties, and the insulator has <u>its</u> properties.
导体有导体的特性，绝缘体有绝缘体的特性。

Whatever <u>its</u> origin is, the e.m.f. of <u>a source</u> is numerically equal to the potential difference between its two terminals with the external circuit open.
不管<u>电源</u>的原动力是什么，<u>其</u>电势在大小上总是等于开路电压。

Without the friction between their feet and the ground, people would not be in a position to walk.

要是没有人的脚与地面之间的摩擦，人就不能走路。

(3) 有时英语句子中代词与其指代物可能离得较远，此时只有正确理解句子，才能很好地去翻译。如：

① 根据语言结构上的呼应关系判断。如：

Light waves are waves of energy that travel through space at the rate of 3,000,000 kilometers per second.

句中，关系代词 that 后的谓语动词 travel 是第三人称复数形式，故可判定其不是指代 energy(尽管它们靠得很近)，而是指代 waves(尽管它离 that 比 energy 远)。因此译为：

光波是以 3 000 000km/s 的速度传播的能量波。

② 根据靠近原则判断。

英文中，其代词出现的位置，大体上有一个原则，就是所谓的"靠近原则"。即代词前最近的一个名词(或名称)，一般是其所指代的词。如：

The two units used most frequently in electricity are ampere and volt. This is the unit of voltage and that of current flow.

电学上最常用的两个单位是安培和伏特，后者是电压单位，前者是电流单位。

③ 有时句中的名词、名称和代词不只一个，"靠近原则"不适用，这时还应该结合思维逻辑上的呼应关系来判断指代关系。如：

An alternating voltage between two points A and B, determined along a specified path L, periodically changes sign, so that if it is assumed to be positive in the direction from A to B, it will be negative in the direction from B to A at the same instant of time.

首先，根据专业背景知识判断什么被 be positive in the direction，通过阅读其前面主句，只可能是 An alternating voltage，故此断定第一个 it 就是指代 An alternating voltage；其次，第二个 it 后面是 be negative in the direction，正好与第一个 it 后面的 be positive in the direction 相对照，故通过逻辑判断，第二个 it 也指代 An alternating voltage。因此译为：

沿某一特定路径 L 上 AB 两点之间的交变电压周期性地改变符号。这样，若假定自 A 至 B 方向的电压为正，那么在同一瞬时自 B 至 A 方向的电压便为负。

2.7.2 虚拟语气的译法

(1) 非真实条件的纯粹虚拟句的译法。

在专业英语中，常常会遇到许多非真实条件的纯粹虚拟的虚拟语气句。翻译这样的句子时，主要是应避免译成真实条件句。如：

What would happen if one broke one of the wires of the electric circuit?

错：如果有人把电路中的一个导线弄断了，会发生什么情况呢？

这样就译成了一般条件句，应该译为：

倘若真的有人把电路中的一根导线弄断了，那会发生什么情况呢？

练习：

If he had time, he would help you.

If there were no gravity, there would be no air around the earth.

If you should move a permanent magnet in and out of a coil of wire, you would be using the magnet and the coil as a simple electric generator.

有时从句中的连词 if 可省略，而将 should, were, had, could 等提前，采用倒装语序的虚拟，翻译是类似的。如：

Were there no electric pressure in a semiconductor, the electron flow would not take place of it.
要是半导体内没有电压，其内部就不会产生电流。
练习：
Had the production process not been made an automatic one, the productivity would not have increased so greatly.

(2) 在专业英语中，有时遇到表示建议、要求或命令等意义的虚拟句，其谓语结构形式为"should + 动词原形"，其含义为"应该"、"要"。如：

Our demand is that correct calculation should be made.
我们要求的是计算要准确。
注意，有时 should 可以省略，但依然是虚拟语气。如：
This requires that the converter connecting the drive to the utility grid be a two-quadrant converter with a reversible DC current.
这就要求连接电动机与公用电网的转换器，应该是能提供可换向直流电的两象限转换器。

Project III   Elevator

3.1   The Lead-in of the Project

In general, a control system is a collection of electronic devices and equipment which are in place to ensure the stability, accuracy and smooth transition of a process manufacturing activity.[1] It takes any form and varies in scale of implementation, from a power plant to a semiconductor machine. As a result of rapid advancement of technology, complicated control tasks accomplished with a highly automated control system, which may be in the form of Programmable Logic Controller (PLC) or possibly a host computer, etc., Besides signal interfacing to the field devices (such as operator panel, motors, sensors, switches, solenoid valves and etc.), capabilities in network communication enable a big scale implementation and process co-ordination besides providing greater flexibility in realizing distributed control system.[2] Every single component in control system plays an important role regardless of size. For instance, as shown in Fig.3.1 the PLC would not know the happenings around it without any sensing devices. And if necessary, an area host computer has to be in place to co-ordinate the activities in a specific area at the shop floor.

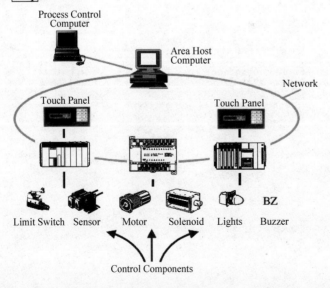

Fig. 3.1   An Application As Small As A Single PLC Controlling A Single or Some Output Devices

猜词断义 & 词义注释

collection:

scale:

implementation
n. 工具,执行

近形记忆

implement
complement
compliment
host
n. 主人,主机
field:

panel
n. 面板,仪表盘
switch   *n.* 开关

词义扩展

switchboard:

co-ordination
n. 协调
flexibility
n. 弹性,灵活机动性
distribute
v. 分散,分配,分发
component
n. 成分,组成部分
regardless of
不管,不顾
shop:

3.2 The Contents of the Project

Many engineering systems, including elevator systems, are nowadays controlled by Programmable Logic Controllers (PLCs). The PLC may be considered as a special-purpose computer with a basic architecture similar to that of any other known computer such as a Central Processing Unit (CPU). It is based on a memory and a number of input and output terminals. The software used for PLC programming is based on a special language known as the ladder diagram. The ladder diagram is an easy programming language since it is based on Boolean logic functions. This makes the task of modifying any system much easier and more cost-effective.

The PLC has many advantages over other control systems. It is known for its flexibility, lower cost, operational speed, reliability, ease of programming, security, and it is easy in implementing changes and correcting errors. One of the applications using PLCs is the control of elevator systems.

猜词断义 & 词义注释

architecture
n. 架构
terminal
n. 终端，终点站
ladder
n. 梯子，阶梯
boolean
n. 布尔
function:

modify
v. 修改，更改
cost-effective
a. 有成本效益的，划算的

3.3 PLC of the Elevator (Task 1)

3.3.1 What is PLC (Text 1)

A PLC consists of a Central Processing Unit (CPU) containing an application program and Input and Output Interface modules, which is directly connected to the field I/O devices. The block diagram of PLC is shown in Fig.3.2. The program controls the PLC so that when an input signal from an input device turns ON, the appropriate response is made. The response normally involves turning ON an output signal to some sort of output devices.

Central Processing Unit

The Central Processing Unit (CPU) is microprocessor that co-ordinates the activities of the PLC system. It executes the program, processes I/O signals & communicates with external devices.

Memory

There are various types of memory unit. It is the area that holds the operating system and user memory. The operating system is actually a system software that co-ordinates the PLC. Ladder program, Timer and Counter Values are stored to the user memory. Depending on user's need, various

猜词断义 & 词义注释

interface
n. 界面，接口
module
n. 模块
response
n. 反应

execute:

communicate:

timer:

types of memory are available for choice.

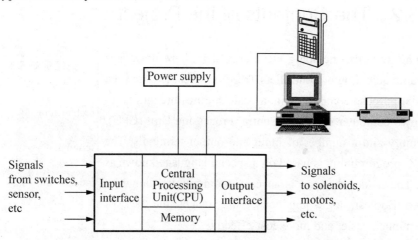

Fig. 3.2 Block Diagram Of PLC

1. Read-Only Memory (ROM)

ROM is a non-volatile memory that can be programmed only once. It is therefore unsuitable. It is least popular as compared with other memory type.

2. Random Access Memory (RAM)

RAM is commonly used for storing the user program and data. The data in the volatile RAM would normally be lost if the power source is removed. However, this problem can be solved by backing up the RAM with a battery.

3. Erasable Programmable Read Only Memory (EPROM)

EPROM holds data permanently just like ROM. It dose not require battery backup. However, its content can be erased by exposing it to ultraviolet light.

4. Electrically Erasable Programmable Read Only Memory (EEPROM)

EEPROM combines the access flexibility of RAM and the non-volatility of EPROM in one. Its contents can be erased and reprogrammed electrically, however, to a limit number of times.

Scan Time

The process of reading the inputs, executing the program and updating the outputs is known as scan. The scan is normally a continuous and sequential process of reading the status of inputs, evaluating the control logic and updating outputs. Scan time specification indicates how fast the controller can react to the field inputs and correctly solve the control logic.

Factors of Influencing Scan Time

The time required to make a single scan (scan time) varies from 0.1ms to tens of ms depending on its CPU processing speed and the length of the user program. The program of PLC is shown in Fig.3.3. The user of remote I/O

volatile
n. 易变的, 反复无常的

back up:

erasable
a. 可消除的, 可抹去的
ultraviolet
n. 紫外线

sequential
a. 顺序的, 连续的
status
n. 身份, 地位, 状态

subsystems increase the scan time as a result of having to transmit the I/O updates to remote subsystem. Monitoring of the control program also adds overhead time to the scan because the controller's CPU has to send the status of coils and contacts to the CRT or other monitoring device.

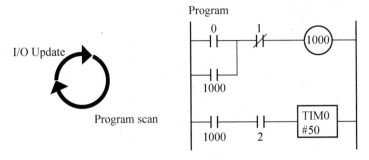

Fig. 3.3 The Program of PLC

3.3.2 The Composition of PLC (Text 2)

In an automated system, the PLC is commonly regarded as the heart of the control system. With a control application program (stored within the PLC memory) in execution, the PLC constantly monitors the state of the system through the field input devices' feedback signal. It will then base on the program logic to determine the course of action to be carried out at the field output devices.

The PLC may be used to control a simple and repetitive task, or a few of them may be interconnected together with other host controllers or host computers through a sort of communication network, in order to integrate the control of a complex process.

Input Devices

Intelligence of an automated system is greatly depending on the ability of a PLC to read in the signal from various types of automatic sensing and manual input field devices.

Push-buttons, keypad and toggle switches, which form the basic man-machine interface, are types of manual input device. On the other hand, for detection of work piece, monitoring of moving mechanism, checking on pressure and or liquid level and many others, the PLC will have to tap the signal from the specific automatic sensing devices like proximity switch, limit switch, photoelectric sensor, and level sensor and so on.[3] Types of input signal to the PLC would be of ON/OFF logic or analogue. These input signals are interfaced to PLC through various types of PLC input module. The input devices of PLC are shown in Fig.3.4.

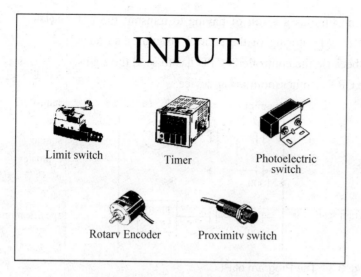

Fig. 3.4 The Input Devices of PLC

Output Devices

An automatic system is incomplete and the PLC system is virtually paralyzed without means of interface to the field output devices. Some of the most commonly controlled devices are motors, solenoids, relays indicators, buzzers and etc. Through activation of motors and solenoids the PLC can control from a simple pick and place system to a much complex servo positioning system. These type of output devices are the mechanism of an automated system and so its direct effect on the system performance.

However, other output devices such as the pilot lamp, buzzers and alarms are merely meant for notifying purpose. Like input signal interfacing, signal from output devices are interfaced to the PLC through the wide range of PLC output module. The output devices of PLC are shown in Fig.3.5.

virtually
adv. 实际上，事实上
paralyze
v. 瘫痪
solenoid
n. 电磁铁
buzzer
n. 蜂鸣器
relay
n. 继电器
pilot lamp
指示灯
notify
n. 通知，告知

Fig. 3.5 The Output Devices of PLC

3.3.3 Examples of the PLC of the Elevators (Text 3)

The objective of the project is the design and implementation of a four-level elevator system controlled by a Programmable Logic Controller (PLC). The inside lock of an elevator is shown in Fig.3.6. The design was not based on a first-come first-served basis, since this approach was not found to be practical. As a practical compromise between energy consumption and speed of response, we decided to combine all requests going in one direction (up or down), and then process them in sequential order.[4] This was achieved in the following manner: if the elevator is going up, all "up" requests are given higher priority than the "down" requests until the elevator reaches the last destination upwards. Then the elevator goes down but now gives priority to all "down" requests over the "up" ones. More details on this will be given in the section "Software design".

猜词断义 & 词义注释
compromise *n.* 妥协，折中

Fig. 3.6 The Inside Look of An Elevator

The objective of the hardware design is to develop the interface circuit between the PLC and the elevator system and the elevator control panel, with both external and internal requests, as shown in Fig.3.7. These requests are produced by push buttons that send continuous signals to the PLC when activated. Each push button is connected to an LED to identify the request placed.

achieve *v.* 实现，完成

Fig. 3.7 Overall Layout of the Control Panel of the Elevator

The block diagram of the system's layout is shown in Fig.3.8, where both the interface between the PLC and the elevator system with the control panel are drawn.

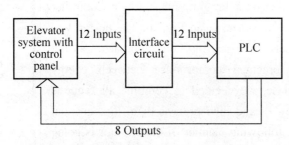

Fig. 3.8 Block Diagram of the System Layout

The 12 inputs and 8 outputs used in this project are listed and defined in Table 3.1.

Table 3.1 List and Definitions of Inputs and Outputs Used

Inputs		Outputs	
Symbol	Function	Symbol	Function
1U	Outer request at level 1 to go up	L1	Indication that the elevator is at level 1
I1	Inner request to go to level 1	L2	Indication that the elevator is at level 2
2D	Outer request at level 2 to go down	L3	Indication that the elevator is at level 3
2U	Outer request at level 2 to go up	L4	Indication that the elevator is at level 4
I2	Inner request to go to level 2	DO	Indication that the door of the elevator is open
3D	Outer request at level 3 to go down		
3U	Outer request at level 3 to go up	A1	Indication that the alarm switch was activated
I3	Inner request to go to level 3		
4D	Outer request at level 4 to go down	L2R	Signal to reset outer requests at level
I4	Inner request to go to level 4	L3R	Signal to reset outer requests at level 3
A1	Alarm switch		
DO	Door open request		

identify
v. 指认，认出

dumb
a. 哑的，简单的

Control Modes

Of the two different control modes: dumb control, or intelligent control, the dumb control is not popular these days because it is not practical. It is usually used for transporting material and equipment in buildings, where all the floors have to be visited sequentially and continuously. On the other hand, the intelligent control responds to requests placed by users by ordering and processing them in an intelligent manner. This type of control is used in most applications requiring modern elevators.

3.3.4 Exercises to the task

I. Brief answer to the question according to the text.

1. Where can we find PLC system?

2. What's the main difference between PLC and computer?

3. Which memory does the USB flash disk use?

4. What influences the scan time?

5. What is the automatic process of PLC?

6. What is a first-come first-served basis?

7. What is the dumb control?

II. Translate the following sentences into Chinese.

[1] In general, a Control System is a collection of electronic devices and equipment which are in place to ensure the stability, accuracy and smooth transition of a process manufacturing activity.

[2] Besides signal interfacing to the field devices (such as operator panel, motors, sensors, switches, solenoid valves and etc.), capabilities in network communication enable a big scale implementation and process co-ordination besides providing greater flexibility in realizing distributed control system.

[3] On the other hand, for detection of work piece, monitoring of moving mechanism, checking on pressure and or liquid level and many others, the PLC will have to tap the signal from the specific automatic sensing devices like proximity switch, limit switch, photoelectric sensor, and level sensor and so on.

[4] As a practical compromise between energy consumption and speed of response, we decided to combine all requests going in one direction (up or down), and then process them in sequential order.

3.3.5 Knowledge Widening: Reading Material

A PLC-based system consists of a CPU with both discrete and analog input and output devices. Connections to input and output devices are made through terminal strips, and these devices cover the full range of AC and DC voltages for inputs and up to 10 amps per point for output devices. Unlike a microcomputer, a PLC does not require a monitor but has the ability to have several types of peripheral devices connected to its view the status of the program that it is running. A microcomputer is one of the peripheral devices used to monitor and program PLCs. Hand-held programming devices may also be used to access and program PLCs. PLCs do not require a monitor or keyboard once they are programmed and running. PLCs run a reduced instruction set of commands designed only to solve a very specific set of programs. PLCs do not have the ability or the need to perform multi-tasking operations because they run only one program at any one time. Although PLCs have the ability to be connected to networks, these networks are usually only for PLCs of the same manufacturer and are extremely specialized. Most PLC designs available currently provide a link to the personal computer systems and mainframe computer systems. PLCs are normally designed for use in harsh industrial environments.

3.4 Sensors of the Elevators (Task 2)

Sensor is a device that when exposed to a physical phenomenon (temperature, displacement, force, etc.) produces a proportional output signal (electrical, mechanical, magnetic, etc.). The term transducer is often used synonymously with sensors. However, ideally, a sensor is a device that responds to a change in the physical phenomenon. On the other hand, a transducer is a device that converts one form of energy into another form of energy. Sensors are transducers when they sense one form of energy input and output in a different form of energy. For example, a thermocouple responds to a temperature change (thermal energy) and outputs a proportional change in electromotive force (electrical energy). Therefore, a thermocouple can be called a sensor and or transducer.

猜词断义 & 词义注释

displacement:

transducer
n. 传感器，换能器
synonymous
a. 同义的
thermocouple
n. 热电偶

3.4.1 The Classification of the Sensors (Text 4)

Linear and Rotational Sensors

Linear and rotational position sensors are two of the most fundamental of all measurements used in a typical mechatronic system. In general, the position sensors produce an electrical output that is proportional to the displacement they experience. There are contact type sensors such as strain gage, LVDT, RVDT, tachometer, etc. LVDT and RVDT are shown in Fig.3.9 and the operating principle of an LVDT is shown in Fig.3.10. The noncontact type includes encoders, hall effect, capacitance, inductance, and interferometer (Fig.3.11)type. They can also be classified based on the range of measurement. Usually the high-resolution type of sensors such as hall effect, fiber optic inductance, capacitance, and strain gage are suitable for only very small range (typically from 0.1 mm to 5 mm). The differential transformers on the other hand, have a much larger range with good

猜词断义 & 词义注释

experience:

gage
n. 测量(仪)
LVDT:
Linear Variable
 differential
Transformer 拉杆式位移传感器
RVDT:
Rotary Variable

resolution. Interferometer type sensors provide both very high resolution (in terms of microns) and large range of measurements (typically up to a meter). However, interferometer type sensors are bulky, expensive, and requires large set up time.

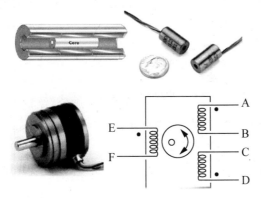

Fig. 3.9 LVDT and RVDT

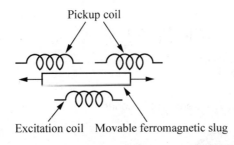

Fig. 3.10 Operating Principle of An LVDT

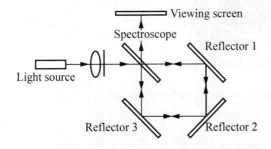

Fig. 3.11 Interferometer

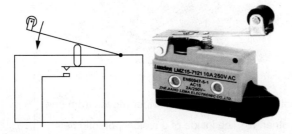

Fig. 3.12 A Typical Microswitch

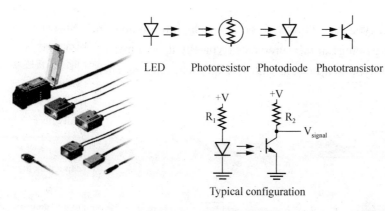

Fig. 3.13   Optoelectronic Circuit Symbols and
A Typical Emitter/Detector Configuration

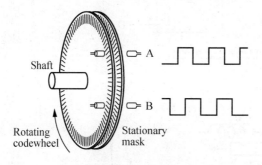

Fig. 3.14   Schematic of An Incremental Encoder

Fig. 3.15   An 8-bit Gray Code Absolute Encoder Disk

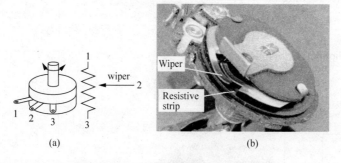

Fig. 3.16   (a) As the shaft of the potentiometer rotates, the wiper moves from one end of the resistive material to the other; (b) The inside of a typical potentiometer, showing the wiper contacting a resistive strip.

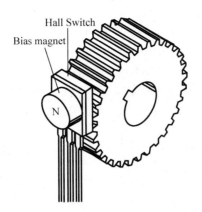

Fig. 3.17 Detecting Gear Teeth in A Ferrous Material Using A Hall Switch and A Bias Magnet

Acceleration Sensors

Measurement of acceleration is important for systems subject to shock and vibration. Although acceleration can be derived from the time history data obtainable from linear or rotary sensors, the accelerometers whose output is directly proportional to the acceleration is preferred.[1] A typical suspended-mass-vibrating string accelerometer is shown in Fig.3.18.

acceleration
n. 加速度

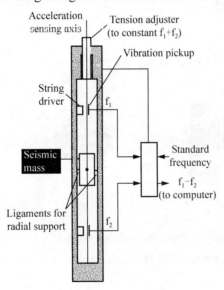

Fig. 3.18 A Typical Suspended-Mass-Vibrating String Accelerometer

Force, Torque, and Pressure Sensors

Among many type of force/torque sensors, such as Fig.3.19 to Fig.3.21 the strain gage dynamometers and piezoelectric type are most common. Both are available to measure force and/or torque either in one axis or multiple axes. The strain gage dynamometers make use of mechanical members that experiences elastic deflection when loaded. These types of sensors are limited by their natural frequency. On the other hand, the piezoelectric

dynamometer
测力计，功率计
piezoelectric
a. 压电的
elastic
a. 有弹性的

sensors are particularly suitable for dynamic loadings in a wide range of frequencies. They provide high stiffness, high resolution over a wide measurement range, and are compact. Piezoelectric sensors for quicker response of varying loads than pneumatic methods, strain gages, etc. The proper sensing technique needs special consideration based on the conditions required for monitoring.

dynamic
a. 有活力的，动的
stiffness
n. 坚硬，硬度

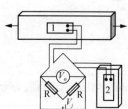

Fig. 3.19 Experimental Setup to Measure Normal Strain Using Strain Gages

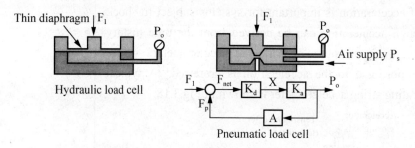

Fig. 3.20 Different Types of Load Cells

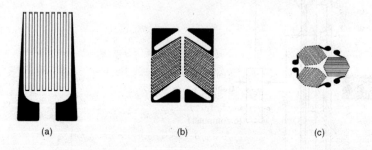

Fig. 3.21 Configuration of Metal-Foil Resistance Strain Gages
(a) Single element; (b) Two element; (c) Three element

3.4.2 Examples of the Sensors of the Elevators (Text 5)

BERO is the trade name used by Siemens to identify its line of "no-touch" sensors. Siemens BERO sensors operate with no mechanical contact or wear. In the following application, for example, a BERO sensor is used to determine if elevators are in the right position.

There are four types of BERO sensors: inductive, capacitive, ultrasonic, and photoelectric. Inductive proximity sensors use an electromagnetic field

猜词断义 &
词义注释

electrostatic
a. 静电的
quantity
n. 数量，大量

to detect the presence of metal objects, like Fig.3.22, for example. Capacitive proximity sensors use an electrostatic field to detect the presence of any object. Ultrasonic proximity sensors use sound waves to detect the presence of objects. Photoelectric sensors react on changes in the received quantity of light. Some photoelectric sensors can even detect a specific color.

Sensor	Objects Detected	Technology
Inductive	Metal	Electromagnetic Field
Capacitive	Any	Electrostatic Field
Ultrasonic	Any	Sound Waves
Photoelectric	Any	Light

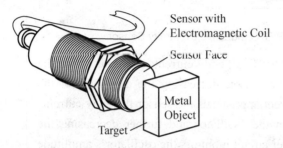

Fig. 3.22 The sensor incorporates an electromagnetic coil which is used to detect the presence of a conductive metal object. The sensor will ignore the presence of an object if it is not metal

incorporate
v. 包括，合并

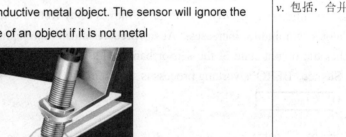

Fig. 3.23 Scanning of the position of elevator cabin with means of a magnet moving along the sensor plint

Siemens BERO inductive proximity sensors are operated using an Eddy Current Killed Oscillator (ECKO) principle. This type of sensor consists of four elements: coil, oscillator, trigger circuit, and an output, as shown in Fig.3.24. The oscillator is an inductive capacitive tuned circuit that creates a radio frequency. The electromagnetic field produced by the oscillator is emitted from the coil away from the face of the sensor. The circuit has just enough feedback from the field to keep the oscillator going.

eddy
n. 旋涡
ECKO:
涡流电流衰减振荡器

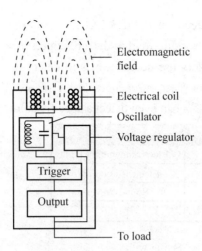

Fig. 3.24 Siemens BERO Inductive Proximity Sensor

When a metal target enters the field, eddy currents circulate within the target. This causes a load on the sensor, decreasing the amplitude of the electromagnetic field. As the target approaches the sensor the eddy currents increase, increasing the load on the oscillator and further decreasing the amplitude of the field. The trigger circuit monitors the oscillator's amplitude and at a predetermined level switches the output state of the sensor from its normal condition (On or Off). As the target moves away from the sensor, the oscillator's amplitude increases. At a predetermined level the trigger switches the output state of the sensor back to its normal condition (On or Off). Siemens BERO's working process is shown in Fig.3.25.

amplitude
n. 振幅

Fig. 3.25 Siemens BERO's Working Process

3.4.3 Exercises to the Task

I. Brief answer to the question according to the text.

1. Are there sensors in our home? Please illustrate some of them.

2. What's the difference between a sensor and a transducer?

3. Why are the interferometer type sensors bulky, expensive, and require large set up time?

4. What is LCD?

5. In the inductive, capacitive, ultrasonic, and photoelectric sensor, which one is preferable for the elevator, and why?

II. Translate the following sentences into Chinese.

Although acceleration can be derived from the time history data obtainable from linear or rotary sensors, the accelerometers whose output is directly proportional to the acceleration is preferred.

3.4.4 Knowledge Windening: Reading Material

For applications within health care, industrial automation, consumer products, and security there is a strong and growing need for wireless, self-powered sensors. Radio Frequency Identification Technology (RFID) is an example of an emerging application with great potential. Sensors with wireless connections and no internal power supply are anticipated to become of great importance in areas like health care, consumer products, and structural health monitoring. Energy tapping, i.e..

The Fig.3.26 illustrates a sensor field where a large number of connected sensor nodes are embedded. Each node will consist of a wireless sensor often without any internal power supply. The sensor interacts with a transceiver which is again connected to an infrastructure, possibly to a so-called sink. The collection of data may be controlled by a managing device.

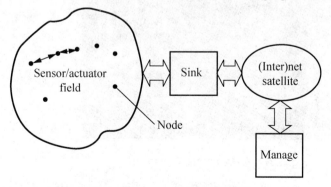

Fig. 3.26 Wireless Sensor Network

3.5 Hydraulic and Pneumatic Elevators (Task 3)

In a mechatronic system, the basic types of power sources include electrical, pneumatic, and hydraulic. Each source of energy and each type of motor has its own characteristics, advantages and limitations. An ac-powered or dc-powered motor may be used depending on the system design and applications. These motors convert electrical energy into mechanical energy to power the elevator. Most new robots and elevators use electrical power supply. Pneumatic actuators have been used for high speed, nonservo robots and are often used for powering tooling such as grippers. Hydraulic actuators have been used for heavier lift systems, typically where accuracy was not also required.

3.5.1 The Hydraulic and Pneumatic System (Text 6)

Hydraulic and pneumatic actuators are normally either rotary motors or linear piston/cylinder or control valves. They are ideally suited for generating very large forces coupled with large motion. Pneumatic actuators use air under pressure that is most suitable for low to medium force, short stroke, and high speed applications. Hydraulic actuators use pressurized oil that is incompressible. They can produce very large forces coupled with large motion in a cost-effective manner. The disadvantage with the hydraulic actuators is that they are more complex and need more maintenance. A pneumatic robot arm is shown in Fig.3.27.

猜词断义 & 词义注释

piston
n. 活塞
valve
n. 阀

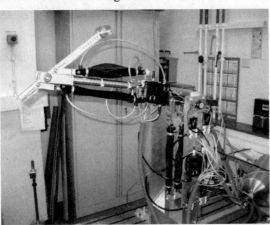

Fig. 3.27 A Pneumatic Robot Arm

All hydraulic systems depend on Pascal's law, named after Braise Pascal, who discovered the law. This law states that pressurized fluid within a closed container such as cylinder or pipe exerts equal force on all of the surfaces of the container.

fluid
n. 流体
container
n. 容器

Project III Elevator

In actual hydraulic systems, Pascal's law defines the basis of the results which are obtained from the system. Thus, a pump moves the liquid in the system. The intake of the pump is connected to a liquid source, usually called the tank or reservoir. Atmospheric pressure, pressing on the liquid in the reservoir, forces the liquid into the pump. When the pump operates, it forces liquid from the tank into the discharge pipe at a suitable pressure.

The flow of the pressurized liquid discharged by the pump is controlled by valves. Three control functions are used in most hydraulic systems: ① control of the liquid pressure; ② control of the liquid flow rate; and ③ control of the direction of flow of the liquid.

Pumps

Pumps transform electrical or mechanical energy into hydraulic energy. They constitute the fluid flow generator of the hydraulic system, as the pressure is determined by the fluid resistance downstream from the generator. External spur gear pump is shown in Fig.3.28. Rotary vane pump is shown in Fig.3.29. Axial piston swash plate pump is shown in Fig.3.30.

intake:

tank:

discharge:

pipe
n. 管子，管道

generator:

downstream
adv. 在下游，顺流地

Fig. 3.28 External Spur Gear Pump

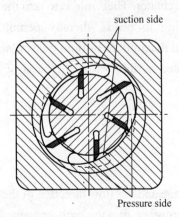

Fig. 3.29 Rotary Vane Pump

suction side
吸油腔

pressure side:

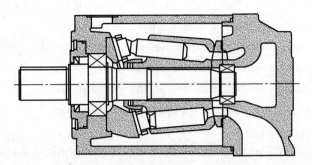

Fig. 3.30 Axial Piston Swash Plate Pump

Hydraulic Rotary Motors

Hydraulic rotary motors convert the hydraulic energy of the liquid under pressure into mechanical energy. These actuators are therefore volumetric hydraulic motors and are distinguished, on the basis of the type of movement generated, similar to what has been said about pumps. However, the operating principle is the opposite of what has been said for pumps. Hydraulic rotary actuator is shown in Fig.3.31.

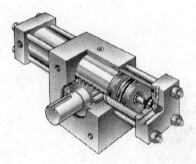

Fig. 3.31 Hydraulic Rotary Actuator

Valves

Valves are the components in hydraulic circuits that carry out the task of regulating the hydraulic power sent to the actuator. Their role is to turn the oil flow on or off or to divert it according to needs, thereby permitting adjustment of the two fundamental physical magnitudes of fluid transmission: pressure and flow rate. They are subdivided as follows on the basis of the operations they carry out.

- directional valves
- on-off valves
- pressure regulator valves
- flow-rate regulator valves

Directional valves determine the passage and the flow direction of the oil current by means of the movement of appropriate moving parts contained in them, actuated from outside. Directional valves, also known as distributors, are distinguished according to the type of mobile element and therefore of their internal structure, by the number of possible connections with external pipes and by the number of switching positions.

On-off valves are unidirectional valves, which permit the fluid to flow in one direction only. Because they impede flow in the opposite direction, they are also called nonreturn or check valves. On-off valves are normally placed in the hydraulic circuit between the pump and the actuator so that, when the generator stops, the fluid contained in the system is not discharged into the reservoir but remains in the piping. This prevents a waste of energy for subsequent refilling and guarantees positioning of the actuator under load.[1]

The function of the pressure regulator valves is to maintain a constant pressure valve downstream from them, independently from variations in the upstream pressure.[2] The regulated pressure value can be set manually, by means of a pilot signal, or by an electrical analog command. In the latter case, pressure regulator valves may operate in closed electrical loops, as they have an internal transducer to measure the controlled pressure. There are some valves symbols, as shown in Fig.3.32.

unidirectional:

impede
n. 阻碍，阻止

subsequent
a. 随后的，接连发生的

pilot:

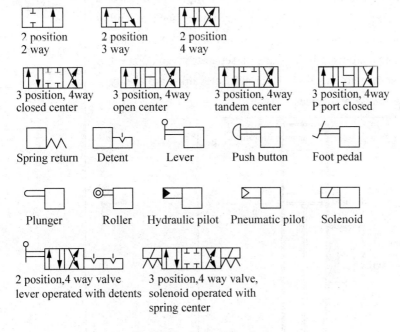

Fig. 3.32 Valves Symbols

Fluid Actuation System

Fig.3.33 illustrates a fluid actuation system. The power part consists of the actuator—a double-acting cylinder in the case in the figure—the front and rear chambers of which are fed by a 4/2 distributor valve, which constitutes the fluid power adjustment interface.

chamber
n. 腔

distributor valve
换向阀

The valve switching command is the order from the control part. This order is sent in accordance with the movement strategy, determined by the desired operating cycle of the cylinder in the control part, on the basis of the feedback signals from the sensors in the cylinder, represented in the figure by the limit switches.

strategy
n. 策略，方法

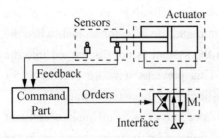

Fig. 3.33 Fluid Power Actuation System

3.5.2 Examples of Hydraulic System of Elevators (Text 7)

There are two types of elevators, hydraulic and traction. The hydraulic elevator consists of a cab attached to the top of a hydraulic jack similar to a jack used for a car lift in a service station. The hydraulic jack assembly normally extends below the lowest floor and is operated by a hydraulic pump and reservoir, both of which are usually located in a separate room adjacent to the elevator shaft, as shown in Fig.3.34. Hydraulic elevators are the type generally used in single-family residences.

猜词断义 & 词义注释

traction
n. 牵引，牵引力
extend:

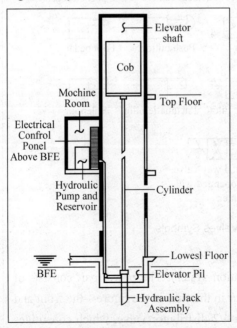

Fig. 3.34 Hydraulic Elevator

The jack assembly for a hydraulic elevator (Fig.3.34), by necessity, will be located below the lowest floor and therefore generally below the BFE. The jack is located in a casing, and while it will resist damage from small amounts of water seepage, total inundation by floodwaters will usually result in contamination of the hydraulic oil and possible damage to the cylinders and seals of the jack.[3] Salt water, because it is corrosive, can be particularly damaging. The hydraulic pump and reservoirs of the hydraulic elevator are also susceptible to water damage, but they can easily be located up to two floors above the jack and above the BFE as shown in Fig.3.34.

Some equipment common to all elevators will be damaged by floodwaters unless protected. The most obvious example is the elevator cab. However, in most elevator control systems, the cab automatically descends to the lowest floor upon loss of electrical power. Installing a system of interlocking controls with one or more float switches in the elevator shaft to always keep the elevator cab from descending into floodwaters will result in a much safer system, as shown in Fig.3.35. Some electrical equipment, such as electrical junction boxes and circuit and control panels, can be located above the BFE as shown in Fig.3.34. Other elevator components, such as doors and pit switches, must be located at or below the lowest floor. Where this becomes necessary, components may sometimes be replaced with more floodwater-resistant models.[4]

BFE
建筑物地基
casing
n. 包装，保护

seepage
n. 漏，渗
inundation
n. 淹没
contamination
n. 污染，污染物
seal
n. 密封
susceptible
a. 易受影响的

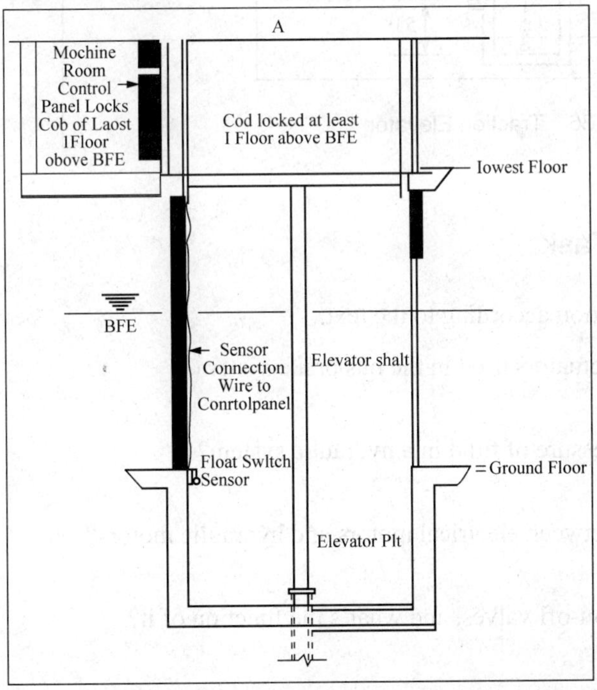

Fig. 3.35 Float and Control Mechanism to Control Cab Descent

junction box
接线盒

The second type is the traction elevator. This is the system that is most commonly associated with elevators. The traction system consists of a cable that is connected to the top of the cab and is operated by an electric motor located in a penthouse above the elevator shaft, as shown in Fig.3.36.

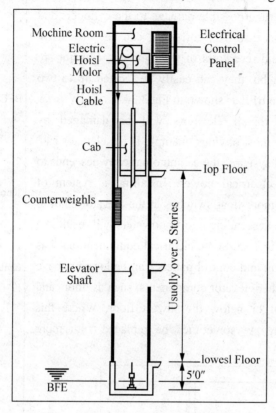

Fig. 3.36 Traction Elevator

3.5.3 Exercises to the Task

I. Brief answer to the question according to the text.

1. Why is the pneumatic actuators used in the bus brake system?

2. What determines the pressure of fluid in a hydraulic system?

3. What's the difference between electrical motors and hydraulic motors?

4. Where can we find the on-off valves, and what's the function of it?

5. What's the jack?

6. How does the elevator resist damage from water seepage?

7. Why does the cab automatically descend to the lowest floor upon loss of electrical power?

II. Translate the following sentences into Chinese.

[1] This prevents a waste of energy for subsequent refilling and guarantees positioning of the actuator under load.

[2] The function of the pressure regulator valves is to maintain a constant pressure valve downstream from them, independently from variations in the upstream pressure.

[3] The jack is located in a casing, and while it will resist damage from small amounts of water seepage, total inundation by floodwaters will usually result in contamination of the hydraulic oil and possible damage to the cylinders and seals of the jack.

[4] Where this becomes necessary, components may sometimes be replaced with more floodwater-resistant models.

3.5.4 Knowledge Widening: Reading Material

With the arrival of programmable controllers, the control design and concept improve tremendously. There are many advantages in using the programmable controllers.

A typical example of the PLC control panel is shown in Fig.3.37.

Fig. 3.37 Typical PLC Control Panel

- Here are the major advantages that can be distinguishably realized.
- The wiring of the system usually reduces by 80% compared to conventional relay control system.

- The power consumption is greatly reduced as PLC consumes much less power.
- The PLC self diagnostic functions enable easy and fast troubleshooting of the system.
- Modification of control sequence or application can easily be done by programming through the console or computer software without changing of I/O wiring, if no additional input or output devices are required.
- In PLC system spare parts for relays and hardware timers are greatly reduced as compared to conventional control panel.
- The machine cycle time is improved tremendously due to the speed of PLC operation is a matter of milliseconds. Thus, productivity increases.
- It costs much less compared to conventional system in situation when the number of I/Os is very large and control functions are complex.
- The reliability of the PLC is higher than the mechanical relays and timers.
- An immediate printout of the PLC program can be done in minutes. Therefore, hardcopy of documentation can be easily maintained.

3.6 Language Study

3.6.1 平行结构

平行结构就是句中表达同样意思的并列的两部分或以同样的语法形式连贯地表现出来的更多的部分。换句话说，就是主语和主语、谓语动词和谓语动词、宾语和宾语、或名词与名词、形容词与形容词、副词与副词、介词短语与介词短语、短语动词与短语动词、从句与从句、主句与主句平行。

平行结构一般由相关连词 and, or, either …or …, neither …nor …, not only …but also… 等引导。

当并列部分的语法形式不同时，就出现了平行结构错误。如：

(1) <u>To design a device</u> and <u>making it</u> are two different jobs. (错误)

(2) <u>Designing a device</u> and <u>making it</u> are two different jobs. (正确)

句(1)中，用动词表达式与动名词两个短语并列作主语不符合英语的表达要求；(2)句中，用两个动名词并列作主语符合英语结构。

(3) Galileo found it difficult to believe <u>that the sun rotates around the earth and the earth to be the centre of the universe</u>. (错误)

(4) Galileo found it difficult to believe <u>that the sun rotates around the earth and that the earth is the centre of the universe</u>. (正确)

句(3)中，并列的两个部分的语法结构不同，为错句；句(4)中，用两个宾语从句并列，故正确。

此外，注意莫犯低级错误：

I don't speak Cantonese and Mandarin. (错误)

I don't speak Cantonese or Mandarin. (正确)

and 连接有肯定意义的两个部分，or 连接有否定意义的两个部分。

又如：

He never swims and runs. (错误)

He never swims or runs. (正确)

3.6.2 专业英语词性的特点

在科技文体中，有些句子英汉两种语言的表达方式不同，不能逐词对译，这时需要转换词性，才能使译文通顺自然。词性转译大体有以下几种情况。

1. 英语动词、形容词、副词译成汉语名词

(1) A voltmeter connected across A B would read 10 Volts.

这里英语动词 read 译为汉语"读数"。整句译为：接在 AB 两点间的电压表的读数应当是 10V。

(2) The instrument is characterized by its compactness, and portability.

这里英语动词 characterized 译为汉语"特点"。整句译为：这个仪器的特点是结构紧凑、携带方便。

(3) The more carbon the steel contains, the harder and stronger it is.

这里英语形容词 harder, stronger 译为汉语"强度、硬度"。整句译为：钢的含碳量越高，强度和硬度就越大。

(4) The cutting tools must be strong, tough, hard and wear resistant.

这里英语形容词 strong, tough, hard 译为汉语"强度、韧性、硬度"。整句译为：刀具必须有足够的强度、韧性、硬度，而且要耐磨。

(5) The image must be dimensionally correct.

这里英语副词 dimensionally 译为汉语"尺寸"。整句译为：图形的尺寸必须正确。

2. 英语名词、介词、形容词译成汉语动词

(1) The application of electronic computers makes for a tremendous rise in labor productivity.

这里英语名词 application 译为汉语"使用"。整句译为：使用电子计算机可以大大提高劳动生产率。

(2) Atomic power for ocean-going vessels is already a reality.

这里英语介词 for 译为汉语"用于"。整句译为：原子能动力用于远洋船只已经成为现实。

(3) Scientists are confident that all matter is indestructible.

这里英语形容词 confident 译为汉语"坚信"。整句译为：科学家们坚信一切物质都是不可毁灭的。

3. 英语名词、副词和动词译成汉语形容词

(1) The maiden voyage of the newly-built steamship was a success.

这里英语名词 success 译为汉语"成功的"。整句译为：那艘新造的轮船的处女航是成功的。

(2) It is a fact that no structural material is perfectly elastic.

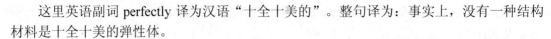

这里英语副词 perfectly 译为汉语"十全十美的"。整句译为：事实上，没有一种结构材料是十全十美的弹性体。

(3) It is a fact that such knowledge is <u>needed</u> before they develop a successful early warning system for earthquakes.

这里英语动词 need 译为汉语"必要的"。整句译为：事实上，这类知识对于他们要发明一种有效的地震早期警报系统是必要的。

4. 英语形容词、名词译成汉语副词

(1) A <u>continuous</u> increase in the temperature of the gas confined in a container will lead to a continuous increase in the internal pressure within the gas.

这里英语形容词 continuous 译为汉语"不断地"。整句译为：不断提高密封容器内气体的温度，会使气体内的压力不断增大。

(2) It is our great <u>pleasure</u> to note that China will sooner join the WTO.

这里英语名词 pleasure 译为汉语"高兴地"。整句译为：我们很高兴地了解到，中国不久就会加入世界贸易组织。

3.7　Practical Skill

3.7.1　获取段落的主题思想

作者写文章时总是围绕一个主题思想来组织写作材料的。许多读者如果在获取主题思想方面有困难时，就可以充分利用这一点。

阅读时，可以把获取主题思想的步骤分为以下 4 步。

(1) 辨认主题名词。

(2) 找出主题句。

(3) 获取主题思想。

(4) 避免不相关的内容。

1. 辨认主题名词

就大多数文章而言，获取主题思想的第一步就是确定一个最能描述作者中心思想的有关某人、某地或者某事的名词。

练习：

试选出主题名词。

(1) Rocks found on the surface of the earth are divided into three classes: igneous, sedimentary, and metamorphic. Molten material becomes igneous rock when it cools. Sedimentary rocks are formed from materials deposited by glaciers，plants，animals，stream, or winds. Metamorphic rocks are rocks that once were igneous or sedimentary but have changed as result of pressure，heat, or the deposit of material from solution.

Topic noun _____

(2) Water is fairly inexpressive and easy to obtain. This makes it a good tool for use in fighting many kinds of fires. Its properties as an extinguishing agent should be studied well.

Topic noun _____

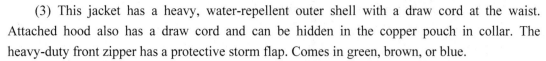

(3) This jacket has a heavy, water-repellent outer shell with a draw cord at the waist. Attached hood also has a draw cord and can be hidden in the copper pouch in collar. The heavy-duty front zipper has a protective storm flap. Comes in green, brown, or blue.

Topic noun _____

2. 找出主题句

一个段落的主题句就是最能表达作者主题思想的句子。主题句通常就是段落中的第一句话，当然有时它也会在后面出现，甚至是段落的最后一句话。

练习：

试画出下面练习中的主题句。

(1) In the early days of big-city post offices, a great deal of time was spent in getting mail from the main station to the substations and from stations to trains. Then compressed air came into use as a means of speeding up the movement of mail from place to place. Long tubes were built under the ground to connect different mail-handling sites, and hollow containers were made to fit the tubes. Mail was put into the containers, the containers were put into the tubes, and compressed air was used to propel the containers to their destinations. Some cities still have many miles of mail tubes. Smaller tubes are used in many libraries, stores, and factories.

(2) Today's marketplace is crowded with sellers competing for your money and your attention by offering different services, prices, specials, bonuses, and quality of goods. There are so many kinds of stores and deals that it is hard to keep them straight. To get the best bargain you need to carefully weigh the advantages and disadvantages of each deal before making your final selection.

(3) The class of drugs known as depressants act to slow down the functioning of the central nervous system. They relax the body and are often used to induce sleep or alleviate pain. When too large a dose is taken, depressant drugs induce a state of drunken intoxication and produce slurred speech, blurred vision, slowed reaction time, and loss of coordination. The depressant drugs are highly addictive and include alcohol, opiates, barbiturates, and minor tranquilizers.

(4) If your car is stopped in a blizzard, by all means stay in it. Trying to walk outside in a blizzard can be extremely dangerous. In blowing and drifting snow, disorientation comes, very rapidly. Being lost in open country during a blizzard can be fatal. If you stay in your car you are most likely to be found and the cams will provide a great deal of protection firm the elements.

3. 获取主题思想

在获取主题思想时，读者通常将主题的一小部分看作主题思想，或者概况内容过多，超出了作者所要表达的主题思想的范围。

练习：

阅读下面各段文章，判断哪句能够正确表达主题思想。

(1) Handling children's anger can be very distressing to adults. Often the distress is the result of being unable to deal with our own anger. Parents, teachers, counselors and others who deal with children need to remember that they may not be very good at dealing with their own anger. As children and many of us were taught that anger was bad and were made to feel guilty for expressing anger.

① Children can be very hard for adults to deal with.

② Our own anger can make it hard to deal with children's anger.

③ Children sometimes make us angry.

④ Teachers must learn to handle their own anger in order to learn how to deal with children's anger.

(2) Lead, cadmium, and mercury are elements that have been found to be harmful to humans. They seem to be completely unnecessary to health. Cadmium, for example, interferes with the functions of iron, copper, and calcium, which are necessary for health. People exposed to large amounts of cadmium may suffer anemia, kidney damage, and bone deficiencies.

① Cadmium is harmful to humans.

② Lead, cadmium, and mercury are harmful to humans and are unnecessary for health.

③ Lead is harmful to humans and has no beneficial properties.

④ Some minerals are harmful to human health.

(3) When the weather is clear, pilots use their eyes to keep the airplane flying straight and level. In low-visibility situations, however, the eye and other orientation senses, such as our sense of balance, are not only useless, they may be totally misleading. The only safe way to fly an airplane in low-visibility conditions is to use instruments which indicate the attitude of the airplane.

① In bad weather, the senses can be misleading.

② Flying an airplane can be very difficult.

③ When visibility is low the only safe way to fly an airplane is by using flight instruments.

④ When the weather is clear, pilots use their eyes to keep the airplane flying straight and level.

(4) Any advertisement that claims a product will result in dramatic changes in your body in a short time should be viewed with suspicion. Often such claims are designed to make the promoter rich at your expense. In some cases these products do nothing at all. In other cases they are positively dangerous.

① Products which are claimed to make dramatic and rapid changes in the body may be useless or dangerous.

② Many products which claim to change your body rapidly do nothing at all.

③ Many products which make tic claims about changing your body in a short time are dangerous.

4. 避免不相关的内容

读者在获取主题思想时容易犯的另一个普遍错误就是头脑中出现一些与文章主题思想不相关的概念，并把它们看作文章的主题思想。在阅读文章之前，读者可能对作者所表述的主题方面有些了解，往往会带着已经了解到的知识和形成的思想去阅读文章，容易主观臆断，受到文章中不相关内容的影响，从而偏离作者的思想主线。总之，读者不能先入为主，不能用自己的想法代替文章的主题思想。

练习：

试选出下列与作者的主题思想相一致的选项。

(1) Movies are actually separate still pictures shown so fast that the human eye cannot detect the break between them. When successive images are presented rapidly enough, we fuse them into a single moving image.

① Movies are extremely popular.

② Modern movie rake much use of slow motion.

③ Motion pictures are separate pictures shown so fast that we see no break between them.

④ Motion pictures require an expensive camera, capable of making very rapid multiple exposures.

(2) Blue dye is only one of the many chemicals that are changed by light. Any chemical which is changed by light is said to be "sensitive to light". If there were no light-sensitive chemicals, we would not be able to make photographs.

① Light-sensitive chemicals are always blue.

② If a chemical, such as blue dye is changed by light, it is said to be "sensitive to light".

③ Blue dye is the only chemical which is changed by light.

④ Without blue dye, there would be no photography.

(3) Spelling skills are very important in modern life. People often form an impression of us based on what we have written. If what we have written is full of misspellings, their impression of us suffers. Some of us may have difficulty learning the principles of good spelling, but if we are to make a favorable impress on our teachers, associates, employers, and other people we communicate with in writing, these principles must be learned.

① Spelling skills are not very important, for some people.

② Spelling skills are very important.

③ Some words are harder to spell than others.

④ Spelling principles are very easy to learn.

(4) Sharks are classified as meat-eating fish. There are about 250 species of sharks in the world's ocean. Most sharks eat live fish. Although they are thought of as dangerous to people, there are fewer than 100 shark attacks in the world each year. Most shark species will not attack humans.

① Sharks have very poor eyesight.

② Sharks are not as dangerous to humans as most people think.

③ In some parts of the world sharks are eaten as food.

④ Shark skeletons are made of cartilage rather than bone.

3.7.2 多重复合句的阅读技巧

多重复合句句子较长，结构较为复杂，往往由一个主句和一个或一个以上的从句组成，主句和从句或从句之间形成多重嵌套。专业英语要求准确详尽地描述客观事实，在一些论述性较强的文章中，多重复合句用得较多，句子也较长。

例句分析如下。

(1) The program controls the PLC so that when an input signal from an input device turns

ON, the appropriate response is made.

主句由 the program controls the PLC 构成，so that 引导结果状语从句，so that 结果状语从句中嵌套 when 引导的时间状语从句。

(2) When we look into the matter carefully, we will find that the world we live in presents an endless variety of fascinating problems which excite our wonder and curiosity.

主句 we will find 有两个从句：时间状语从句 when …在前面，宾语从句 that …在后面。宾语从句中又有两个定语从句：第一个定语从句是 we live in 插在它中间，第二个定语从句是 which excite our wonder and curiosity 跟在它后面。

(3) Galileo's greatest glory was that in 1609 he was the first person to turn the newly invented telescope on the heavens to prove that the planets revolve around the sun rather than around the Earth.

主句为 Galileo's greatest glory was that …，引导一个表语从句，表语从句内又嵌套宾语从句 that the planets revolve around the sun rather than around the Earth。

遇到多重复合句之类的长句难句时，不要囫囵吞枣，而是要耐心地层层分析、层层剥离，把一个复杂的句子，拆成一个个分句进行分析。首先要找出谓语(谓语的形式比较明显，容易发现)，然后再找出它的主语。英语句子不像汉语那样经常省略主语，而是由主语和谓语一起构成句子的核心。其次要找出连接词。英语和汉语的另一个不同就是汉语句子的分句之间常常没有连接词，而英语句子的分句之间一般都有连接词。找到了连接词就找到了分句间的界限和它们之间的关系。

练习：

试分析下列多重复合句。

(1) The construction of such a satellite is now believed to be quite realizable (可实现的), its realization being supported with all the achievements of contemporary science, which have brought into being not only materials capable of withstanding severe stresses involved and high temperatures developed, but new technological processes as well.

(2) It also means that governments are increasingly compelled to interfere in these sectors in order to step up production and ensure that it is utilized to the best advantage: for example, they may encourage research in various ways, including the setting up of their own research centers; they may alter the structure of education, or interfere in order to reduce the wastage of natural resources or tap resources hitherto unexploited; or they may co-operate directly in the growing number of international projects related to science, economies and industry, such as the International Atomic energy Agency the European Iron and Steel Community or the various Common Markets.

Project IV MP4 Player

4.1 The Lead-in of the Project

Fig.4.1 shows two models of the iPod Video. There are 80GB and 30GB models and the later revision had a thinner back case. The insides are almost identical, as shown in Fig.4.2, so Apple will only be covering the different back case pictured above.

猜词断义 & 词义注释

identical: _____

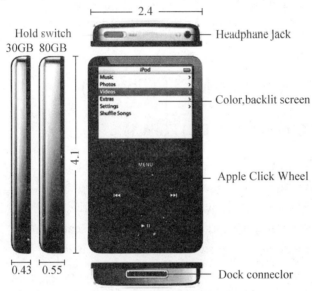

Fig. 4.1 The Aspect of iPod Video

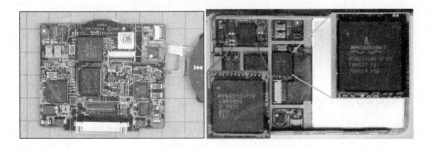

Fig. 4.2 Inner Chips of iPod Video

The new Apple iPod Video employs Broadcom's BCM2722 multimedia/video processor. Apple's choice of the Broadcom multimedia/video processor supports an extension of the capabilities of prior-generation iPods into video playback, while the latent features of the BCM2722 suggest the possibility of a further expansion of the iPod family tree, including potentially the introduction of iPods that support image capture.

4.2 The Contents of the Project

When all the circuitry for a digital computer is contained on one integrated circuit, the unit is called a microcomputer. Even though there are self-contained memory and I/O circuits contained in a microcomputer, external circuits of the same type may be added, especially memory. As a result, there are many variations between microprocessors and microcomputers. Memory, I/O, signal conditioning, timing and control many times are added to adapt the particular IC to an application, or to a market requirement. A particular type of microcomputer, now called a microcontroller unit (MCU), has been adapted to the industrial control market.

猜词断义 & 词义注释

integrated circuit
集成电路
variation:

4.3 What is MCU (Task 1)

4.3.1 Analog-to-Digital Converters (ADC) (Text 1)

As shown in Fig.4.3, the digital data from the ADC, represented in codes, is manipulated by computing networks to alter, modify and redefine the data, but it emerges from the computing networks again as a series of digital codes, again timed by the timing network.[1] The codes are presented to the DAC to be converted back to an analog signal. The circuit discussion begins with a DAC.

猜词断义 & 词义注释

timing network
定时网络

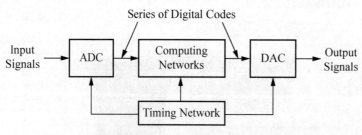

Fig. 4.3 Computing Network Manipulates Digital Data

The input portion of Fig.4.3 is an ADC, an analog-to-digital converter. One of the earliest ADCs was the counting ADC shown in Fig.4.4. It is made up of a binary counter that counts pulses from a central clock. The counters binary output is fed to two units—a DAC and a latch. Each unit has the number of input or output bit lines to cover the number of bits required from the ADC.

latch
n. 锁存器

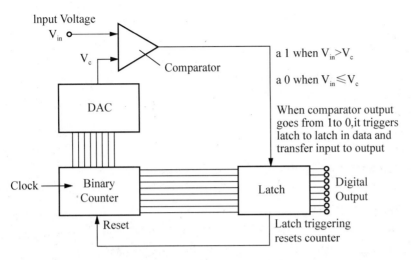

Fig. 4.4 An 8-bit Counting ADC

Notice the DAC in the loop. This is the reason that the discussion of the DAC came first. The binary code input to the DAC produces an analog voltage that feeds one input of a comparator. The analog input voltage to be converted to a digital output is the other comparator input. When the input from the DAC is lower than the analog input, the comparator will be a high voltage (a digital 1); when the input from the DAC is equal to or greater than the analog input, the comparator output is a low voltage (a digital 0). When the comparator output changes from a high voltage to a low voltage, it triggers the latch to latch in the binary values from the bit lines of the counter. Thus, the output of the latch is the binary code matching the value of the input analog voltage.

The A to D process works like this. The counter is reset to a count of zero. The DAC output is zero as a result. If the analog input voltage, V_{in}, is some positive value, the comparator output will be a 1. As the clock increments the counter, the output of the DAC will increase in steps, each a small positive voltage. If the DAC output is a lower positive voltage than V_{in}, the counter continues to count and increases the DAC output voltage until it is greater than V_{in}. This triggers the comparator, its output goes to 0 to latch in the binary code at the output to the ADC and reset the counter. Resetting the counter to zero causes the comparator output to go to a 1 and the ADC is ready for another conversion. One of the disadvantages of the counting ADC is the time for conversion. The conversion time can be as great as $2^n - 1$ clock cycles, where n is the number of bits of the binary output of the ADC.

increment
n. 增加,增长

Example: Maximum Conversion Time for Counting ADC

What is the maximum conversion time for an 8-bit, 12-bit and 16-bit counting ADC when the clock frequency is 1 MHz?

Solution:

The maximum conversion time is $2^n - 1$ clock cycles; therefore, since the period of a 1 MHz clock is 1 μs,

N	$2^n - 1$	Max. Conversion time
8	255	255 μs = 0.255 ms
12	4095	4095 μs = 4.095 ms
16	32767	32767 μs = 32.767 ms

4.3.2 Introduction of MCU (Text 2)

Previous paragraphs have sensed the analog signal, conditioned the signal and converted it from analog to digital. The processing of the digital signal to modify, calculate, manipulate, change the form of the signal or to route the signal to particular channels may be needed to accomplish a task predetermined by the application that is being fulfilled.[2] The total system is designed to perform a task, and the digital processor is a very important part of the system.

Fig.4.5 is a diagram of a generalized central processing unit (CPU). The main components are the program counter, the instruction register, the instruction decoder, the data address register, the arithmetic and logic unit (ALU), the timing and control circuits, and the permanent and temporary storage. As discussed previously, a digital code, called an instruction, organized in sequence into a program, is sent to the CPU to instruct it to execute a particular operation. The instruction came from a memory address contained in an instruction address register called the program counter. The program is stored in memory one address after another in sequence so the program counter holding the address can be incremented by one to step through the program instructions one step after the other. Thus, the name for the address register is the program counter. Each instruction address from the program counter addresses the next step in the program as the task proceeds.

Traditionally, increased processing throughput has been achieved by increasing the processor clock frequency. Unfortunately, increasing the clock rate has a direct effect on power consumption which may be unacceptable in some portable applications. An alternative to increasing the clock frequency is to modify the processor architecture to increase the amount of computation that can be done with each cycle.[3]

Some of the factors that affects a CPU efficiency to execute a particular function include: ① the number of cycles used to move data into and out of the processor (load/store operations); ② the execution efficiency of individual instructions in the pipeline; ③ branches; ④ the programming

猜词断义 & 词义注释

sense:

condition v. 制约，影响，决定

route v. 沿特定路线发送，沿特定方向移动

register n. 寄存器

permanent
a. 永久的，永恒的

temporary
a. 临时的，暂时的

词义拓展

contemporary:

program counter 程序计数器，也称为指令地址寄存器

throughput
n. 吞吐量

consumption
n. 消耗

portable:

近形记忆

alternative
alternate

model; and ⑤ program code density.

Several steps can be taken to improve the computational throughput of the CPU.

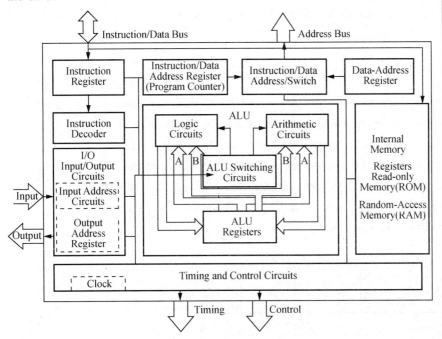

Fig. 4.5 A Generalized CPU

Reduce the amount of load/store cycles. More than 30% of the instructions executed in RISC (Reduced Instruction Set Computing) architecture are load or store instructions, each of which takes one or more cycles. Reducing the number of load/store cycles can have a substantial effect on processor throughput.

Streamline repetitive operations. Some algorithms, such as those for multimedia, contain operations that are repeated thousands of times on streams of data. For example, some algorithms contain many repetitive operations that must be executed on every pixel of an image during MPEG-4 encoding. Performing these operations on multiple data simultaneously (Single Instruction Multiple Data or SIMD) results in a linear reduction in cycles required to process the data stream.

Maximize utilization of pipeline resources. Some arithmetic operations take a single cycle while others take several cycles. For example, a division operation can take 32 cycles to execute. If the processor must wait for a multi-cycle operation to complete before issuing a new instruction, the other resources in the pipeline will be under-utilized.

Improve code density. Since memory is relatively inexpensive, few people worry about code density. However, with processors that rely on an instruction cache for fast performance, code density can have a direct effect on performance. If the code is smaller, more instructions can be stored in the cache, resulting in fewer caches "misses" and fewer cycle-intensive fetches from external memory. Reducing the traffic on the main system bus can also significantly reduce power consumption.

bus
n. 总线

4.3.3　Examples of MCU inside MP4 Players (Text 3)

Atmel has developed a high-performance 32-bit RISC processor core with an instruction set architecture that vastly increases the computational throughput per cycle while also delivering ultra-low power consumption. The AVR32 core, as shown in Fig.4.6, minimizes penalties from load/store and branch operations and maximizes pipeline throughput, allowing complex algorithms to be executed with a much lower clock frequency and power consumption than conventional processors.

猜词断义 & 词义注释

penalty
n. 损失，出错

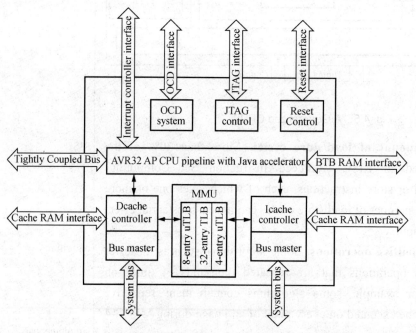

Fig. 4.6　AVR32 Architecture

On target algorithms, the AVR32 achieves 35% more throughput per instruction cycle than an ARM11 core. It can execute 30 frame per second (fps) quarter-VGA MPEG-4 decoding with a clock frequency of just 100MHz compared to the 150 to 175 MHz required in the ARM11 architecture, as shown in Fig.4.7.

frame:

Minimizes cycles expended for load/store operations. The AVR32 architecture has load/store instructions supporting byte (8bit), half-word

(16bit), word (32bit) and double word (64bit) widths. The instructions are combined with various pointer arithmetic to efficiently access tables, data structures and random data. Instructions for loading bytes and half-words all have optional sign or zero extension of the data value.

pointer
n. 指针
access:
―――――

一词多义

access:
―――――

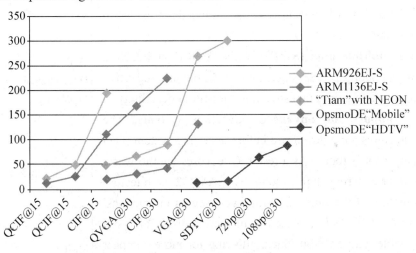

Fig. 4.7 ARM® Processor Core MPEG-4 Decoding

Multiple pipelines support out-of-order execution. Generally, processors execute instructions one at a time, as they enter the pipeline. If a particularly complex instruction requires multiple clock cycles, the pipeline is stalled until that instruction is complete. Available computational resources are left idle during this instruction. The AVR32 has extensive logic in the pipeline that allows it to accomplish more processing per cycle. The AVR32 has three pipelines (load/store, multiplier and ALU) that allow arithmetic operations on non-dependent data to be executed out of order, as shown in Fig.4.8.

stall
v. 熄火，抛锚
idle
a. 空闲的，闲着的

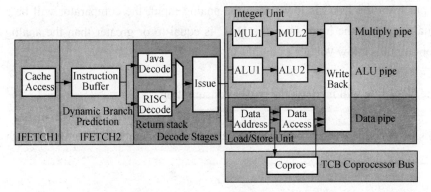

Fig. 4.8 Multiple Pipeline Supports

Another cycle-saving feature of the AVR32 is the data forwarding between the pipeline stages. Instructions that finish execution before the

data forwarding
数据前送

write back stage are immediately forwarded to the beginning of the pipelines if there are instructions waiting for the results. For instance when an add instruction finishes in the ALU1 pipeline stage, the result is forwarded back to the MUL1, ALU1 and Data Address stages. This allows the result to be used one cycle after the add was issued instead of waiting three cycles to pass it to the write back stage.

Single-instruction multiple data (SIMD) in the AVR32 architecture can quadruple the throughput of DSP algorithms that require repetitive operation on a stream of data (e.g. motion estimation for MPEG decoding).

Instruction set support for advanced operating systems. The majority of CPU architectures were developed before operating system (OS) use became as pervasive as it is today. As a result, CPU cores tend to waste cycles calling the OS or external applications. The AVR32 architecture specifically supports the use of the Linux OS with cycle-saving instructions. These include an Application Call (ACALL) instruction that calls sub routines from a jump table with an 8-bit index, allowing for more compact code, and a System Call (SCALL) instruction that issues a call to the operating system routine. The AVR32 comes fully-featured with an advanced MMU and security modes to support advanced operating systems such as Linux.

DSP:
Digital Signal Processing
数字信号处理

ACALL
程序调用指令
SCALL
系统调用指令

MMU:
Memory Unit

4.3.4 Exercises to the Task

I. Write a T in front of a statement if it is true and write an F if it is false according to the text.

1. The microprocessor and microcomputer, now called microcontroller unit (MCU), has been adapted to the industrial control.

2. When the input from the DAC is lower than the analog input, the comparator will be a high voltage (a digital 0); when the input from the DAC is equal to or greater than the analog input, the comparator output is a low voltage (a digital 1).

3. Increasing the clock rate will increase the power consumption.

4. During MPEG-4 encoding, RISC performs these repetitive operations on multiple data simultaneously.

5. AVR32 need more clock frequency to execute instruction than an ARM11.

6. Out-of-order execution means disordering to execute the instructions.

II. Translate the following sentences into Chinese.

[1] As shown in Fig.4.3, the digital data from the ADC, represented in codes, is manipulated by computing networks to alter, modify and redefine the data, but it emerges from the computing networks again as a series of digital codes, again timed by the timing network.

[2] The processing of the digital signal to modify, calculate, manipulate, change the form of the signal or to route the signal to particular channels may be needed to accomplish a task predetermined by the application that is being fulfilled.

[3] An alternative to increasing the clock frequency is to modify the processor architecture to increase the amount of computation that can be done with each cycle.

4.3.5 Knowledge Widening: Reading Material

The ARM926EJ-S processor is a member of the ARM9 family of general-purpose microprocessors. The ARM926EJ-S processor is targeted at multi-tasking applications where full memory management, high performance, low die size, and low power are all important.

The ARM926EJ-S processor supports the 32-bit ARM and 16-bit Thumb instruction sets, enabling the user to trade off between high performance and high code density. The ARM926EJ-S processor includes features for efficient execution of Java byte codes, providing Java performance similar to JIT, but without the associated code overhead.

The ARM926EJ-S processor supports the ARM debug architecture and includes logic to assist in both hardware and software debug. The ARM926EJ-S processor has a Harvard cached architecture and provides a complete high-performance processor subsystem, including:
- an ARM9EJ-S integer core;
- a Memory Management Unit (MMU);
- separate instruction and data AMBA AHB bus interfaces;
- separate instruction and data TCM interfaces.

The ARM926EJ-S processor provides support for external coprocessors enabling floating-point or other application-specific hardware acceleration to be added. The ARM926EJ-S processor implements ARM architecture version 5TEJ.

The ARM926EJ-S processor is a synthesizable macrocell. This means that you can optimize the macrocell for a particular target library, and that you can configure the memory system to suit your target application. You can individually configure the cache sizes to be any power of two between 4KB and 128KB.

The tightly-coupled instruction and data memories are instantiated externally to the ARM926EJ-S macrocell, providing you with the flexibility of optimizing the memory subsystem for performance, power, and particular RAM type. The TCM interfaces enable nonzero wait state memory to be attached, as well as providing a mechanism for supporting DMA.

4.4 Semiconductor Materials (Task 2)

4.4.1 What is Semiconductor (Text 4)

A conductor is an element whose electrons can move freely and an insulator is one whose electrons are stuck tightly in place. An atom, you recall if you have learn, has a nucleus of protons and neutrons. This nucleus has a positive charge. Whizzing around that nucleus is a cloud of electrons, normally just enough to make the atom's electric charge neutral.

Each electron has an energy level which could refer to how fast it is moving, and these energy levels are almost digital in nature. An electron could have an energy of "1" or "2" but never "1.25". This discrete separation of energy levels is known as energy quanta.

Each orbital shell is associated with a particular energy level. Only electrons with the correct amount of energy can live in a given shell. If you add a quantum of energy e to an electron by, perhaps, banging on it with a hammer or shining a light on it, the electron can no longer stay in its current shell but must jump to a higher energy shell (Fig.4.9).

猜词断义 & 词义注释

stick:

proton　*n.* 质子
neutron　*n.* 中子
whiz　*v.* 飞驰
neutral　*a.* 中性的
digital in nature:

discrete　*a.* 分离的，不相干的
quanta　*n.* 量子
orbital　*a.* 轨道的
shell　*n.* 壳层
bang　*v. n.* 撞击
hammer　*n.* 锤子

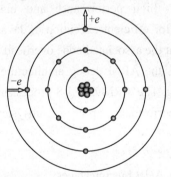

Fig. 4.9　Silicon Atom

Each orbital shell can hold a limited number of electrons and no more. The inner shells of an atom are normally all full. We work with the outer shells because they are often not full. If we add energy to an atom, an electron will jump from an outer shell to an even higher energy shell. Similarly, that electron will drop back down to its regular level when it loses its energy.

The "normal" outer shell of an atom is the valence and the energy level of that shell is its valence band. The next band out is the conduction band. When an electron is in the conduction band, it is very loosely bound to the atom and can be easily pushed into a neighboring atom's conduction band.

work with:

The amount of energy needed to jump an electron from the valence to the conduction band is the band gap (Fig.4.10).

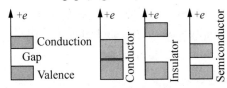

Fig. 4.10 Valence and Conduction Bands

Conductors have a very small band gap so that the energy available at room temperature kicks a bunch of the conductor's electrons into the conduction band. An insulator has a large band gap. It takes a lot of energy to kick an electron out of its valence band and into the loosely held conduction band. Semiconductors have a medium-sized band gap and are mostly insulators.

room temperature:

4.4.2 Application of Semiconductor Materials (Text 5)

Silicon (Si, element 14) is a semiconductor. At room temperature, silicon conducts a little bit. The energy available during normal operating conditions kicks some of its valence electrons into the conduction band. Not many, maybe one in a billion, but enough to create a perceptible current.

The colder the silicon is, the less it will conduct because the electrons lose their energy and fall back into the valence band. A simple component, the thermistor, takes advantage of this feature, changing its resistance based on the temperature.

The conduction behavior of a silicon semiconductor can be adjusted by alloying it with small amounts of impurities, or dopants. Silicom crystal is shown in Fig.4.11.

猜词断义 & 词义注释

one in a billion:

perceptible
a. 可感受到的

component:

thermistor
n. 热敏电阻
impurity *n.* 杂质
dopant *n.* 掺杂物

Fig. 4.11 Silicon Crystal

Since only the outer shell interacts with the neighboring atoms, we simplify the atom and draw only this outer shell and its four electrons. Silicon creates covalent bonds with four of its neighbors, meaning they share electrons in the valance shell. The valence shell in silicon has four electrons but has room for four more. It is these empty slots in the shell that are filled by electrons from neighboring atoms. This creates a tight bond between the atoms and keeps the electrons firmly in place.

What if you added some phosphorus (P, element 15) to the silicon? Phosphorus has five electrons in its valence shell, but will still form covalent bonds with silicon. Fig.4.12 shows this, though it is hard to see. With five electrons but only four of them tied in a covalent bond, there is an unbound electron. This electron is free to jump into the conduction band, giving this alloy more free electrons.

interact:

covalent bond
共价键
slot:

phosphorus
n. 磷

unbound
a. 束缚的

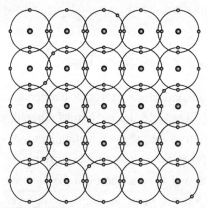

Fig. 4.12   N-type Semiconductor (Silicon and Phosphorus)

A semiconductor with these free electrons is an N-type semiconductor. Note that the material still has a neutral charge, the same way that copper has a neutral charge. There are simply more loose electrons available to move when a voltage differential is created.

What if you added some boron (B, element 5) to the mix? Boron has only three electrons in its valence shell, but will still form covalent bonds with silicon. Fig.4.13 shows this. In this case, there are a number of covalent bonding positions that are not filled by the boron. These holes are places where a free electron can get stuck. This type of alloy is a P-type semiconductor. Again, it is electrically neutral. It is interesting to note that electron holes are mobile in the same way that free electrons are. As such, they are considered charge carriers. In most explanations, electron holes are said to carry a positive charge.

boron   n. 硼

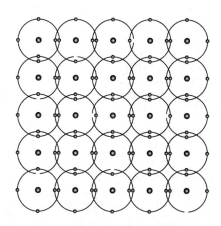

Fig. 4.13 P-type Semiconductor (Silicon and Boron)

A transistor behaves like a variable resistor or, using the water analogy, a water faucet. The basic transistor is the bipolar junction transistor, or BJT. Transistors come in two flavors, NPN and PNP. Note that transistors are not digital, but are analog switches.

As the name suggests, an NPN transistor consists of three pieces of material, a thin P-type semiconductor with N-type semiconductors on either side (Fig.4.14). This is like two diodes placed together back to back (Fig.4.15). The transistor's schematic symbol even reflects this two-diode shape. Using just the block diagrams that show the depletion zone, let's do a quick tour through the transistor's operation. The sequence is shown in Fig.4.16. Fig.4.16(a) shows the raw N-P-N configuration. Note the depletion zones on both sides of the P section.

transistor
n. 三极管
bipolar
a. 有两极的
junction
n. 接口
diode   *n.* 二极管

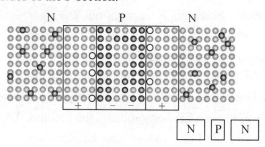

Fig. 4.14 NPN Transistor

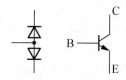

Fig. 4.15 NPN Transistor Symbol (Two Diodes)

depletion
n. 损耗，减压

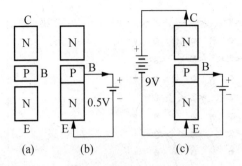

Fig. 4.16 NPN Transistor Operation

In transistor terminology, the center of the transistor is the base and is marked with a B. One of the ends is the emitter (E) and the other is the collector (C). If you connect the emitter and collector into a circuit right now, no current would pass through the transistor because the depletion zones insulate these sides from each other.

What if you were to apply a small, say half-volt, charge between the base and the emitter (Fig.4.16(b))? These two sections, by themselves, are a diode and you would have forward biased it. The insulating layer between the emitter and base is reduced just enough so that it can conduct.

Now, what if you connect a larger charge, say 9V, between the emitter and collector (Fig.4.16(c))? The emitter-base diode is not directly affected, since we aren't letting more than a half volt of charge out of the base. The collector develops a large positive charge as its electrons escape, and there is plenty of negative charge at the emitter from the large battery.[1]

There is, however, still that insulating layer between the base and the collector. Doesn't that stop the current? Interestingly enough, no. The base layer is thin enough, and the charge difference between the base and collector is large enough, that most of the electrons zoom through the emitter and jump across the gap into the collector.[2] Current flows from the emitter to the collector as long as the voltage differential across the emitter-base junction keeps that insulating layer thin. If you remove the base voltage, the emitter-collector current stops. If you increase the base voltage, the emitter-base insulator is even thinner and more electrons make it across to the collector. The emitter-collector current increases.

The name transistor is short for transfer resistor. The voltage at the base of the transistor controls the current flow across the rest of it. It is, in fact, a voltage-controlled variable insulator. As fundamental as transistors are, I don't recommend using them unless you are interested in designing low-level circuits. For most electronic switch applications, the MOSFET is a better device. If you are looking to amplify a signal, you are probably better off buying a commercially designed amplifier on an integrated circuit.

base:

emitter:

collector:

bias v. 加偏压

say:

MOSFET:
全氧半场效晶体管
Metal-Oxide-
Semiconductor
Field-Effect
Transistor

4.4.3 Exercises to the Task

I. Write a T in front of a statement if it is true and write an F if it is false according to the text.

1. Each electron has an energy level, and the separated energy level is known as energy quanta.

2. The amount of energy is needed to push an electron into a neighboring atom's conduction band.

3. The conduction behavior of a silicon semiconductor can be adjusted by itself.

4. Silicon creates covalent bonds with three of its neighbors, so the empty slot is negative.

5. The NPN-type transistor and the PNP-type are the same typical transistor.

6. The author considers the transistor used for amplifier is appropriate.

II. Translate the following sentences into Chinese.

[1] The collector develops a large positive charge as its electrons escape, and there is plenty of negative charge at the emitter from the large battery.

[2] The base layer is thin enough, and the charge difference between the base and collector is large enough, that most of the electrons zoom through the emitter and jump across the gap into the collector.

4.4.4 Knowledge Widening: Reading Material

The MOSFET

The MOSFET (pronounced "MOSS-fet") stands for metal-oxide-semiconductor field-effect transistor. This type of component can be constructed with a channel of N-type material, or with a channel of P type material. The former type is called an N-channel MOSFET; the latter type is called a P-channel MOSFET.

A simplified cross-sectional drawing of an N-channel MOSFET, along with the schematic symbol, is shown in Fig.4.17(a) and (b). The P-channel cross-section drawing and symbol are shown at (c) and (d).

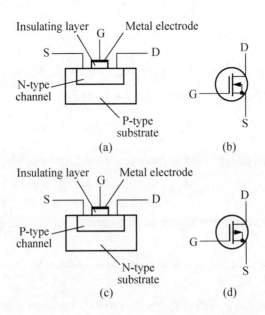

Fig. 4.17 N-Channel and P-Channel MOSFET

(a) Pictorial Diagram of N-channel MOSFET; (b) Schematic Symbol of N-channel MOSFET;
(c) Pictorial Diagram of P-channel MOSFET; (d) Schematic Symbol For P-channel MOSFET

The Insulated Gate

When the MOSFET was first developed, it was called an insulated-gate FET or IGFET. This is perhaps more descriptive of the device than the currently accepted name. The gate electrode is actually insulated, by a thin layer of dielectric material, from the channel.

The input impedance for a MOSFET is even higher than that of a JFET when the input is applied at the gate electrode. In fact, the gate-to-source resistance of a typical MOSFET is comparable to that of a well-designed capacitor; it is practically infinite.

A family of characteristic curves for a hypothetical N-channel MOSFET is shown in Fig.4.18. Note that the curves rise steeply at first, but then, as the positive drain voltage increases beyond a certain threshold, the curves level off much more quickly than they do for the JFET.

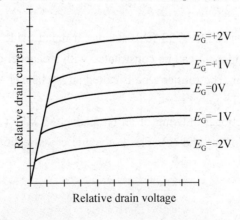

Fig. 4.18 A Family of Characteristic Curves for A Hypothetical N-channel MOSFET

Project IV MP4 Player

4.5 Circuit of the MP4 Player (Task 3)

4.5.1 Introduction of Direct Circuit (Text 6)

Ohm's Law

The law of electricity most used in electronic circuit design is Ohm's Law. It is named in honor of George Simon Ohm, who formulated the relationship between voltage, current and resistance in the 19th Century. Ohm's Law states:

"The current in an electrical circuit is directly proportional to the voltage applied to the circuit, and inversely proportional to the resistance." In equation form, Ohm's Law is

$$I = \frac{E}{R}$$ where: I is current in amperes

$$E = I \times R$$ E is voltage in volts

$$R = \frac{E}{I}$$ R is resistance in ohms

A simple aid for remembering Ohm's law is shown in Fig.4.19(a). Just cover the letter in the circle that you want to find and read the equation formed by the remaining letters. When the current is unknown, but the voltage and resistance are known, the basic equation to be solved for I is found by using the aid of Fig.4.19(b). The result is

$$I = \frac{E}{R}$$

Similarly, knowing the current and resistance, the voltage can be calculated by using the equation shown in Fig.4.19(c):

$$E = I \times R$$

Fig.4.19(d) shows the aids when the current and resistance are in values other than amperes and ohms, respectively.

Resistor Networks

It is a rare circuit that has just one resistor in it. You will usually have several resistors in different configurations in the circuit. How do you calculate the overall resistance of these circuits?

First, why would you want to calculate the resistance of a resistor network? Because if you know the resistance of a circuit and the voltage it is operating at, both of which are usually known values, you can calculate the current consumed by the circuit using equation: $I = \dfrac{V}{R}$. Knowing how much current a circuit needs, you can decide what kind of power supply it needs as

猜词断义 & 词义注释

law: _____

in honor of
为了向……表示敬意

be directly proportional to
与……成正比

be inversely proportional to:

respectively
adv. 各自地，分别地

well as how much power, typically released as heat, it is going to use.[1]

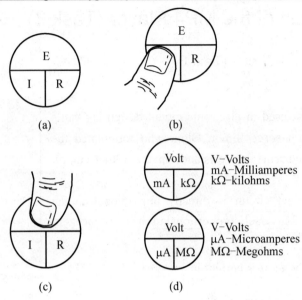

Fig. 4.19 Ohm's Law Circle
(a) Basic; (b) Finding current; (c) Finding Voltage;
(d) Special cases for mA, kΩ and μA , MΩ

The power consumption of a circuit, in watts, is determined by equation: $P = I^2 \times R$. For the second form of the equation, we replace V with its Ohm's Law equivalent $I \times R$:

$$P = I \times V$$

A small difference in current can make a big difference in power consumption. The calculation of resistance depends on how the resistors are wired together.

When devices are in series, it means that they are connected end-to-end, as shown in Fig.4.20. Resistors in series add together to make a larger resistor.

end-to-end:

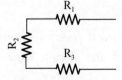

Fig. 4.20 Series Resistors

When devices are in parallel, they are connected side-by-side, as shown in Fig.4.21. Because current has more than one path through the circuit, there is less resistance in a parallel circuit than in one of the resistors in the circuit. For two resistors, the total resistance is:

side-by-side:

$$R = \frac{R_1 \times R_2}{R_1 + R_2}$$

If there are more than two resistors, the general calculation is:

$$R = \frac{1}{\frac{1}{R_1} + \frac{1}{R_2} \cdots \frac{1}{R_N}}$$

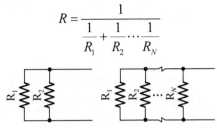

Fig. 4.21 Parallel Resistors

Printed Circuit Board

If a circuit is going to be of any use, the lines and components in the schematic need to be translated into physical reality. Most electronic circuits that you find in the wild are assembled on printed circuit boards (PCBs), or just circuit boards. The circuit board for our schematic is shown in Fig.4.22.

of:

PCB 印制电路板
copper *n.* 铜
photoresist
光阻材料，光致抗蚀剂
mask:

Fig. 4.22 Printed Circuit Boards

Most PCBs are created photographically. The special fiber board begins its life covered on one or both sides with copper. A photoresist mask is applied to this and then a picture of the circuit is projected onto it. Most of the mask is then washed off, leaving mask over just the traces. A strong acid is used to dissolve the rest of the copper off of the board. When that is done, holes can be drilled for the components and the board is done.

The traces on the board are wires. Flat wires, but still the same thing as the wires you are used to. The pads are round or oval areas where components are inserted into the board and soldered into place. The process of soldering is described later.

Cheap circuit boards have copper on just one side, or maybe on both sides, but no copper in the holes. Better circuit boards have plated holes, where copper is plated into the holes on the board. This copper plating

trace *n.* 迹线，描绘图
acid *n.* 酸
dissolve:

drill *v.* 钻
pad *n.* 焊接区，焊接点
oval *a.* 椭圆的
solder *v.* 焊接

plate *v.* 电镀

connects to the solder pad and makes it easier to solder components into the board. Plated holes are also stronger and the pads are less likely to "lift" off the board. The copper is held onto the board with glue, but too much heat during soldering can melt the glue and cause the pad and traces to lose their grip on the board.

If there is copper on both sides of the board, plated holes also do a good job of connecting the pads on the top and bottom sides of the board. There may even be plated holes in the board that aren't for components, used to connect traces between the front and back. These are called vias.

Some circuit boards have more than two layers of copper. These multilayer boards are like several two-layer circuit boards glued, or laminated together. In these cases the vias are critical for connections between one layer and the next.

While a professional circuit board is created using Computer Aided Design (CAD) software, you can also make them by hand using either a chemical photoresist or stick-on resist pads and traces. I don't personally recommend these kits, since good results can be hard to achieve and the chemicals are particularly nasty.

glue n. 胶水
grip:

via n. 通路[孔]

laminate
v. 层压制成

critical:

4.5.2 What is Integrated Circuit (IC) (Text 7)

An integrated circuit (IC) is a collection of electronic devices such as transistors, diodes, and resistors that have been fabricated and electronically interconnected on a small flat chip of semiconductor material.

Semiconductors are fabricated from a wafer of silicon shaped as a disk. Wafers (varying from 75 mm to 150 mm in diameter, and less than 1 mm thick) are sliced from an ingot of single crystal silicon. The most widely used single-crystal growing method is the Czochralski process (Fig.4.23). Controlled amounts of impurities are added to molten polycrystalline silicon to achieve the required doping. Other contamination is avoided as this will adversely affect the silicon's electrical properties. A single silicon crystal ingot, 1 m long and 50~150 mm in diameter, can be fabricated using the Czochralski process. The ingot is then shaped into a cylinder and sliced into wafers which are polished.

Lithography is the process by which the geometric patterns that define devices are transferred from a reticle to the silicon wafer surface.

The reticle is the masking unit, and computer aided design (CAD) techniques play a major role in its design and generation. Lithography ensures that these areas are precisely placed and sized. The SiO_2 acts as a barrier (or mask) to doping impurities. Dopant atoms are able to pass into the

猜词断义 &
词义注释

wafer
n. 华夫饼干，威化饼干，晶片
ingot n. 锭
slice v. 切
cystal n. 晶体
Czochralski
卓克拉尔斯基，又称为提拉法
impurity
n. 混合物
polycrystalline
a. 多晶的
doping
n. 半导体混合物
adverse
a. 不利的

wafer where there is an absence of SiO_2. Lithography is the process used for selectively removing the SiO_2. The SiO_2 is covered with an acid resistant coating except where diffusion windows are required. The SiO_2 is removed using an etching technique. The acid resistant coating is normally a photosensitive organic material known as photo-resist which can be polymerized by ultraviolet (UV) light. If the UV light is passed through a mask containing the desired pattern, the coating is polymerized where the pattern is to appear. The unpolymerized areas may then be removed with an organic solvent. Electron beam lithography (EBL) is used to avoid diffraction and achieve very high accuracy line widths.

lithography
n. 光刻法
reticle
n. 光掩模板,光罩

etch
v. (用酸)蚀刻图案
diffusion

polymerize
v. 聚合

organic
a. 有机的
solvent
n. 溶剂
a. 溶解的

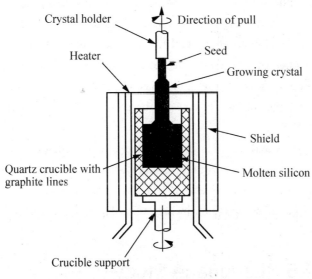

Fig. 4.23 The Czochralski Process

4.5.3 Exercises to the Task

I. Write a T in front of a statement if it is true and write an F if it is false according to the text.

1. Because current has only one path through the circuit, there is more resistance in a series circuit than in one of the resistors in the circuit.

2. A strong acid is used to dissolve the rest of photoresist mask of the board.

3. Cheap circuit boards have copper on just one side, but plated holes also do a good job of connecting the pads on the top and bottom sides of the board.

4. Molten polycrystalline silicon need be contaminated to achieve the required doping.

5. When the SiO_2 acts as the reticle, Dopant atoms aren't able to pass into the wafer.

6. The SiO_2 is removed using ultraviolet (UV) light.

II. Translate the following sentences into Chinese.

Knowing how much current a circuit needs, you can decide what kind of power supply it needs as well as how much power, typically released as heat, it is going to use.

4.5.4 Knowledge Widening: Reading Material

It is interesting to note that almost all electronic components can be constructed from thin layers of doped semiconductors and insulating oxides. These layers can be created fairly easily, with methods not entirely unlike developing photographs. This means that we can take a single slab of silicon and turn it into a bunch of different electronic components, all microscopic in size. And these components, still using various photographic masking techniques, can be connected with films of metal wires. An entire electronic circuit can be constructed at microscopic scale. And this is an integrated circuit (IC).

There are many different types and families of integrated circuit. Analog ICs can create amplifier and filter circuits, among others. Digital ICs perform all of the various logical operations. Some ICs convert between analog and digital signals. Large-scale ICs can put hundreds, thousands, even millions of components in one chip. The central processing unit in your computer is one such chip.

4.6 Language Study

4.6.1 陪衬对比表示法

当在专业英语中遇到深奥难懂或者枯燥乏味的概念时，可以采用比较熟悉的概念或事物作为陪衬或进行对比的方法，以理解文章所表达的含义或记住这些概念。如：

Most strong earthquakes in lonely outposts are not dangerous. On the other hand, even a fairly minor one in a city can cause great damage.

即使从没见过 lonely outpost，也可以根据 on the other hand 来猜出它的含义。通过对比可以看出 lonely outpost 肯定与 city 非常不同，所以意思一定是没有什么人居住的地方。

在阅读过程中如果特别留意这些表示陪衬和对比的词语，对文章的理解就会更深入，也可以节省查字典的时间。

常见的表示对比的词有 while、however、unlike、but、although、in contrast 和 on the other hand 等。如：

(1) Earthquakes occur most frequently in the western part of the United States. However, they also occur in all parts of North America.

(Contrast: earthquake locations. Explanation: You probably already know that earthquakes occur in the West. You probably do not know that they also occur in Nova Scotia.)

(2) Amaranth and other wild plants can be hard to farm because, unlike corn, wheat, and oats, they do not have a known harvest time.

(Contrast: harvest tunes for various grains. Explanation: The reason amaranth is hard to farm is that it doesn't have a predictable harvest time.)

(3) Most eye surgery is still performed in the traditional manner. But more and more conditions are beginning to be treated with lasers, making true surgery unnecessary.

(Contrast: surgical methods. Explanation: The reality of the situation is that lasers have not made eye surgery a thing of the past.)

(4) The English system of measurement is based on multiples of twelve. In contrast, the metric system is always based on multiples of ten.

(Contrast: systems of measurement. Explanation: See just how different two systems of measurement can be.)

(5) Having an advanced degree in science does not help a teacher teach. On the other hand, it is impossible to get a science teaching position without having an advanced degree in science.

(Contrast: methods of preparing for teaching. Explanation: Absurdity of situation pointed out.)

4.6.2 专业英语中的否定

1. 全部否定

英语中表示全部否定的词有 no、nobody、none、nowhere、neither、nor 等，这类词一般表示全部否定。

Nothing in the world moves faster than light.
世界上不存在比光的速度更快的事物。

There is no sound evidence to prove this.
没有充分的证据证明这一点。

除了上述否定句之外，有一类否定语气更强烈，一般称为绝对否定。表示绝对否定的词有 never、not …at all、cannot possibly、by no means、in no way、none、nothing、not nearly、short of 等。

He could not possibly have done the experiment alone.
他根本不可能独立完成那个实验。

In this case, the cutting tool, that is, the drill, turn fast, but the work piece doesn't move at all.
在这种情况下，切削刀具，即钻头，快速运转，但工件却根本不动。

Never have I seen a bridge so magnificent.
我从未见过这么宏伟的大桥。

2. 部分否定

这类否定句通常是由 not 与 every、all both、always、each、many、much、often 等构成的，或 not 与句子的谓语连用，表示"不全是"，"不总是"，"并非都"等。

Not each transistor in the box is out of order.
盒子里的晶体管并非每个都是坏的。

Friction is not always a disadvantage. In many instances it is highly important.
摩擦并不总是不利的，在许多情况下，它是非常重要的。

除此以外，还有一种部分否定形式，这种形式往往用一些副词来表示，如 scarcely、hardly、rarely、seldom、barely、few、little 等。

At the same time, it is noticed that the sound becomes gradually weaker, until it scarcely audible although the bell is still ringing.
同时人们会注意到，尽管电铃仍在响，但是声音逐渐变弱，直至几乎听不见。

3. 意义上的否定

一些单词或者词组本身含有"缺陷、缺少、脱落、排除、忽略、不知"等否定含义。

1) 某些动词及动词词组

如 deny、fail、neglect、lack、ignore、refuse、miss、exclude、prevent …from、save …from、protect …from、keep …from 等。

The value of loss in this equation is so small that we can overlook it.
在此方程中，损耗值太小，可以忽略不计。

He was prevented from coming yesterday.
昨天他因病没来。

As rubber prevents electricity from passing through it, it is used as insulating material.
由于橡胶不导电，所以被用做绝缘材料。

2) 某些抽象名词

Perhaps more important for today's engineering applications is the lack of large physical and virtual memories on PCs.
对于当今的工程应用来说，也许更为重要的是 PC 上缺少大容量的物理内存和虚拟内存。

A few instruments are in a state of neglect.
一些仪器处于无人管理状态。

3) 某些形容词及形容词词组

如 free from、far from、inferior to、few、little、short of、last、least、ignorant 等。

Support is much less advanced for distributed computing than for distributed file systems.
对分布式计算提供的支持比对分布式文件系统提供的支持落后得多。

These elements are shielded so that they are free from the influence of magnetic field.
这些元件被屏蔽起来以防受到磁场的影响。

4) 某些介词及介词词组

如 beyond、against、above、instead of、out of、except、without、in place of 等。

Without control one is apt to be beyond control.
没有理智容易变得不受约束。

The machine seems to be out of gear.
机器似乎出故障了。

5) 某些固定搭配

如 would rather …than、too …to、rather than、yet to、more than、but that 等。

An explosion is nothing more than a tremendously rapid burning.
爆炸只不过是非常急速的燃烧。

During the day, MW signals are too heavily absorbed by the D regions to be heard over long distances.
中波信号在白天被 D 区吸收得很厉害，因而，在距离远的地方都收听不到。

4.7 Practical Skill

4.7.1 获取细节

在专业英语文章中，作者要表达的主观意见或建议都体现在文章的细枝末节中，要使阅读有效，就必须学会辨认这些细节。

判断画线的英文是否是细节。

(1) The climate of this area is typical of desert conditions. Summer temperatures often do not <u>vary widely from day to night</u>.

(2) Farming was the main occupation of the people of this area; using irrigation <u>they grew corn</u>, beans, and squash.

(3) All of the <u>drugs classed as opiates are physically addicting</u>, and when they are taken regularly the user develops a tolerance for them, so that larger and larger doses are necessary to achieve the same results.

(4) People all over the world dream about the same amount each night. <u>People vary, however, in how well they remember their dream.</u>

在很多情况下，还要能够区分哪些是重要细节，哪些是次要细节。想记住所有的细节是不可能的，但是在阅读过程中要尽量发现重要的细节并记住它们。

判断下列各段中的语句哪些是最重要的细节。

(1) (a) <u>Only Congress can declare war.</u> (b) <u>A declaration of war cannot be made by the president alone.</u> (c) Usually the declaration is a joint resolution adopted by at least a majority of both houses and signed by the president.

(2) (a) <u>Children are very curious by nature.</u> (b) <u>They often like to smell, touch, and taste things while exploring their environment.</u> (c) <u>Your home contains many products that are beneficial if used properly but may be dangerous or even fatal to children.</u> (d) <u>Children are often unaware of the dancers of these products.</u>

(3) (a) <u>Standing or sitting for long time is hard on anyone's circulation.</u> (b) <u>This is because</u>

blood accumulates in the lower legs and around the ankles. (c) and distends the veins in these areas. (d) This is especially harmful for people suffering from varicose veins.

4.7.2 长难句的翻译

长难句翻译的一般步骤如下。
(1) 确定有几个主谓结构，即包含几个分句。
(2) 根据句中的连词、关联词、标点符号及句意，初步确定各分句的并列或主从关系。
(3) 确定主句，再确定分句。
(4) 根据上下文译成汉语。

关键是抓住句子结构的特点和语句所表达的中心内容，弄清逻辑上和结构上的主次，全面理解后再进行翻译。如：

(1) Another important communications applications, appeared in 1990s, are local area networks (LANs) and wide area networks (WANs), systems that allow multiple computers to communicate over short or long distances.

主语为 another important communications applications，谓语为 appeared、are，systems that …是 LANs 和 WANs 的同位语。

故翻译：另一种重要的通信应用是 20 世纪 90 年代出现的局域网和广域网。这些系统使多个计算机能在或长或短的距离内进行通信活动。

(2) Typically, when a customer places an order, that order begins a mostly paper-based journey from in-basket to in-basket around the company, often being keyed and rekeyed into different departments' computer systems along the way.

主语为 that order，前面是 when 时间状语从句，谓语为 begins，often being keyed and rekeyed 为伴随状语。

故翻译：在一般情况下，当一位顾客预定了一份订单后，那张订单就会在公司里被传阅，并经常以这种方式被发送和再转发到不同部门的计算机系统中。

练习：

将下列长句译成汉语。

(1) Manufacturing processes may be classified as unit production with small quantities being made and mass production with large numbers of identical parts being produced.

(2) The input and output units are often slower in operation than the rest of the computer, which makes it necessary to store unworked and partly processed data in the storage unit.

(3) Traffic management systems are becoming smarter and researchers hope that Internet, coupled with satellite global positioning systems, will prove to be a fantastic tool to advise car users on how to avoid congested routes.

Project V　Mechanical Design and Manufacture

5.1　The Lead-in of the Project

Making parts and putting them together is manufacturing. If you make parts and put them together to make a product, you are manufacturing. The manufacturing industry is important in our society and economy. An economy is a system for producing and distributing products and services. Many people work in manufacturing. They help produce products, and they buy products with the money that they earn. The more products people buy, the more products are manufactured. And this allows more people to work. Manufacturing is also important to the economy in another way. A piece of material is worth more after it is been changed into a useful product. That is value added. Value is increased by the manufacturing process. The manufacturing streamline is shown in Fig.5.1.

猜词断义 & 词义注释

manufacture
v. 制造
economy
n. 经济

Fig. 5.1　Manufacturing Streamline

5.2　The Contents of the Project

Over the years, manufacturing technology has achieved great progress with significant development of technology in other areas. Modern manufacturing technology can be defined as the technology which is, combined with mechanical, electronic information and modern management technology applied in whole life cycle of product to achieve T (low lead time), Q (high quality), C (low cost) and S (good service) purposes. Following is not a complete list of all new technologies that are used in manufacturing but some representative samples.

FMS stands for flexible manufacturing system. As the name suggests, the system can accommodate to certain changes in product types or the order of operations. FMS consists of three major categories: ① computer controlled system; ② automatic materials handling system; ③ numerically controlled machine tools. It can be considered to fill the gap between transfer lines which have high rates of production but one type of particular part and CNC machines which have low production rates but various types of parts.[1] The relative position of FMS in manufacturing is illustrated in Fig.5.2.

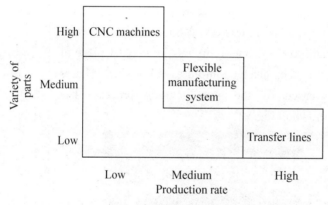

Fig. 5.2 The Relative Position of FMS in Manufacturing

5.3 Basic Knowledge (Task 1)

5.3.1 CIMS (Text 1)

CIMS stands for Computer Integrated Manufacturing System. If FMS is the manufacturing system on the shop level, CIMS is the one on the enterprise level. Although CIMS can include many advanced manufacturing technologies such as robotics, Computer Numerical Control (CNC), Computer Aided Design (CAD), Computer Aided Manufacturing (CAM), Computer Aided Engineering (CAE), and Just-In-Time (JIT) production, it goes beyond these technologies.

CIMS is a new way to do business that includes a commitment to total enterprise quality, continuous improvement, customer satisfaction, use of a single computer database for all product information that is the basis for manufacturing and production decisions in every department, removal of communication barriers among all departments, and the integration of enterprise resources.[2]

5.3.2 What is Mechanical Design (Text 2)

Mechanical design is the process of designing and/or selecting mechanical components and putting them together to accomplish a desired function. Of course, machine elements must be compatible, must fit well together, and must perform safely and efficiently. The designer must consider not only the performance of the element being designed at a given time but also the elements with which it must interface.

To illustrate how the design of machine elements must be integrated with a mechanical design, let us consider the design of a speed reducer for the small tractor. Suppose that, to accomplish the speed reduction, you decide to design a single-reduction, worm gear speed reducer. You specify a worm gear, a worm, a shaft, four bearings, and a housing to hold the individual elements in proper relation to each other, as shown in Fig.5.3. You should recognize that you have already made many design decisions by rendering a sketch.

Fig. 5.3 A Speed Reducer

First, you chose a worm and worm-gear rather than spur gears, helical gears, or bevel gears. In fact, other types of speed reduction devices such as belt drives, chain drives, or many others could be appropriate. The arrangement of the worm and worm-gear, the placement of the bearings so that they straddle the worm and worm-gear, and the general configuration of the housing are also design decisions.[3] The design process cannot rationally proceed until these kinds of decisions are made. When the overall design is conceptualized, the design of the individual machine elements in the speed reducer can proceed. The design process model is shown in Fig.5.4.

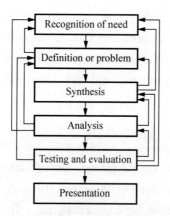

Fig. 5.4   Design Process Model

5.3.3   Tolerances and Fits (Text 3)

Quality and accuracy are major considerations in making machine parts. Interchangeable parts require suitable accuracy to fit together. Both of dimensions of parts given on engineering drawings and manufactured dimensions should be exactly the same the fit properly. Unfortunately, it is impossible and unnecessary to make things to an exact shape or dimension. Most dimensions have a varying degree of accuracy and means of specifying acceptable limitations in dimensional variance that an object will tolerate and still have its function.[4]

Size usually includes nominal, basic, design, and actual size, etc..

Nominal size generally identifies the overall size of an object without any error.

Basic size is the size from which the limits of size are derived by the application of allowances and tolerances.

Design size is the size from which you derive the limits of size by the use of tolerances.

Actual size is the manufactured size of the object that may be larger or smaller than the nominal size.

The indicating object size is shown in Fig.5.5.

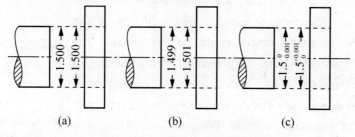

Fig. 5.5   Indicating Object Size
(a) Basic size;   (b)Actual size;   (c)Design size

猜词断义 &
词义注释

Tolerance is the total permissible variation in the size of a part or the total amount of a specific dimension that may vary from a minimum limit to a maximum limit.

Unilateral tolerances indicate variation from the basic size in one direction.

Bilateral tolerances indicate variation from the basic size in both directions.

The indicating tolerance is shown in Fig.5.6.

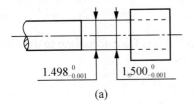
(a)

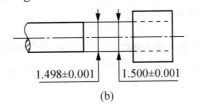
(b)

Fig. 5.6 Indicating Tolerance

(a) Unilateral tolerance;   (b) Bilateral tolerance

Allowance is the intentional difference between the maximum material limits of mating parts (a hole and a shaft). This is a minimum clearance (positive allowance) or maximum interference (negative allowance) between mating parts.

Fit is the general range of tightness resulting from the application of a specific combination of allowance and tolerances in the design of mating parts.[5] How mating parts or assemblies fit together with component parts could be referred to as different fits: clearance fit, interference fit, or transition fit.

Clearance fit is a fit that always enables a clearance between the hole and shaft in the coupling. The low limit size of the hole is greater or at least equal to the upper limit size of the shaft.

Transition fit is a fit where (depending on the actual sizes of the hole and shaft) both clearance and interference may occur in the coupling. Tolerance zones of the hole and shaft partly or completely interfere.

Interference fit is a fit always ensuring some interference between the hole and shaft in the coupling. The upper limit size of the hole is smaller or at least equal to the lower limit size of the shaft.

The difference among dearance fit, transition fit, and interference fit is shown in Fig.5.7.

---

permissible
a. 允许的

unilateral
a. 单边的

bilateral:

allowance:

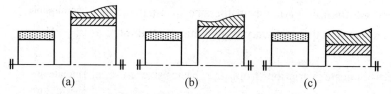

Fig. 5.7 The Difference Among Clearance Fit, Transition Fit, And Interference Fit
(a)Clearance fit;   (b)Transition fit;   (c)Interference fit

5.3.4 Exercises to the Task

I. Write a T in front of a statement if it is true and write an F if it is false according to the text.

1. When people buy products, the value is added to it.

2. FMS can accommodate to certain changes in product types or the order of operations.

3. The design process cannot rationally proceed before design is conceptualized.

4. Actual size is the size from which you derive the limits of size by the use of tolerances.

5. Clearance fit is a fit that always enables a clearance between the hole and shaft in the coupling.

II. Translate the following sentences into Chinese.

[1] It can be considered to fill the gap between transfer lines which have high rates of production but one type of particular part and NC machines which have low production rates but various types of parts.

[2] CIM is a new way to do business that includes a commitment to total enterprise quality, continuous improvement, customer satisfaction, use of a single computer database for all product information that is the basis for manufacturing and production decisions in every department, removal of communication barriers among all departments, and the integration of enterprise resources.

[3] The arrangement of the worm and worm-gear, the placement of the bearings so that they straddle the worm and worm-gear, and the general configuration of the housing are also design decisions.

[4] Most dimensions have a varying degree of accuracy and means of specifying acceptable limitations in dimensional variance that an object will tolerate and still have its function.

Project V Mechanical Design and Manufacture

[5] Fit is the general range of tightness resulting from the application of a specific combination of allowance and tolerances in the design of mating parts.

5.3.5 Knowledge Widening: Reading Material

A solid is defined by its surface boundaries. Designers typically specify a component's nominal dimensions such that it fulfils its requirements. In reality, components cannot be made repeatedly to nominal dimensions, due to surface irregularities and the intrinsic surface roughness.

Some variability in dimensions must be allowed to ensure manufacture is possible. However, the variability permitted must not be so great that the performance of the assembled parts is impaired. The allowed variability on the individual component dimensions is called the tolerance.

The term tolerance applies not only to the acceptable range of component dimensions produced by manufacturing techniques, but also to the output of machines or processes. For example, the power produced by a given type of internal combustion engine varies from one engine to another. In practice, the variability is usually found to be modeled by a frequency distribution curve, for example the normal distribution (also called the Gaussian distribution). One of the tasks of the designer is to specify a dimension on a component and the allowable variability on this value that will give acceptable performance.

5.4 Material Forming Processes (Task 2)

Mechanical working processes are used to achieve optimum mechanical properties in the metal. Metal working reduces any internal voids or cavities present to make the metal dense. The impurities present in the metal also get elongated with the grains and in the process get broken and dispersed throughout the metal. This decreases the harmful effect of the impurities and improves the mechanical strength.

The metal working processes are traditionally divided into hot working and cold working processes. The division is on the basis of the amount of heating applied to the metal before applying the mechanical force.

5.4.1 Turning (Text 4)

The turning process, which is the best known and most widely used mass-reducing process, is employed to manufacture all types of cylindrical shapes by removing material in the form of chips from the work material with a cutting tool (Fig.5.8(a)). The work material rotates and the cutting tool is fed longitudinally. The cutting tool is much harder and more wear resistant

猜词断义 &
词义注释

turning *n.* 车削
longitudinally

than the work material. A variety of types of lathes are employed, some of which are automatic in operation. The lathes are usually powered by electric motors which, through various gears, supply the necessary torque to the work material and provide the |feed| motion to the tool.

A wide variety of machining operations or processes based on the same metal-cutting principle are available. Among the most common are milling and drilling carried out on various machine tools. By varying the tool shape and the pattern of relative work-tool motions, many different shapes can be produced (Fig.5.8(b)and (c)).

adv. 纵向地
feed:

resistant:

mill
n.v. 铣
drill
n.v. 钻

联想记忆

longitude
latitude
altitude

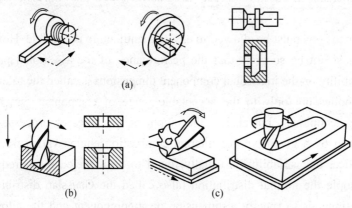

Fig. 5.8 Turning
(a) Turning; (b) Drilling; (c) Milling

5.4.2 Forging (Text 5)

Forging is the operation where the metal is heated and then a force is applied to manipulate the metal in such a way that the required final shape is obtained.[1] This is the oldest of the metal working processes known to mankind since the copper age. Forging is generally a hot working operation though cold forging is used sometimes.

There are four types of forging methods which are generally used.

Smith forging is the traditional forging operation done openly or in open dies by the village blacksmith or modem shop floor by manual hammering or by power hammers, as shown in Fig.5.9.

猜词断义 &
词义注释

forging   *n.* 锻造
die   *n.* 模具
smith   *n.* 铁匠
blacksmith
n. 锻工

Fig. 5.9 Smith Forging

Drop forging is the operation done in closed impression dies by means of drop hammers. Here the force for shaping the component is applied in a series of blows. The metal is heated to a suitable working temperature and placed in the lower die cavity. The upper die is then lowered so that the metal is forced to fill the cavity. Excess material is squeezed out between the die faces at the periphery as flash, which is removed in a later trimming process. It's shown in Fig.5.10.

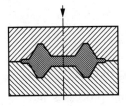

Fig. 5.10　Drop Forging

Similar to drop forging, the press forging is also done in closed impression dies with the exception that the force is a continuous squeezing type applied by the hydraulic presses.

Unlike the drop or press forging where the material is drawn out, in machine forging, the material is only upset to get the desired shape.

5.4.3　Rolling (Text 6)

Rolling is a process where the metal is compressed between two rotating rolls (different shapes) for reducing its cross sectional area.

Rolling is normally a hot working process unless specifically mentioned as cold rolling. The metal is taken into rolls by friction and subsequently compressed to obtain the final shape. The thickness of the metal that can be drawn into rolls depends on the roughness of the roll surface. Rougher rolls would be able to achieve greater reduction than smoother rolls. But, the roll surface gets embedded into the rolled metal thus producing rough surface.

Rolling is extensively used in the manufacturing of plates, sheets, structural beams, and so on. Fig.5.11 shows the rolling of plates or sheets. An ingot is produced in casting and in several stages it is reduced in thickness, usually while hot. Since the width of the work material is kept constant, its length is increased according to the reductions. After the last hot-rolling stage, a final stage is carried out cold to improve surface quality and tolerances and to increase strength.[2] In rolling, the profiles of the rolls are designed to produce the desired geometry.

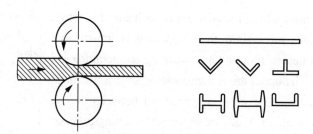

Fig. 5.11 Rolling

5.4.4 Casting (Text 7)

The first casings were made during the period 4000~3000 B.C., using stone and metal molds for casting copper. Various casting processes have been developed over a long time, each with its own characteristics and applications, to meet specific engineering and service requirements.

The traditional method of casting metals is in sand molds and has been used for millennia. Simply stated, sand casting consists of ① placing a pattern having the shape of the desired casting in sand to make an imprint; ② incorporating a gating system; ③ filling the resulting cavity with molten metal; ④ allowing the metal to cool until it solidifies; ⑤ breaking away the sand mold; and ⑥ removing the casting (Fig.5.12).

猜词断义 & 词义注释

casting n. 铸造
millennia n. 一千年
imprint n. 印记，印痕
incorporate v. 开设，组建
gating n. 浇铸系统，浇口
solidify v. 硬化，凝固
core n. 铸芯
withstand v. 承受，经受
collapsibility n. 拆卸
aggregate n. 聚合体

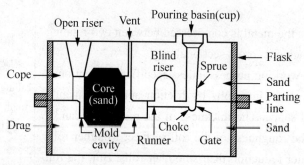

Fig. 5.12 Schematic Illustration of A Sand Mold

For castings with internal cavities or passages, such as those found in an automotive engine block or a valve body, cores are utilized. Cores are placed in the mold cavity before casting to form the interior surfaces of the casting and are removed from the finished part during shakeout and further processing. Like molds, cores must possess strength, ability to withstand heat, and collapsibility; therefore, cores are made of sand aggregates.

The investment-casting process, also called the lost-wax process, was first used during the period 4000 to 3000 B.C. The pattern is made of wax or of a plastic (such as polystyrene) by molding or rapid prototyping techniques. The sequences involved in investment casting are shown in Fig.5.13. The

investment-casting n. 精密铸造
wax n. 蜡
lost-wax:

pattern is made by injecting molten wax or plastic into a metal die in the shape of the pattern. The pattern is then dipped into the slurry of refractory material such as very fine silica and binders, including water, ethyl silicate, and acids. After this initial coating has dried, the pattern is coated repeatedly to increase its thickness.

slurry
n. 浆
refractory
a. 难熔的
silica
n. 二氧化硅
binder
n. 黏合剂
ethyl *n.* 乙酯
silicate *n.* 硅酸盐

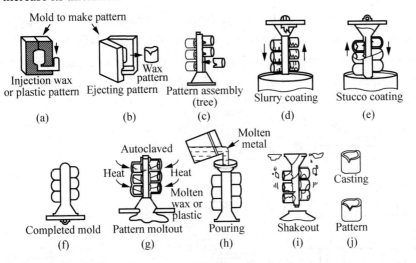

Fig. 5.13 Schematic Illustration of Investment Casting (Lost-Wax Process)

5.4.5 Exercises to the task

I. Write a T in front of a statement if it is true and write an F if it is false according to the text.

1. Turning, Drilling, and Milling are mass-reducing process.

2. Drop forging is the traditional forging operation done openly or in open dies by the village blacksmith.

3. Rougher rolls would provide more friction and be able to achieve greater reduction than smoother rolls.

4. Sand casings were used for casting copper long ago.

5. During the period 4000 to 3000 B.C., the investment-casting pattern is made of a plastic by molding or rapid prototyping techniques.

II. Translate the following sentences into Chinese.

[1] Forging is the operation where the metal is heated and then a force is applied to manipulate the metal in such a way that the required final shape is obtained.

[2] After the last hot-rolling stage, a final stage is carried out cold to improve surface quality and tolerances and to increase strength.

5.4.6　Knowledge Widening: Reading Material

By applying a stress that exceeds the original yield strength of metallic material, we have strain hardened or cold worked the metallic material, while simultaneously deforming it. This is the basis for many manufacturing techniques, such as wire drawing. Fig.5.14 illustrates several manufacturing processes that make use of both cold-working and hot-working processes.

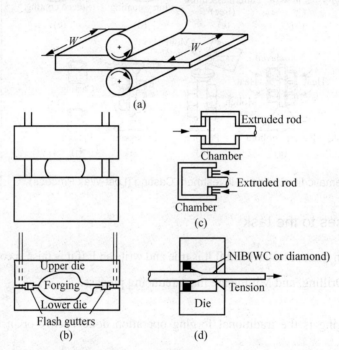

Fig. 5.14　Metal Forming Processes That Make Use of Cold Working As Well As Hot Working
(a) Rolling; (b) Forging (open and closed die); (c) Extrusion; (d) Wire drawing

Many techniques are used to simutaneously shape and strengthen a material by cold working (Fig.5.14). For example, rolling is used to produce metal plate and sheet. Forging deforms the material into a die cavity, producing relatively complex shapes such as automotive crankshafts or connecting rods. In drawing, a metallic rod is pulled through a die to produce a wire or fiber. In extrusion, a material is pushed through a die to form products of uniform cross-sections, including rods, tubes, or aluminum trims for doors or windows. Deep drawing is used to form the body of aluminum beverage cans. Stretch forming and bending as well as other processes are used to shape material. Thus, cold working is an effective way of shaping metallic materials while simultaneously increasing their strength. We can obtain excellent dimensional tolerances and surface finishes by the cold working processes. Note that many of the processes such as rolling, can be conducted using both cold and hot working.

5.5 Components of CIMS (Task 3)

5.5.1 Computer Numerical Control (Text 8)

What is Computer Numerical Control, or CNC? Simply put, Computer Numerical Control is the automated control of machine tools by a computer and computer program. In other words, a computer rather than a person will directly control the machine tool.[1] The axial movements of CNC machine tools are guided by a computer, which reads a program and instructs several motors to move in the appropriate manner. The motors in turn cause the table to move and produce the machined part.

Before Computer Numerical Control (CNC), the motions of the machine tool had to be controlled manually or mechanically. Today, conventional machine tools have been largely replaced by CNC machine tools. The machines still perform essentially the same functions, but movements of the machine tool are controlled electronically rather than by hand. CNC machine tools can produce the same parts over and over again with very little variation. They can run day and night, week after week, without getting tired. These are obvious advantages over conventional machine tools, which need a great deal of human interaction in order to do anything. CNC machine tools, as shown in Fig.5.15, are highly productive. They are also expensive to purchase, set up, and maintain. However, the productivity advantage can easily offset this cost if their use is properly managed.

猜词断义 & 词义注释

table:

essentially
基本上，本质上

offset:

Fig. 5.15　CNC Machine Tools

Principles of CNC Machines

The basic elements and operation of a typical CNC machine are shown in Fig.5.16. The functional elements in CNC machine and the components involved are described here.

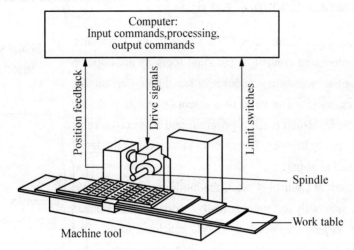

Fig. 5.16 Major Components for Position Control on An CNC Machine

- Data input: The numerical information is read and stored in computer memory.
- Data processing: The programs are read into the machine control unit for processing.
- Data output: This information is translated into commands (typically pulsed commands) to the servomotor (Fig.5.17). The servomotor then moves the table (on which the work piece is mounted) to specific positions through linear or rotary movements by means of stepping motors, leadscrews, and other similar devices.
- Types of control circuits: An CNC machine can be controlled through two types of circuits that are open-loop and closed-loop. In the open-loop system (Fig.5.17(a)), the signals are sent to the servomotor by the controller, but the movements and final positions of the work table are not checked for accuracy. The closed-loop system (Fig.5.17(b)) is equipped with various transducers, sensors, and counters that accurately measure the position of the work table. Through feedback control, the position of the work table is compared against the signal, and the table movements terminate when the proper coordinates are reached.
- Position measurement: That can be classified as direct and indirect methods (Fig.5.18). Various sensors are based mainly on magnetic and photoelectric principles. In direct measuring systems, a sensing device reads a graduated scale on the machine table or slide for linear

terminate
v. 结束，终结

coordinate:

a graduated scale:

movement (Fig.5.18(a)). In indirect measuring systems, position is measured by rotary encoders or resolvers (Fig.5.18(b))

resolver
n. 解算器

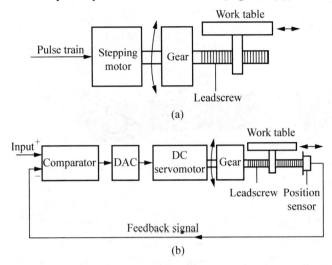

Fig. 5.17 Types of Control Systems
(a) An open-loop control system; (b) A closed-loop control symtem

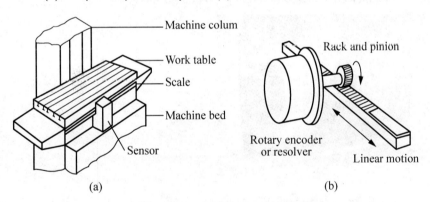

Fig. 5.18 Position Measurement Methods
(a) Direct method; (b) Indirect method

Common Types of CNC Machines

CNC Lathe

The CNC lathe, as shown in Fig.5.19, is a common sight in job shops and production facilities.[2] CNC lathes have some unique advantages over their conventional counterparts. They can cut circular arcs that were all but impossible to cut on a conventional lathe without special tooling.[3] CNC lathes also excel at threading.

counterpart
n. 竞争对手
arc n. 弧，弧线

thread:

CNC Mill

A CNC mill, as shown in Fig.5.20, performs the same types of operations as a conventional mill, but these operations of a CNC mill are executed automatically rather than by hand.

Fig. 5.19 CNC Lathe

Fig. 5.20 CNC Mill

CNC Grinder

A CNC grinder is shown in Fig.5.21. Surface grinders and cylindrical grinders were probably the last frontier for CNC systems.[4] The tight tolerances required in grinding meant they had to wait for the motion control technology to catch up.[5] Today, the positioning systems are capable of the 50 millionths of an inch tolerances that are common in precision grinding.

grind
n.v. 磨

50 millionths:

Fig. 5.21 CNC Grinder

CNC Machining Center

A CNC machining center is an advanced, computer-controlled machine tool that is capable of performing a variety of machining operation on different surfaces and different orientations of a workpiece without having to remove it from its workholding device or fixture. CNC machining centers are usually considered good, all-purpose machine tools, and they are really the workhorses of job shops and low-volume production. They are agile machines and can be easily adapted to a great variety of workpieces.

workhorse:

agile
a. 敏捷的，灵巧的

The Vertical Machining Center (VMC) and Horizontal Machining Center (HMC), as shown in Fig.5.22 and Fig.5.23, are probably the most common CNC machine tool found in shops today, and their operations have good visibility.

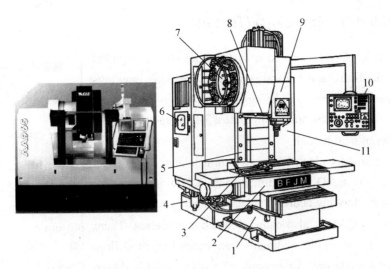

Fig. 5.22 Vertical Machining Center (VMC)
1—Bed; 2—Saddle; 3—Worktable; 4—Servo motor; 5—Traveling column;
6—Machine control unit; 7—Tool storage; 8—Tool-interchange arm(Fig.5.24);
9—Headstock; 10—Control panel; 11—Power supply unit

Fig. 5.23 Horizontal Machining Center (HMC)

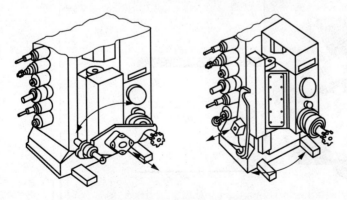

Fig. 5.24 Tool-interchange Arm

5.5.2 Computer Aided Design (CAD) (Text 9)

Computer Aided Design(CAD)refers to a system that uses computers with advanced graphics hardware and software to create precision drawings or technical illustrations. If the system is being used to design parts to be manufactured, the designer can draw and manipulate a 3-D image of the part without having to build a physical model.

CAD systems can be broadly classified as two-dimensional (2-D) CAD and three-dimensional (3-D) CAD. Two-dimensional CAD systems are basically glorified electronic drawing boards, replacing paper, pencil, and the T-square. Three-dimensional CAD is also called geometric modeling. There are three methods of modeling in three dimensions; wireframe modeling, surface modeling, and solid modeling. An example of a wire model is shown in Fig.5.25. The intended purpose of the image dictates the appropriate model. A solid model is shown in Fig.5.26. A surface model is shown in Fig.27.

猜词断义 & 词义注释

3-D:
Three-dimension
三维

glorified
a. 被美化了的
T-square
n. 丁字尺
model
v. 建模

intend
v. 想要，打算，计划

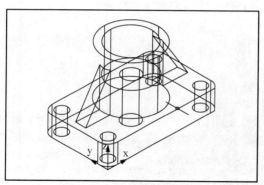

Fig. 5.25　A Wire Model

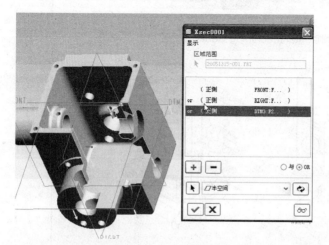

Fig. 5.26　A Solid Model

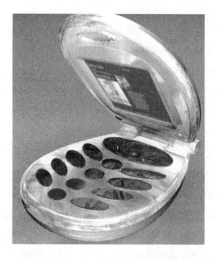

Fig. 5.27 A Surface Model

Wireframe, the simple 3-D modeling, represents objects by line elements that provide <u>exact</u> information about edges, corners, and surface discontinuities. With these models, there is no way to distinguish between the inside and the outside of the object. Surface modeling, on the other hand, defines <u>precisely</u> the outside the object being modeled. Surface models connect various types of surface elements by line segments. Solid models make use of topology, the interior volume and mass of object is defined. Surface models appear similar to solid models, but the interior of the surface model is empty.

Every CAD system has a set of elements or primitives out of which the designs are created.

5.5.3 Computer Aided Manufacturing (CAM) (Text 10)

Computer Aided Manufacturing (CAM) centers around four main areas: NC, process planning, robotics, and factory management.

Numerical Control in CAM

The importance of NC in the CAM area is that the computer can generate a NC program directly from a geometric model or part. At present, automatic capabilities are generally limited to highly symmetric geometries and other specialized parts. However, in the near future some companies will not use drawings at all, but will be passing part information directly from design to manufacturing via a database.[6] As the drawings disappear, so will many of the problems, since computer models developed from a common integrated database will be used by both design and manufacturing.

Process Planning

Process planning involves the detailed planning of the production sequence from start to finish. What is relevant to CAM is a process planning system that is able to produce process plans directly from the geometric model database with almost no human assistance.[7]

Industrial Robots

Many advances are being made to integrate robots into the manufacturing system, as in on-line assembly, welding, and painting.

Factory Management

Factory Management uses interactive factory data collection to get timely information from the factory floor. At the same time, it uses this data to calculate production priorities and dynamically determine what work needs to be done next to ensure that the master production schedule is being properly executed. The system can also be directly modified to satisfy a specific need without calling in computer programming experts.

interactive
a. 交互的
timely
a. 实时的
priority
n. 优先权
dynamically
adv. 动态地

5.5.4　Exercises to the Task

I. Write a T in front of a statement if it is true and write an F if it is false according to the text.

1. Computer Numerical Control (CNC) completely substitutes the machine controlled by hand.

2. In direct measuring systems, position is measured by rotary encoders or resolvers.

3. CNC lathes have many advantages over conventional lathes.

4. CNC machining center performs a variety of machining operation on different surfaces without having to remove it from its work table.

5. Two-dimensional CAD systems are electronic drawing boards.

6. Solid models connect various types of surface elements by line segments.

7. In the near future automatic capabilities are not generally limited to highly symmetric geometries and other specialized parts.

II. Translate the following sentences into Chinese.

[1] In other words, a computer rather than a person will directly control the machine tool.

[2] The CNC lathe, as shown in Fig.5.19, is a common sight in job shops and production facilities.

[3] They can cut circular arcs that were all but impossible to cut on a conventional lathe without special tooling.

[4] Surface grinders and cylindrical grinders were probably the last frontier for CNC systems.

[5] The tight tolerances required in grinding meant they had to wait for the motion control technology to catch up.

[6] However, in the near future some companies will not use drawings at all, but will be passing part information directly from design to manufacturing via a database.

[7] What is relevant to CAM is a process planning system that is able to produce process plans directly from the geometric model database with almost no human assistance.

5.5.5 Knowledge Widening: Reading Material

CAPP

Computer Aided Process Planning (CAPP) can be defined as the functions which use computers to assist the work of process planners. The levels of assistance depend on the different strategies employed to implement the system. Lower level strategies only use computers for storage and retrieval of the data for the process plans which will be constructed manually by process planners, as well as for supplying the data which will be used in the planner's new work.

In comparison with lower level strategies, higher level strategies use computers to automatically generate process plans for some work pieces of simple geometrical shapes. Sometimes a process planner is required to input the data needed or to modify plans which do not fit specific production requirements well. The highest level strategy, which is the ultimate goal of CAPP, generates process plans by computer, which may replace process planners, when the knowledge and expertise of process planning and working experience have been incorporated into the computer programs. The database in a CAPP system based on the highest level strategy will be directly integrated with conjunctive systems, e.g. CAD and CAM. CAPP has been recognized as playing a key role in CIMS (Computer Integrated Manufacturing System).

5.6 Language Study

5.6.1 专业英语的时态特点

就时态而言，因为专业科技文献所涉及的内容(如科学定义、定理、方程式或公式、图表等)一般并没有特定的时间关系,所以在专业文献中大部分都使用一般现在时,时态形式比较单一。由于科技文章一般重在客观地叙述事实,所以它们的用法也不如普通英语那样丰富多彩。

1. 一般现在时

一般现在时是机电科技文章中最常见的时态,表示现在、经常或习惯的动作或状态和普遍现象、常识或客观真理。它主要有 3 种用法:①叙述过程;②叙述客观事实或科学定理;③通常或习惯发生的行为。如:

CIMS stands for Computer Integrated Manufacturing System.

CIMS 表示计算机集成制造系统。

2. 一般将来时

表示将要发生的动作或存在的状态,即将来打算做的事情。常用 will, be to, be about to。如:

The software will also automatically calculate the proper feeds and speeds to be used during the machining, create a tooling list, and define the tool path.

在加工、创建刀具清单并定义刀具轨迹时,该软件同样也可以自动地计算出所适用的进给量与切削速度。

3. 现在完成时

表示过去发生的动作造成目前的结果和对现在造成的影响或表示从过去延续至今的动作、状态和习惯等。如:

Today, conventional machine tools have been largely replaced by CNC machine tools.

如今,普通机床在很大程度上已经被计算机数控机床所取代。

至于一般过去时、过去完成时也在专业英语中经常出现,如科技报告、科技新闻、科技史等。其他时态,如过去将来时、完成进行时等,在专业英语中很少出现。

5.6.2 专业英语的语态特点

在科技文章中,被动语态用得十分频繁,这是由于:①科技文章重在客观地叙述事实,表达力求严谨和清楚,避免带有主观成分和感情色彩;②科技文章描写行为或状态本身,由谁或由什么作为行为或状态的主体显得不重要,状态的主体没有必要指出,有时也根本指不出来。如:

(1) The parts must be manufactured within the specified limits.

零件必须在指定的公差内制造。

(2) Screws have been used as fastener for a long time.

螺钉长期以来作为紧固件来用。

(3) Extrusion is named for the manufacturing process which forms material by forcing it through a shaped opening.

拉伸是由制造过程来命名的,即在具有一定形状的开口上施加作用力来制成材料。

被动语态使用频繁的另一个原因是便于向后扩展句子,而不至于使句子显得头重脚轻。如:

In the digital computer, the numbers to be manipulated are represented by sequences of

Project V Mechanical Design and Manufacture

digits which are first recorded in suitable code, then converted into positive and negative electrical pulses, and stored in electrical or magnetic registers.

在上面的句子中，被动行为的主体是 sequences of digits, which 连接的定语从句作为它的定语，如果这个句子用主动句表示，把 sequences of digits 改为句子的主语，整个句子会显得非常笨拙，违背了英语造句的一般原则。

另外，现在完成时态的被动语态使用频率也比较高。如：It has been shown that …，在使用主动语态时，主语也经常不是人，而是表示"研究"、"资料"、"证据"等名词。如：Preliminary data from our study suggest that …，There is evidence to suggest that …等。

了解专业英语中语态的特点，有助于学习者掌握其文体特点，提高阅读理解和写作能力。

5.7 Practical Skill

5.7.1 what 及 what 从句的译法

英语中 what 的用法很多，因而译法也很多。要译好 what 或 what 从句需要首先了解 what 的词性、功能和词义。一般来说，what 可以用作代词、连词、副词和形容词等。因此，what 可以充当主语、宾语、表语和定语等句子成分，而 what 从句则可作让步或方式等状语从句。在翻译实践中，人们一般通过增词、语用引申、语言单位推移和省略等方法来实现对 what 及 what 从句的语义表达。

1. 直译

(1) 在 what 及 what 从句作宾语、表语或主语时，直接加"什么"。如：

What does your husband do? 你丈夫做什么工作？

Let me see what you've chosen. 让我看看你选了什么。

(2) what 从句作让步状语时，原文从句中谓语动词通常倒装，what 可译为"不管……什么……"或"不论……什么……"。如：

Say what he will, in his heart he knows that he is wrong.

不管他说什么理由，在内心他知道自己错了。

2. 词义引申

在翻译实践中，what 在辞典上找不到适当的词义，如果生硬地搬用词义，肯定会造成译文生涩，甚至产生误解。这时必须根据上下文逻辑关系，从词的基本含义出发加以引申，从而以恰当的汉语表达出原文的正确含义。如：

What did you do with my umbrella? 你把我的伞放到哪里去了？

We must decide what to do with her. 我们必须决定如何来应付她。

What，no salt? 怎么，没盐了？

It's a good film，what? 这是部好电影，不是吗？

What will be，will be. 要发生的事总是要发生的。

3. 语言转移

语言转移就是词性的转换、结构关系的变化与衔接手段的增减。

(1) what 作为疑问代词或连接代词，what 从句可以充当宾语、表语或介词宾语。有时采取从句转换为短语的方法进行翻译。如：

I don't care what she thinks. 我并不关心她心里所想的事情。

It was clear enough what she meant. 她内心的打算是很显然的。

(2) what 作关系代词，汉译时也采用同样的方法。如：

They did what they could to console her. 他们尽量安慰她。

(3)"what+名词"可译为"所有……的"或"一切……的"等，这种结构相当于 all the ...that 或 that ...which。如：

We will give you what help is possible. 我们一定给你们一切可能的帮助。

Lend me what reference books you have on the subject.

把你所有的关于这题目的参考书都借给我。

(4) what little (few) ...则表示"虽少但是全部……"或"所仅有的……"等含义。翻译时也采用同样的方法。如：

What few friends I have here have been very kind to me.

我在这里仅有的几个朋友一直对我很好。

4. 特殊结构译法

(1) what ...is to ...方式状语从句，可译为"犹如……一样"或"好比……一样"等。翻译从句时要结合主句的内容，与主句结构相呼应。如：

Air is to us what water is to fish. 我们离不开空气，犹如鱼儿离不开水一样。

(2) what with ...and ...或 what with ...and what with …短语，可译为"由于……种种原因"，"或因……或因……"。一般将短语后内容以排比或并列的形式译出。如：

What with writing letters，lecturing and attending to the duties of my office, I am so busy that I scarcely have time to eat.

由于写信、做报告和处理办公事务等种种原因，我几乎没有吃饭的时间。

(3) what 用于一些成语或固定词组中，必须根据固定含义进行翻译，不能望文生义。下面英语句子中画线部分为成语或固定词组，注意译文句子中画线部分的对应含义。如：

They will send you food supplies and <u>what not</u> by direct mail.

他们将直接向你邮递食物<u>等</u>物品。

Ask someone <u>who knows what's what</u>. 向<u>在行</u>的人请教。

5.7.2 一词多译

由于英汉两种语言在遣词造句上的差异，对英语原文中的同一个词，汉译时的表达可有多种形式，这就是所谓的英汉翻译中的一词多译现象。一词多译现象的出现有多种情况，以下是不同情况下的一词多译法。

1. 多主一表，表语一词多译

<u>Tensile strength</u>, <u>elasticity</u>, <u>tear and abrasion resistance</u> and <u>compression set</u> are <u>relatively low</u>.

抗拉强度<u>较低</u>，弹性及抗撕裂与耐磨损性<u>较差</u>，压缩永久变形<u>较小</u>。原句中的表语 relatively low 由于主语的不同，因此应分别译为"较低"、"较差"和"较小"。如若译为：抗拉强度、弹性、抗撕裂、耐磨损性和压缩永久变形<u>较低</u>。就不符合汉语用词习惯了。

2. 一动多宾，动词一词多译

You cannot build a ship, a house, or a machine tool if you don't know how to make a design or how to read it.

如果你不知道怎样制图或识图，你就不可能建船、盖房或造机床。句中动词 build 有 3 个不同的宾语，即 a ship，a house 和 a machine tool，根据汉语动宾搭配习惯，应将同一个动词 build 分别译成"建"、"盖"和"造"。

3. 一动多宾，宾语一词多译

The current increases faster than resistance decreases, leading to more heating and less heat radiation and resistance.

电流增大的速度比电阻下降的要快，这便导致发热增加、热辐射减弱、热传导阻力减小。

4. 一定多中(中心词)，定语一词多译

Engine must breathe freely to provide maximum power and performance.

发电机必须通风良好，以便提供最大动力，发挥最佳性能。

句中定语 maximum 有两个被其修饰的中心词 power 和 performance，为了符合汉语的搭配习惯，应将同一个定语 maximum 分别译成"最大"和"最佳"。

5. 多定一中(中心词)，中心词一词多译

Making a visual inspection of the vessel to conform that there are no material or dimensional defects.

对容器进行检查，以确保其材料没有缺陷，尺寸符合要求。

试比较：对容器进行外观检查，以确保材料或尺寸没有缺陷。

Project VI Modern and New Technology

6.1 The Lead-in of the Project

In the future, growth in mechatronic systems will be fueled by the growth in the constituent areas. Advancements in traditional disciplines fuel the growth of mechatronics systems by providing "enabling technologies". For example, the invention of the microprocessor had a profound effect on the redesign of mechanical systems and design of new mechatronics systems. We should expect continued advancements in cost-effective microprocessors and microcontrollers, development in sensor and actuator which enabled by advancements in applications of MEMS, adaptive control methodologies and real-time programming methods, networking and wireless technologies, mature CAE technologies for advanced system modeling, virtual prototyping, and testing.

6.2 The Contents of the Project

Microelectromechanical Systems (MEMS) is an enabling technology for the cost-effective development of sensors and actuators for mechatronics applications. Already, several MEMS devices are in use in automobiles, including sensors and actuators for airbag deployment and pressure sensors for manifold pressure measurement. Integrating MEMS devices with CMOS signal conditioning circuits on the same silicon chip is another example of development of enabling technologies that will improve mechatronic products, such as the automobile.

6.3 Microelectromechanical Systems (MEMS) Technology (Task 1)

6.3.1 Introduction of Microelectromechanical Systems (Text 1)

In the United States, the technology is known as Microelectromechanical Systems (MEMS); in Europe, it is called Microsystems Technology (MST). A question asking for a more specific definition is certain to generate a broad collection of replies with few common characteristics other than "miniature".[1] But such apparent divergence in these responses merely

猜词断义 & 词义注释

MEMS 微机电系统

reflects the diversity of applications this technology enables, rather than a lack of commonality. MEMS is simultaneously a toolbox, a physical product, and a methodology, all in one.

(1) It is a portfolio of techniques and processes to design and create miniature systems, as shown in Fig.6.1.

Fig. 6.1 Microrobot

(2) It is a physical product often specialized and unique to a final application—one can seldom buy a generic MEMS product at the neighborhood electronics store.

(3) "MEMS is a way of making things", reported by the Microsystems Technology Office of the United States. These "things" merge the functions of sensing and actuation with computation and communication to locally control physical parameters at the microscale, yet cause effects at much grander scales.[2]

Compared with conventional devices, the new principle actuators provide much quicker response, smaller size, higher resolution, and a higher power-to-weight ratio. For instance, the minimum size of an electromagnetic motor is generally limited to about 1 cm, as motors smaller than this will not provide adequate torque and efficiency. One of the smallest electromagnetic motors to be fabricated is shown in Fig.6.2. A micromotor with a diameter of 1.9mm typically generates a torque of only 7.5 μNm and rotational speeds of 100,000 rpm. An optional microgearbox with a reduction ratio of 47% can be used with this motor so that the drive can deliver an enhanced torque of up to 300 μNm. Use of this gearbox, however, reduces the efficiency of the motor significantly. Further, as the size of electromagnetic motor is reduced the winding wire thickness must also be reduced, which leads to a significant increase in the electrical resistance and Joule heating.[3]

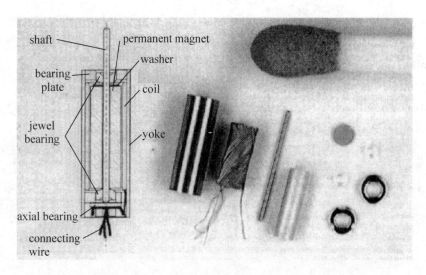

Fig. 6.2 An Electromagnetic Micromotor with A Diameter of 1.9 mm

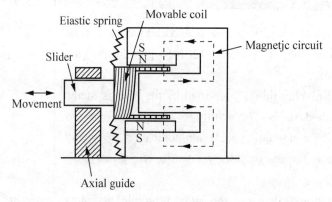

Fig. 6.3 Schematic Representation of A Voice Coil Motor

6.3.2 Ink-Jet Printed Nanoparticle Microelectromechanical Systems (Text 2)

Nanoparticles typically measure 1 to 100 nm in diameter and consist of clusters of metallic, semiconducting, or insulating atoms. Because of their small size, nanoparticles exhibit a melting point as low as 1000℃ below the bulk material. The lower melting point is a result of comparatively high surface-area-to-volume ratio in nanoparticles, which allows bonds to readily form between neighboring particles. Nanoparticles can be made into a colloid that can be printed like ink.

An ink-jet printer patterns material by expelling tiny droplets of liquid ink from an orifice one at a time as it is moved in two dimensions approximately 1 mm above a substrate. Each droplet takes ballistic trajectory to the substrate on command by a pressure impulse, often by a deformable piezo crystal, from within a small chamber attached to the orifice (Fig.6.4).[4] The pattern of droplets left behind on the substrate constitutes the printed

---

猜词断义 & 词义注释

nanoparticle
n. 纳米粒子
cluster
n. 一丛，一群，一束，一串
exhibit:

同义记忆

comparative
comparable

output. Ink-jet printing is additive, reducing waste and processing steps compared to subtractive fabrication methods. It is data-driven, requiring no masks, reducing turnaround time over lithographic processes. Ink-jet printing is less limited by substrate composition and morphology, and can accommodate a greater number of layers and range of materials than can lithography and subsequent semiconductor-based batch processing. State of the art ink-jet print heads will allow minimum feature sizes lower than 20 μm. In sum, ink-jet printing presents a number of advantages as a fabrication technology. Coupled with the novel use of nanoparticles as the building material, the process enables a practical route to a desktop fabrication system for electronic circuitry or MEMS.

colloid n. 胶体
droplet n. 水滴
orifice
n. 孔，洞口
approximately
adv. 大约
substrate
n. 底面，底层
ballistic
a. 发射的
trajectory
n. 轨道，导轨
impulse
n. 冲动，推动
deformable
a. 可变形的
piezo a. 压电的
chamber
n. 房间，盒，腔
additive
a. 加的，附加的
n. 添加剂，叠加色
subtractive
a. 减的
turnaround
n. 回转
morphology
n. 形态学
lithographic
a. 平版印刷的，平版的
lithography:

batch
n. 一批，批量处理

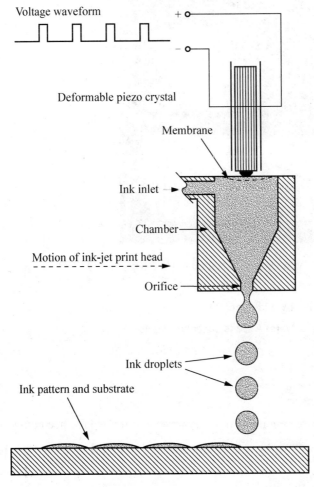

Fig. 6.4 Diagram of the Piezo Drop-on-demand Ink-jet Printing System

In the print head, a piezocrystal expands in response to an electrical driving signal, deforming a membrane, causing a pressure impulse within the ink chamber, expelling a single droplet from the orifice. The chamber is refilled through the inlet by capillary action at the orifice. Multiple droplets deposited onto the substrate leave the printed pattern.

An ink-jet printed droplet of nanoparticle silver on a glass slide after being sintered, as shown in Fig.6.5, imaged by Atomic Force Microscope(AFM).

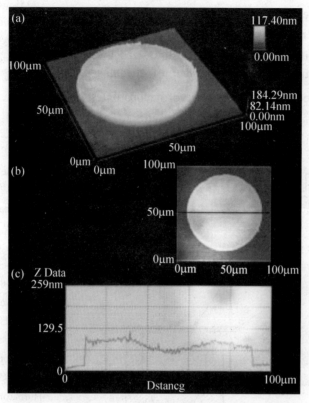

Fig. 6.5　An Ink-jet Printed Droplet of Nanoparticle Silver on
A Glass Slide after Being Sintered
(a) An isometric view, amplified by a factor of 80 in the vertical dimension;
(b) An overhead view; (c) A cross-sectional profile

6.3.3　Exercises to the Task

I. Write a T in front of a statement if it is true and write an F if it is false according to the text.

1. Such apparent divergence merely reflects the diversity of applications and this technology is a lack of commonality.

2. The smallest electromagnetic is fabricated to deliver torque and efficiency.

3. Ink-jet printing adds colors to form every pattern.

II. Translate the following sentences into Chinese.

[1] A question asking for a more specific definition is certain to generate a broad collection of replies with few common characteristics other than "miniature."

[2] These "things" merge the functions of sensing and actuation with computation and communication to locally control physical parameters at the microscale, yet cause effects at much grander scales.

[3] Further, as the size of electromagnetic motor is reduced the winding wire thickness must also be reduced, which leads to a significant increase in the electrical resistance and Joule heating.

[4] Each droplet takes ballistic trajectory to the substrate on command by a pressure impulse, often by a deformable piezo crystal, from within a small chamber attached to the orifice (Fig.6.4).

6.3.4 Knowledge Widening: Reading Material

We designed a high power electrostatic motor and generator using electrets and their circuits, and revealed that the motor/generator with a rotor of 6 mm diameter has a potential output of 30.4 W at 1 Mrpm by calculation.

Electrostatic motors are suitable to MEMS technology from the fabrication point of view, because they consist of thin-film components. Many types of electrostatic motors are reported, but they have low output. By using electrets which store charge to generate voltage on the rotor, much higher power than that of conventional ones is expected. The schematic structure of the electret motor is shown in Fig.6.6. Periodical potential is generated on the rotor by periodically placing ground electrodes on the electret, and torque is produced by applying voltage on stator electrodes. This motor also works as a generator, if the phase of stator voltage is changed to brake the rotor.

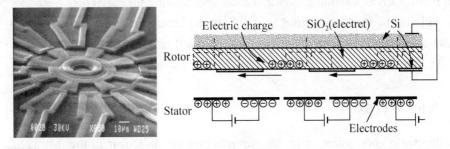

Fig. 6.6 Electrostatic Motor

6.4 Future Robots (Task 2)

6.4.1 Swarm Robots (Text 3)

The robots you see in the movies are built in our own image. A single machine with flexible manipulators (arms, hands, and fingers) capable of traversing most forms of terrain and with a single, complex control system (brain).

Industrial robots are almost the direct opposite of this. They are special purpose machines specialized for a single task, they tend to be fixed in position, and their control system is little more than a script reader playing back preset instructions.[1]

There is a third approach to robots, almost alien in nature. Their inspiration is in the complex communities and behaviors of ants and bees.[2] A single ant is not very complex. Building an ant brain is a far more approachable task than building a human brain. Ants in groups have more complex behavior than an ant by itself. Much like a brain has behavior beyond that which could be anticipated by looking at a single neuron.[3]

This thinking brings us to swarm robotics. Each robot is a small, inexpensive, and simply programmed unit. It has the ability to communicate with neighboring robots and it is deployed with a large number of its siblings. Any small subset of these robots can be destroyed or lost and the swarm can still fulfill its job. The robots are inexpensive so there can be a bunch of them, and since there are a bunch of them, any one of them is expendable.

This configuration of robots, the swarm, lends itself to exploration. Exploration of space leaps to mind, but there are also important exploration tasks on Earth, such as swarming over a disaster area looking for survivors. Swarms will also be used in wartime, to scout out the urban landscape and report on conditions. Swarms of flying robots, another topic that has generated a lot of interest lately, are especially useful for scouting.

6.4.2 Agents (Text 4)

As the world goes online, many of our activities are no longer in the realm of the physical but involve traversing and manipulating our new electronic realities. There will be online tasks that we don't want to do ourselves because they are hard, tedious, or otherwise better left to

---

猜词断义 & 词义注释

swarm
n. 蚁群，一群
traverse
v. 横穿，横越
terrain n. 地形
script
n. 一系列指示
community
n. 社区，公众
inspiration
n. 灵感，好主意
approachable:

anticipate v. 预料
neuron
n. 神经元
deploy v. 实施，展开，部署
sibling n. 同胞
subset n. 子集
expendable:

lend:

leap v. 飞快移动
scout v. 侦查
urban a. 城市的
landscape:

猜词断义 & 词义注释

agent
n. 代理，特工

automation. And some of these tasks will take a fair level of intelligence.

What is needed is an electronic "robot" with many of the traits of its physical counterpart.[4] The ability to travel around its environment, in this case the Internet. The ability to sense and manipulate this environment. And the ability to match incomplete or unclear patterns and to make action decisions based on them.

Such a virtual robot is known as an agent. Agents tend to operate in swarms, interacting with other agents with perhaps different capabilities. Agents lack the physical dimension, so there is none of that pesky, expensive hardware to worry about. They are robots in their most abstract form, pure information.

People have been creating simulated robots in simulated environments almost as long as we have been building computer-driven robots. It is easier and faster to perform experiments in the computer before committing the design to solid form. But those are still just simulations of a robot whose ultimate operation is to be in the physical world. An agent's environment is the world of information.

realm
n. 领域，王国

tedious
a. 乏味的

pesky
a. 犯人的

commit:

6.4.3 Exercises to the Task

I. Write a T in front of a statement if it is true and write an F if it is false according to the text.

1. Building an ant brain is a far easier task than building a human brain.

2. Because of swarms' low cost, they are very suitable to swarm over a disaster area looking for survivors.

3. In the realm of electronics, we could traverse and manipulate realities.

4. Agents' environment is the world of information, for those are still just simulations of a robot whose ultimate operation is to be in the physical world.

II. Translate the following sentences into Chinese.

[1] They are special purpose machines specialized for a single task, they tend to be fixed in position, and their control system is little more than a script reader playing back preset instructions.

[2] Their inspiration is in the complex communities and behaviors of ants and bees.

[3] Much like a brain has behavior beyond that which could be anticipated by looking at a single neuron.

[4] What is needed is an electronic "robot" with many of the traits of its physical counterpart.

6.4.4　Knowledge Widening: Reading Material

Active Park Assist, as shown in Fig.6.7, uses an ultrasonic-based sensing system and Electric Power Assist Steering (EPAS) to position the vehicle for parallel parking, calculate the optimal steering angle and quickly steer the vehicle into a parking spot.

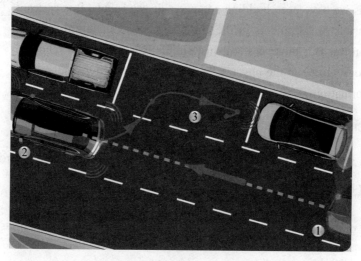

Fig. 6.7　Active Park Assist

(1) The driver activates the system by pressing a center console button, which activates ultrasonic sensors that measure and identify a feasible parking space.

(2) The system then prompts the driver to accept parking assistance. The steering system then takes over and steers the car into the parking space hands-free. The driver still shifts the transmission and operates the gas and brake pedals.

(3) A visual and/or audible driver notification advises the driver about the proximity of other cars and objects and provides instructions.

While the steering is all done automatically, the driver remains responsible for safe parking and can interrupt the system by grasping the steering wheel.

Project VI Modern and New Technology

6.5 Opto-Mechatronic Systems (Task 3)

6.5.1 Introduction of Opto-Mechatronic Systems (Text 5)

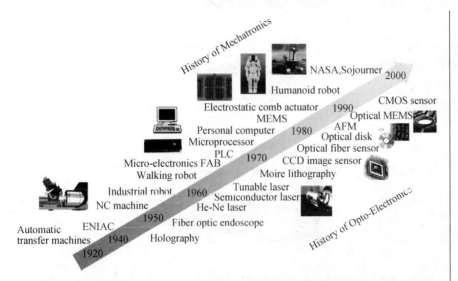

As seen from a historical perspective, the electronic revolution accelerated the integration of mechanical and electronic components, and later the optical revolution effected the integration of optical and electronic components. This trend enabled a number of conventional systems that had low-level autonomy and very low-level performance to evolve into ones having improved autonomy and performance.[1]

Fig.6.8 illustrates the practical systems currently in use that evolved from their original old version. Until recently, the PCB inspection was carried out by human workers with the naked eye aided by a microscope, but it was enabled by a visual inspection technique.[2] The functions of the chip mounter, which originally were mostly mechanical, are now being carried out by integrated devices and include part position estimators, visual sensors, and servo control units. The Coordinate Measuring Machine (CMM) appeared as a contact for the first time, followed by noncontact digital electromagnetic, and then the optical type. In recent years, the CMM has been intensely researched in the hope that it may be introduced as an accurate, reliable, and versatile product that uses sensor integration technique.[3] The washing machine shown in Figure 6.9 also evolved from a mechanically operated machine into one with optical sensory feedback and intelligent control function.

猜词断义 & 词义注释

optical
a. 光的
revolution
n. 革命
inspection
n. 检查，检测
naked
a. 裸的
mounter
n. 安装工，装配工
originally:

estimator
n. 估算仪，测算仪
CMM
坐标测量仪
versatile
a. 多才多艺的，多用途的，多功能的

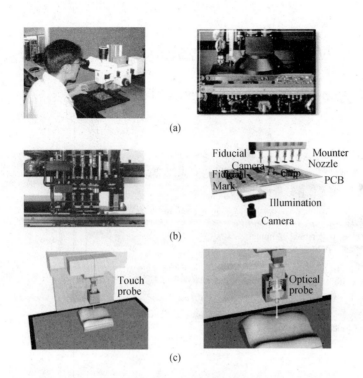

Fig. 6.8 Illustrative evolutions

(a) PCB inspection; (b) Chip/SMD mounting; (c) Coordinate measuring machine

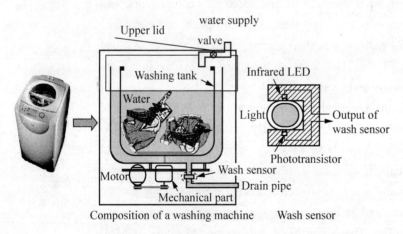

Fig. 6.9 Modern Washing Machine with Optical Sensory Feedback

The technology associated with the developments of machines/processes/systems has continuously evolved to enhance their performance and to create a new value and new function. Mechatronic technology integrated by mechanical, electronic, and computer technologies has certainly played an important role in this evolution. However, to make them further evolve toward systems of precision, intelligence, and autonomy, optics and optical engineering technology had to be embedded into mechatronic systems, compensating for the existing functionalities and

enhance:

compensate
v. 补偿
functionality
n. 功能性，实用性

element:

creating new ones. The opto-mechatronic system is, therefore, a system integrated with optical elements, mechanical elements, electronic elements, and a computer system.

The major functions and roles of optical components or elements in opto-mechatronic systems can be categorized into several technological domains, as shown in Fig.6.10.

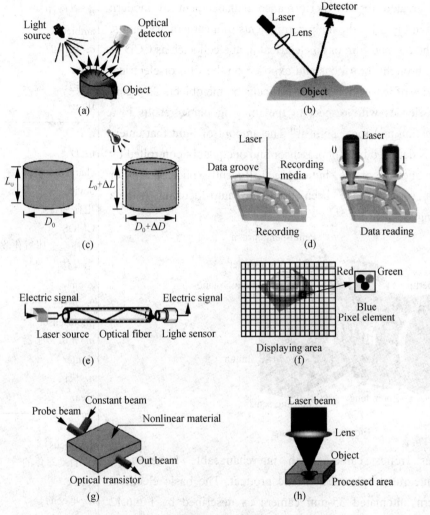

Fig. 6.10 Basic Roles of Optical Technology
(a) Illumination; (b) Sensing; (c) Actuating; (d) Data memory; (e) Data transmission; (f) Data display; (g) Computing; (h) Material property variation

6.5.2 Practical Opto-Mechatronic Systems (Text 6)

Examples of opto-mechatronic systems are found in many control and instrumentation, inspection and testing, optical, manufacturing, consumer, and industrial electronics products as well as in MEMS, automotive,

instrumentation
n. 仪表

bioapplications, and many other fields of engineering. Below are some examples of such applications.

Cameras is typical device that are operated by opto-mechatronic components. For example, a smart camera is equipped with an aperture control and a focusing adjustment with an illuminometer designed to perform well independent of ambient brightness. With this system configuration, new functionalities are created for the performance enhancement of modern cameras. As shown in Fig.6.11, the main components of a camera are lenses, one aperture, one shutter, and film or an electrical image cell such as CCD or CMOS. Images are brought into focus and exposed on the film or electrical image cell via a series of lenses that zoom and focus on the object. Changing the position of the lenses with respect to the imaging plane results in a change in magnification and focal points.[4] The amount of light that enters through the lenses is detected by a photosensor and adequately controlled by changing either the aperture or the shutter speed. Recently, photosensors or even CMOS area sensors have been used for auto-focusing with a controllable focusing lens.

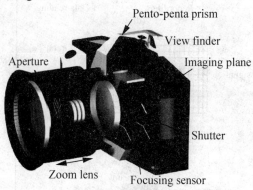

Fig. 6.11 Camera

The autofocus, reflex camera with interchangeable lenses is a multi-functional, integrated opto-mechatronic product. The basic electrical design of a modern automated 35-mm camera as described by Fig.6.12 consists of a microcontroller embedded in the camera body and another microcontroller located in the lens housing. The two embedded controllers are able to communicate when the lens assembly is firmly attached to the camera body.

As the photographer begins to press the shutter button (initial position), the microcontroller in the camera body calculates both the shutter speed and aperture settings from the output of the meter sensor and displays the result on both the viewfinder and external LCD display panel.[5]

Project VI Modern and New Technology

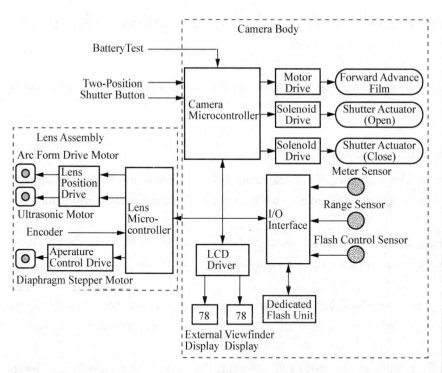

Fig. 6.12 The Electronic Subsystems of An Automatic Camera

While adjusting the shutter speed and aperture based on current lighting conditions, the microcontroller in the camera body determines whether the projected image is focused on the photographic film. After passing through the camera lens, the light reflected from the object in the field-of-view strikes the two 48-bit linear arrays of photodetectors. The spacing of the signals measured by the detector arrays will be at a known value when the image is correctly focused on the photographic film. However, if the image is out of focus, then the measured spacing will deviate from the expected value and the magnitude of the deviation is used to generate an error signal. The error signal is fed to the lens microcontroller in order to produce a control signal to drive the DC motors that adjust the focus of the lens assembly.

project
v. 投射

strike:

spacing
n. 间隔，间距
array
n. 阵列
deviation
n. 偏离
magnitude:

6.5.3 Exercises to the task

I. Write a T in front of a statement if it is true and write an F if it is false according to the text.

1. The Coordinate Measuring Machine (CMM) appeared as not only a contact but also noncontact digital electromagnetic type.

2. Mechatronic technology will be integrated by mechanical, electronic, optical, and computer technologies.

3. What includes optical elements, mechanical elements, electronic elements, and a computer system is an opto-mechatronic system.

4. Auto-focusing means changing the position of the lenses with respect to the imaging plane automatically.

II. Translate the following sentences into Chinese.

[1] This trend enabled a number of conventional systems that had low-level autonomy and very low-level performance to evolve into ones having improved autonomy and performance.

[2] Until recently, the PCB inspection was carried out by human workers with the naked eye aided by a microscope, but it was enabled by a visual inspection technique.

[3] In recent years, the CMM has been intensely researched in the hope that it may be introduced as an accurate, reliable, and versatile product that uses sensor integration technique.

[4] Changing the position of the lenses with respect to the imaging plane results in a change in magnification and focal points.

[5] As the photographer begins to press the shutter button (initial position), the microcontroller in the camera body calculates both the shutter speed and aperture settings from the output of the meter sensor and displays the result on both the viewfinder and external LCD display panel.

6.5.4　Knowledge Widening: Reading Material

A three-dimen sional contacting probe or sensor, commonly known as a Coordinate Measuring Machine (CMM), measures the three-dimensional geometric surface dimensions of objects. The CMM shown in Fig.6.13 uses the principle of typical opto-mechatronic technology, it adopts an opto-mechatronic sensing principle with the aid of a device that scans the motion of the measuring machine. The probe is composed of a seven-fiber array and a concave mirror mounted on a stylus that contacts the object to be measured. The infrared light emitted by one of the fibers is reflected by the mirror. The reflected light is then detected by the optical fiber array and modulated by the position and orientation of the mirror, which changes with the position of the stylus. Nano CMM is another typical example of a system that accommodates optical elements into the conventional system to enhance system measurement performance.

Project VI　Modern and New Technology

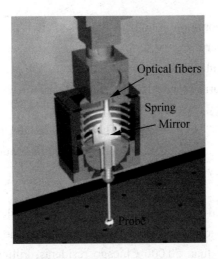

Fig. 6.13　Optical-based Coordinate Measuring Machine

6.6　Language Study

记忆事实

只有记住事实，人们才可以用它。在下面的练习中，阅读完一段后，马上就做选择，不要回顾原文。

练习：

You my deduct the full amoum of certain medical and dental expenses you paid for yourself, your spouse, and any person who is your dependents. You may not deduct amounts paid for you by insurance.

(1) What amount of medical expenses can you deduct? _____.

a. Half of the amount you paid

b. The full amount you paid

c. 20 percent of the mount you paid

d. 75 percent of the mount you paid

(2) You may not deduct medical expenses you paid for_____.

a. yourself

b. your spouse

c. one of your dependents

d. someone who is not your dependent

(3) You may be duct_____.

a. dental expenses but not medical expenses

b. medical expenses but not dental expenses

c. only dental expenses you paid for yourself

d. both medical and dental expenses

Magnesium can be found in all the tissues of the body but is mainly located in the bones.

Magnesium deficiency is uncommon in humans but is sometimes seen in alcoholics and in some patients recovering from surgery.

(1) The paragraph is about_____.

    a. copper   b. phosphorus   c. calcium   d. magnesium

(2) Magnesium deficiency in humans is_____.

    a. uncommon   b. a major health risk in the United States

    c. related to heart attacks   d. extremely common but not dangerous

(3) Magnesium deficiency is sometimes seen in_____.

    a. children   b. alcoholics

    c. adults over 65 years old   d. people with German measles

Thunderstorms and tornados struck the middle portion of the United States on Thursday, knocking out power to more than 50,000 Chicago residents, killing one man, and injuring 25 people.

(1) A power outage was experienced by residents of _____.

    a. detroit   b. minneapolis   c. toledo   d. chicago

(2) What part of the country did the bad weather strike?

    a. East   b. West   c. South   d. Central

(3) How many people were injured?

    a. 25   b. 19   c. 15   d. 10

(4) On what day of the week did the storm hit?

    a. Monday   b. Saturday   c. Thursday   d. Friday

6.7 Practical Skill

增减翻译法

由于英汉两种语言语法结构的差异、词类差异及修辞手法的不同，在翻译过程中往往会出现词量增补或减少的现象。增减翻译法包括加词译法、减词译法、句子的分译与合译。

1. 加词译法

为了确切表达原文，在译文中有时需要增加原文中无其形而有其意的某些词。词的增补主要包括重复英语省略的某些词、给动作名词加汉语名词、增加概括性的词、增加解说性的词、增加加强上下文连贯性的词语、语法加词、虚拟语气加词、分词独立结构和分词短语的加词等。

(1) High voltage is necessary for long transmission while low voltage for safe use.

远距离输电需要高压，安全用电则<u>需要低压</u>。(增加英语句子省略的词)

(2) The lower the frequency is, the greater the refraction of a wave will be.

频率越低，波的折射<u>作用</u>就越强。(给动作名词加汉语名词)

(3) This report summed up the new achievements made in electron tubes, semiconductors and components.

这篇报告总结了电子管、半导体和元件<u>三方面</u>的新成就。(增加概况性的词)

2. 减词译法

在英语中，有些词如冠词、介词、连词和代词等，在汉语中要么没有，要么用得不多，主要是因为汉语可以借助词序来表达逻辑关系。因此，英汉翻译中的词量减少主要出现在英语冠词、介词、代词、连词以及关系代词的省略翻译上。

(1) The alternating current supplies <u>the</u> greatest part of the electric power for industry today.
如今交流电占了工业用电的绝大部分。(冠词的省略)

(2) Because they are neutral electrically，<u>they</u> are called "neutrons".
由于它们呈电中性，所以被称为"中子"。(代词的省略)

(3) Because copper possesses good conductivity，<u>it</u> is widely used in electrical engineering.
因为铜具有良好的导电性，所以被广泛地应用于电力工程。(代词的省略)

(4) They have found a method <u>for</u> solving this problem.
他们已经找到了解决这个问题的方法。(介词的省略)

(5) Check the circuit <u>before</u> you begin the experiment.
检查好线路后再开始做实验。(连词的省略)

3. 分译法

单词的分译：有的英文句子虽然不长，但字对字译出来很别扭，或容易发生误解，这时往往可把单词译成一个分句或单句。

短语的分译：英语中能提出来分译的短语通常有分词短语、介词短语、动词不定式短语或名词短语。

句子的分译：把英语中的从句译成分句，或把一个简单句拆开，将其译成两个或两个以上的句子，以及在翻译复合句过程中增加分句或句子的数量。

(1) The <u>price</u> limits its production.
由于它价格昂贵，所以限制了其批量生产。(名词的分译)

(2) The time could have been <u>more profitably</u> sent in raking a detailed investigation.
如果当初把时间花在细致的调查上，那么<u>好处就更大了</u>。(副词的分译)

(3) <u>Computers being used</u>, the complicated problem was solved quickly.
<u>由于使用了计算机</u>，复杂的问题才得到了迅速解决。(分词独立结构的分译)

(4) <u>The wrong power-line connections</u> will damage the motor.
<u>如果电源接错了</u>，那么电动机就会被损坏。(名词短语的分译)

4. 合译法

合译法是把两个或两个以上单句合译成一个单句，或把主从复合句及并列句合译成一个单句，这种译法同样是由英汉两种语言在句子结构、修辞及习惯用法方面的差异所决定的。合译法可省略一些重复的词语或句子成分，从而使译文更加紧凑，符合汉语习惯。

(1) Generally speaking, the typical metal conducts electricity and heat. It slows lustrous surface，usually with white，or so-called metallic luster. It is ductile and malleable.
一般来说，典型的金属能导热导电，其表面有光泽，并具有延展性和可锻性。(简单句的合译)

(2) Welding is used where a tight seal is desired and weight increases cannot be tolerated.
在要求接缝紧密而又不允许增加重量的地方就可使用焊接。(复合句——地点状语从句

的合译)

(3) Sulphuric acid enters into the manufacture of explosives, dyestuffs and drugs; it is useded in sugar refining and in the preparation of fertilizers.

硫酸被用来制造炸药、染料、药物、食糖和化肥等。(并列句的合译)

练习:

(1) Some of the gases in the air are constant in amount, while others air not.

(2) An elementary form of radar, shown in Fig.2, consists of an antenna, a transmitter, and an energy-detecting device, or receiver.

(3) A wire lengthens while it is heated.

(4) Semiconductor is a new kind of material which has found a good use in industry.

(5) The degree to which they impede the flow of current is called resistance.

Project VII Job Application in Mechatronic Trades

7.1 Job Advertisement (Task 1)

Siemens PML Software (Shanghai) Limited

Located in Pudong Economic & Technological Development Zone of Shanghai City, Siemens PML Software (Shanghai) Co., Ltd. is a division of Siemens Automation and Drives (A&D), leading global provider of product lifecycle management (PLM) software and services with 5.5 million licensed seats and 51,000 customers worldwide. According to the rapid expansion in the Eastern China, our company is searching for highly qualified and motivated candidates for the following position based in Shanghai.

1. Secretary Assistant (2 person)

Responsibility:
- Administration work
- Arranging license applications
- Maintaining office accounts and general secretarial duties, etc.

Requirement:
- University graduate preferably with degree in business administration
- Good command of spoken and written English, Shanghainese and Mandarin
- Good PC knowledge e.g. Word, Excel, Outlook (E-mail), Chinese Word Processing
- Possess a pleasant personality and positive work attitude and be willing and able to work diligently without supervision
- Ideally below 30 years of age and good character
- Minimum 2 years working experience in operating a small office independently

We provide:

The right candidates with guaranteed salary ($12/hr), car allowance, comm., profit sharing, plus Health Insur/Dent/Lif.

The applicants are invited to E-mail your resume (in both English and Chinese), copies of certificates, a recent photo, current and expected salaries

---

猜词断义 & 词义注释

Siemens 西门子
division n. 分公司
seat n. 席位
responsibility 工作职责
license n. 营业执照
accounts n. 账号，账目

Shanghainese 上海话
Mandarin 浦东话

pleasant personality:

diligent a. 勤奋的
guarante v. 保证

and contact details within 10 days. Please indicate the position name on the bottom left of the envelope.

E-mail: staffing-cn@ugs.com

2. PLC Engineer (5 person)

Responsibility:
- Consulting customizing training
- Understand and analyze customers' requirement
- Manage the project implementation
- Summarize project and documentation
- Support for sales activities

Requirement:
- College education or above, major in Mechanical/Electrical/Electronic Engineer or relevant field
- Self-motivated and hard-working
- Good at oral and written English, can communicate with foreigner
- Familiar with WINCC, PCS7, SIMATIC S7-400
- More than three years experience in engineering institute
- Knowledge of technical English will have an added advantage
- Training will be given to the right candidate

Others:
- Frequent travel is needful for this role

We offer:
- Attractive salary & benefit
- Excellent career prospects to the right candidates
- Training opportunities abroad

Please send a full resume (in both English and Chinese) with a photo, copy of university results, past employment reference letters and contact phone number to: Personnel Manager, GPO BOX 88, Pudong Economic & Technological Development Zone of Shanghai City.

allowance
n. 津贴
comm.
交通，通信
profit sharing
利润分红
Health Insur/Dent/Lif
健康/牙科/生命保险
envelope
n. 信封
consulting
a. 接受咨询的，担任顾问的
customizing
a. 按客户的要求做的
implementation
v. 执行
summarize
v. 总结，概括
major
v. 主修
relevant
a. 相关的
oral
n. 口语的
institute
n. 机构
GPO: general post office
邮政局

7.2　Letters of Application (Task 2)

1. Secretary Assistant

Dear Sir or Madam:

In response to your advertisement in today's newspaper, I wish to apply for the position of secretary assistant in your esteemed company. I consider that I am totally competent to meet the requirements which you have specified.

猜词断义 & 词义注释

esteem
v. 尊敬
esteemed:

I am twenty-six years of age. After graduating from high school I took a three years' business course in one of the best commercial school in Shanghai. Since graduating from business school I have worked for three years in a lawyer's office, where I am at present employed. My salary for the past three years has been over 1,500 yuan per month, and I should not make a change for less.

I believe I would make a capable secretary assistant for the following reasons.

I am alert, adaptable, and keen-minded; an efficient typist; can write clearly, concisely, and entertainingly; can speak Shanghainese and Mandarin very well.

My resume is enclosed and I would welcome the opportunity to meet with you personally. Thank you for your consideration.

Sincerely yours,
Li Hong

competent
a. 胜任的

alert
a. 机敏的
adaptable
a. 有适应能力的
keen-minded
热心的
concise
a. 简明的
entertaining
a. 生动有趣的

2. PLC Engineer

Dear Sir or Madam:

Referring to your advertisement in *21 Century Human Resource* of May 17 for an PLC engineer, I feel I can fill that position.

I graduated from Shanghai Technical Institute of Electronics & Information this year, and majored in Mechatronic Engineeing.

The reason why I feel I can fill the position of PLC Engineer are as follows.

- I am adaptable, self-motivated and hard-working.
- I have practical experience in repairing electronic devices and maintaining CNC lathes.
- I can speak Shanghainese and Mandarin very well.
- I am familiar with English for Mechatronic Engineering.

Hope you will consider this application favorable and I wish to assure you that I should make every effort to be worthy of the confidence you may place in me. Enclosed herewith are two copies of my diplomas and a copy of my resume for your reference.

Thank you in advance for your consideration and courtesy.

Yours faithfully,
Li Ming

motivate
v. 激发
self-motivated

7.3 Resume (Task 3)

Resume

Name: Li Ming **Born:** Feb.1, 1987
Place of Birth: Xuhui, Shanghai **Sex:** Male
Height: 175cm **Weight:** 67kg
Health: Excellent **Marital Status:** Single
Tel: 021-57132333 **E-mail:** Li@126.com
Current Address: Room 1201, Building 8, Lane 567, West Nanjing Road, Shanghai China
Objective: PLC Engineer
Education:

2008—2011 Dept. of Mechanical Engineering, Shanghai Technical Institute of Electronics & Information, Diploma in Mechnatronic Engineering (2011)

Major courses taken include:

college physics, basic technology of analogue electron, basics of C programming, microcomputer principles and application, basic technology of digital electron, advanced mathematics, engineering graphics, engineering mechanics, electric circuits principles, principles and applications of PLC, hydraulic control technology, measurement and test, CNC programming principles and applications, CAD/CAM, etc.

English Qualification:

National College English Test Band 4 Certificate, 2009

Computer Proficiency:

National Computer Level Test-Rank Two Certificate, 2009

Mastery of C programming skills

Sound knowledge and experience in Office, AutoCAD and MasterCAM

Extracurricular Activities:

Succeeded in organizing the English Speech Contest of First College Cultural and Artistic Festival and praised by relevant leaders

Minister of Practical Department

Editor of campus life, a weekly

Technical Qualifications And Special Skills:

Senior Electronic Assembling Worker

Tourist guides' qualification

Sixth class electrician certificate

Typing proficiency: 50 wpm

Rewards:

Scholarship from the college in 2009 and 2010

Title of excellent leader of the Student Union, 2010

Project VII Job Application in Mechatronic Trades

Experience:

Devices Repairing and Assembling Worker

Repaired electronic devices in Community Service Centre

Apprentice in Shanghai Electric Group Maintaining Automatic Streamline, summer holiday in 2010

References:

Will be furnished upon request.

7.4 Interview (Task 4)

A: May I come in?

B: Yes, please.

A: How do you do, sir? My name is Li Ming. I'm coming for an interview as requested.

B: Glad to meet you. I'm Tom. Have a seat please.

A: Thanks, and I'd like to apply for the job as a PLC engineer.

B: We have received your letter in answer to our advertisement. I would like to talk with you regarding your qualification for this job. Just relax, and let's have a chat, shall we?

A: Yes. It's a great pleasure for me to have this opportunity for interview.

A: Why do you want to join us?

B: I'm very interested in the PLC engineering and very fond of solving various engineering problems. I think it would be very exciting and challenging to work for your company. Equally important, I want to expand our horizon and reach to a new summit of my life. I know your company enjoys a rather good reputation in this field.

A: Have you applied for a similar post to any other companies?

B: Yes, I applied to ABC Company the other day, in case you may not accept me, but I still prefer to work for you.

A: What kind of personalities do you think you have?

B: I think I am initiative and responsible. I am easy-going and friendly to everybody. I would not like to go ahead of people and lead them. Instead, I'd rather cooperate with others, and get the job done by working together.

A: What do you think is the most important thing for you to be happy?

B: I think the most important thing is to build a career. If my career is successful and promising, I will feel very happy.

A: What are your plans for the future?

> 猜词断义 &
> 词义注释
>
> expand
> our horizon
> 开阔视野
>
> initiative
> a. 自发的，主动的

B: I'd like to continue working as long as your company needs me. If I feel I am making progress in the work, I would stay until I reach the age limit.

A: What attitude do you take towards work?

B: In general, I hold a positive attitude towards work. Seize the day, seize the hour. So even if it's hard at the time, I try to get things done that day and not to let them go.

A: What is your expected salary?

B: Since this will be my first job and I don't have much experience, I feel hesitant to suggest salary. I'd rather leave that to you, sir.

A: How can we contact you?

B: This is my phone number. Please call me if necessary.

A: We will inform you of the result within one week. Thank you for coming.

B: Thanks. I am looking forward to that.

7.5 Exercise: Translate the Following Paragraphs

Interview

Place: Personnel Manager's Office in a company

Characters: (Interviewer) Mike Anderson, Personnel Manager of a company (Applicant) Chenzhuo

I: Come in, please. Good morning, I am Mike Anderson, personnel manager of our company.

A: How do you do? My name is Chen Zhuo.

I: Sit down please and make yourself at home.

A: Thank you very much.

I: As I know you have applied to work in our company. Would you please introduce yourself?

A: I'm 23 years old and was born in Huangshi. I can speak and write English fluently and know how to operate the computer and NC machines. I have been an assistant engineer for half a year in a famous company one year ago. So, I am sure that I am quite efficient in technical work, like NC programming, operation, maintenance and debugging.

I: OK, I would infer that you are an excellent student in your college. Could you tell me more details about your major and English courses?

A: All right. Though I am a student in the Department of Mechanical and Electrical Engineering, I studied many English Courses including English Reading and Comprehension, Oral English, English Writing and professional English. Most of the courses are taught in English, some are even taught by foreign teachers.

Project VII Job Application in Mechatronic Trades

I: By the way, do you have any experience as a leader at the school?

A: Yes, I was the monitor of our class. I have organized many social activities.

I: Besides all these, what do you like to do in your spare time?

A: I have a great interest in travel, reading and sports such as swimming, tennis and so on.

I: I am very glad to hear that. Travel and sports are also my hobbies. Why do you choose our company?

A: Your company is one of the largest NC machine manufacturers in East China. As you see in my resume, I specialized in CAD/CAM in college, so I expect to develop my capabilities in your company. On the other hand, the position for which I applied is quite challenging. That's the reason why I like to come to your company. I hope to display my talents fully here.

I: If I accept you, how much do you expect to be paid?

A: At least ¥1,500 a month.

I: That will be no problem.

A: OK. When can I get the reply about my application?

I: I think you will know the final result within a week. It's my pleasure to have a talk with you.

A: Me too. It takes your much time. Good bye.

I: Goodbye.

Appendix Translation

项目一 汽 车

1.1 项目引入

汽车是一种在陆地上行驶的机动车辆。相对于卡车或者公共汽车来说，如图 1.1 所示，汽车通常指的是一种四轮车辆，载客 2 到 6 人，以及少量货物，而卡车主要是设计用于运送货物的，由更大型重型零部件制造而成。公共汽车(或者说多用途公共汽车和长途客车)则是一种公共交通工具，为较大载客量而设计，当然有时也可以装载少量货物。

图 1.1 汽车和卡车

汽车是现代机电一体化技术发展的产物。过去，有许多功能都是纯机械或是纯电子技术的，例如启动电机和电池充电系统。比如，在使用传感器和微控制器之前，由一个机械式配电器控制火花塞的点火，以点燃压缩混合油气。但是就燃油效率而言，这种机械式的燃油控制方式是不够理想的。电子点火系统是 20 世纪 70 年代晚期引入汽车中的第一套机电系统中的一个系统。电子点火系统是由曲轴位置传感器，凸轮轴位置传感器，空气流量、气门位置、气门位置变化率传感器和专门控制火花塞点火时机的微控制器组成的，如图 1.2 所示。

图 1.2 电子点火系统

1.2 项目内容

机电一体化通过使用多个学科的知识来解决一些技术问题，包括机械工程技术、电子学和计算机技术。

过去，传统的工程师往往只会使用某一个学科的知识来解决这些技术问题(例如，一位机械工程师会使用一些机械工程方法来解决手头的技术问题)。

后来，由于技术难度的加大，以及更多先进产品的出现，科学家和工程师们需要找到一种新颖的方法以满足科研和产品开发的需求，这就促使他们在不同的知识和技术领域寻找解决方案，以便开发出新的产品(例如，机械工程师试图使用电子技术来解决机械问题)。

微处理器的发展对于科学家和工程师们是极大的鼓舞。正因为如此，他们才能够以更开阔的视角考虑问题的解决方案，选择更高效的手段，于是基于这种多学科技术的融合可以获得新的产品。

1.3 任务一 什么是机电一体化？

1.3.1 文章一 机电一体化简介

20世纪70年代，"机电一体化"这个术语首先在日本产生。经过25年的不断发展，机电一体化技术已经硕果累累。那么什么是机电一体化呢？

(1) 机电一体化技术是一套方法，可以起到优化机电产品设计的作用。机电一体化mechatronics一词是由mechatronics这个单词的开头几个字母mecha和electronics这个单词的结尾几个字母tronics首尾连接而成的。也就是说，在技术发展和产品开发的过程中，越来越多的电子技术将被运用到机械技术中去，紧密结合、融为一体，无所谓谁先谁后。一个机电一体化系统不仅仅是电子与机械系统的结合，也不仅仅是一个控制系统，更多的是所有这些的高度集成，如图1.3所示。

图1.3 机电一体化系统的主要组成部分

(2) 机电一体化技术是一种复杂的应用技术，用于实现对物理系统的操控。

现在，在家里、办公室里、学校里、商店里，以及工业应用中都随处可见机电一体化系统。

常见的机电一体化系统包括以下几种。

- 家用电器，例如冰箱和冷柜、微波炉、洗衣机、吸尘器、洗碗机、烤箱、定时器、搅拌机、榨汁机、音响、电视机、电话机、割草机、数码相机、VCD、摄像机，以及其他许许多多现代化的同类设备。
- 民用系统，例如空调系统、安保系统、全自动门禁系统。
- 办公设备，例如激光打印机、硬盘驱动器、液晶显示器、磁带驱动器、扫描仪、复印件、传真机，以及其他计算机外部设备。
- 零售业设备，例如自动标签系统，条形码编码机，以及超市中的相关设备。
- 银行系统，例如收银机、自动取款机。
- 生产制造设备，例如数控机床、搬运机器人、焊接机器人、自动导航车辆、以及其他工业机器人。
- 航空系统，例如驾驶室控制和仪表系统、飞行控制器、着陆系统，以及其他飞行器子系统。

1.3.2 文章二 基本机械装置简介

复杂机器都是由一些运动部件组成的，例如斜面、杠杆、齿轮、凸轮、曲轴、弹簧、传动带和各类轮系。机器在外力的作用下，将一定类型的运动传递到特定位置。有些机器只是将一种运动转换成另一种运动，例如将旋转运动转换为直线运动。虽然机器看似在不停地变化，但是它们都是由一些简单的基本机械装置构成的。机械装置即是一组连接(或者说是机器中由零件构成的一个系统)，能完成预定的动作。因此，机械装置与机器的区别在于是否对外做功。本文中将要讨论的机械装置包括斜面、杠杆、轮和轴。

斜面——楔

要在做功相同的情况下将一个物体提升到给定的高度,斜面如图 1.4 所示,可以通过增加距离的方法减小作用力的大小,使工作变得更省力。试想将两倍于自己体重的重物提升到 4 英尺高的架子上,或者将同样质量的重物滚上一个平缓的斜坡,后者将更省力一些。

图 1.4　斜面

斜面一般用在切割设备(如斧子)上。通常两个斜面背对背地形成楔形,如图 1.5 所示。向下运动被垂直分离到刃面上。拉链是一组楔的组合,下部两个楔用于关闭拉链,上部的一个楔用于打开拉链。

图 1.5　斜面效果图

杠杆

最简单可能也是人们最熟悉的机器就是杠杆。跷跷板就是杠杆的一种常见形式,它靠两端的重量来保持平衡。如图 1.6 到图 1.8 所示,杠杆一般分为 3 种类型,它们的支点、作用力和负载的相对位置各有不同。

(1) 第一种杠杆的示例有称、撬杠和剪刀等。

图 1.6　杠杆(1)

(2) 在第二种杠杆中负载位于支点和作用力之间,示例有:手推车,启瓶器和核桃夹等。

图 1.7　杠杆(2)

(3) 在第三种杠杆中作用力位于负载和支点之间,示例有:锤子、鱼竿和镊子等。

图 1.8　杠杆(3)

大多数机器都会用到杠杆,或是一些杠杆的组合,或是几种不同类型杠杆的组合。

轮轴

无论是斜面还是杠杆都是以增加力的作用距离为代价来达到省力的目的的。轮轴同样也是这样,作用在轴上的力和运动可以把运动放大,但是作用在转轮圆周上会更省力。实际上,可以认为转轴只是一种环形杠杆,如图 1.9 所示。许多常见的机械装置都使用轮轴,例如螺丝刀、方向盘、扳手和水龙头等。

图 1.9　轮轴类似于环形杠杆

1.3.3　文章三　电子技术基础

电流和电压

大多数机电一体化系统都包含有许多电子器件和电路,因此,了解电荷(Q)、电场(E)、磁场(B)和电压(V)这些概念是非常重要的。本文并不会详细讨论它们的大小问题,而是采用近似的方法进行处理。用电子学来处理以上物理量可能更切合实际。

在电学中电荷是电量的基本单位,通常用电荷数来表示构成物质的基本粒子的电量。因此,重要的是得电子数或者失电子数,而质子的电荷数可忽略不计。

电流(I)用运动电荷的总和来表示：$I(t) = \dfrac{dQ}{dt}$，即单位时间内流过某一截面的正电荷数。而实际上运动着的电荷是负电子，所以这些电子的运动方向与电流方向相反。电流的国际单位是安培(A)。对于大多数电路来说，用安培作为量纲数值太大，所以往往用毫安(mA)或微安(μA)来表示。

导体中存在电流是由于导体两端有电势差。电子由低电位流向高电位，而电流正好相反。

通常用静电势能(V)作为电荷流动的动因，而不是用电场(E)，这样更为简便。通常电场 E 的广义矢量特性并不重要。在电场中，一定距离内的电势可以表示为：$dV = -E \times dx$。

正电荷由高电位向低电位流动。电位也可以称为电势差，或者不确切地说，也可以称为电压：$V = V_{21} = V_2 - V_1 = \int_{V_1}^{V_2} dV$。

电势差的国际单位是伏特(V)。直流(DC)电路分析用于处理电流和电压方向不随时间变化的电路问题，而交流(AC)电路分析则用于处理电压和电流信号随时间变化的电路问题，交变电流在一个周期内的平均值为零。

外接电源

电荷在外电场的作用下在导体中流动。最终，由于电荷的重置内电场与外电场相互抵消，结果造成零电流。为了保证有一个稳定的电压降(和电荷流动)，需要存在一个电动势(EMF)，即外接电源(电池、电力供电和信号发生器等)。

人们所关心的电动势基本上分为以下两类。

- 理想的电压源，无论电流如何变化，它能使电压始终保持恒定(电流有可能为无穷大)。
- 理想的电流源，无论电压如何变化，它能使电流始终保持恒定(电压有可能为无穷大)。

因为电池不可能产生无限大的电流，所以采用一种理想的电池模型，就是把它看做由一个内电阻和一个理想电压源(零电阻)串联而成。在实际应用时，总是将电动势近似看做理想电动势，并与其他电路元件连接在一起。

只要电池连续供电并且电路始终导通，电子将在电路中不断流动。就像水在管道内流动一样，电子在电路中连续的定向流动称为电流。只要电压源朝着一个方向"推动"电子，电流在电路中就会朝一个方向流动。这种电子的单向流动被称为直流电(Direct Current，DC)。

接地

电压的大小总是相对于某个参考点来衡量的。电压(或者说电势差)通常是指两个点之间的差值，而某点处的电压则以接地点作为参考。同样，电流流过导体时，将从高电势流向低电势(而不是停留在导体中)。按照严格的定义，地面是地球的主要部分(有时指接地线)。地面就像是一个巨大的电池。它能存储或输出大量的电荷，而其本身的电性不变。

1.4　任务二　与汽车有关的工程力学

目前，几乎所有的汽车都是由发动机、底盘、车身和电子设备组成的，如图 1.11 所示。

图 1.11　汽车的构造

发动机用于为车轮提供动力。为了承受燃烧所产生的压力和热量，发动机必须足够坚固。

底盘由传动系统和运动机构组成。这些运动机构包括转向系统、刹车系统和悬挂系统。传动系统负责将动力从发动机传递到车轮。转向系统用于控制汽车的方向。刹车系统用于减速和停车。悬挂系统用于吸收路面振动和帮助驾驶员在崎岖道路上驾驶车辆。

这些主要系统的部件都安装在钢架上，钢架上覆盖有汽车车身板件。汽车的外形就是由这些板件形成的，并且这些板件能够保护内部零件免受外界损坏。而且在交通事故中，这些板件还可以为乘客提供一定的保护。

电子设备包括电池、发电机、仪表、灯光、导线、收音机和空调。汽车通过许多电路将电流从电池输送到各部件，这样电子设备才能正常工作。

作为一种机电产品，汽车经常承受着工作应力，有超过材料承受极限的风险。材料力学的目的就是分析和减小这一风险。

1.4.1 文章四 轴向拉压

静力学回顾
……
结构受力图
……
分离体受力图
……
接合点法
……
应力分析
……
设计
……

1.4.2 文章五 扭转与剪切

在机械工程中，承受扭转载荷的转轴是最常使用的结构。如图1.11所示，一根标准的后轮驱动轴主要用来传递扭矩。这类轴的横截面通常是空心圆环，将动力由变速箱传递到差速器，差速器可以使各车轮转动起来。本文将讨论这些轴，因为它们可以反映出剪应力和剪应变起到的作用。

……
例题
……
解答
……

1.5 任务三 与汽车有关的工程材料

在日常生活中，我们每天都会接触到相当数量的工程材料：金属、塑料和陶瓷是通常用来描述这些材料的一些术语。加工材料的尺寸有大有小，小到硅晶片中的材料，大到悬架上的钢板。各种材料是人类文明的真实写照，是人类劳动的结晶，对人类文明的特征具有决定性的影响，就如工业革命时期的铸铁一样。材料使用的正确与否，会对材料将来的发展产生显著的影响。我们应该认识到全球能源使用和环境控制问题刻不容缓、复杂多变，这些问题都会对材料领域产生深远的影响。

就人们所用到的各类主要材料而言，首先了解如图1.14所示的类型很有用。图中用几个扇面表示金属、陶瓷和聚合物。这些材料如今都可以制成非晶体形态，所以图中的圆心部分表示玻璃。将两种或者两种以上不同特性的材料结合起来使用的方法已经有100多年的历史了，这样可以产生重要的复合材料，碳纤维增强型聚合物和金属基复合材料就是很好的例子。

图1.14 材料的基本分类

1.5.1 文章六 金属材料

金属材料包括金属合金。从严格意义上讲，金属专指铁、金、铝和铅这几个元素。金属的定义随着研究领域的不同而不同。化学家所使用的金属的定义就不同于物理学家所使用的。

金属元素可以通过不同的金属特性来定义，如延展性、硬度、韧性、导热导电性和热膨胀性。

金属指的是一个大类。相对于非金属，金属元素的核外电子数通常小于4个，而非金属元素的核外电子数一般为4~7个。金属原子一般要比非金属大得多。

合金是由金属元素和其他元素构成的。钢是一种铁合金，它是由铁、碳和一些其他元素构成的。铝锂合金要比传统的铝合金轻10%。

人们所使用的材料3/4以上是金属，极少使用纯金属元素。不使用纯金属有许多原因。纯金属不是太硬就是太软，或是因为稀少而昂贵，但是主要原因通常是纯金属不能满足工程需要，只有将金属和其他元素混合起来才能达到工程所需要的性能。于是，人们较多使用这些混合形式(合金)。因此，金属这个名称也可以用于表示含有金属的材料。金属又可以细分为黑色金属和有色金属。图1.5中列出了几种贵重金属。

图1.15 贵重金属

铸铁

铸铁是将生铁和焦炭以及石灰石放入一个称为冲天炉的熔炉中熔融得到的。它主要是铁和碳的合金。碳在铸铁中的含量为1.7%~4.5%。铸铁中也包含有少量的硅、锰、磷和硫。

铁矿石由非金属元素比如氧或硫与铁元素构成。将铁矿石和来自于焦炭的一氧化碳(一种从煤炭中得到的碳形式)一起加热后，铁就会与氧元素分离开。加入石灰石保持这些杂质为液态，于是铁就可以从这些杂质中分离出来，如图1.6所示。

图 1.16 熔炼

钢

钢是一种铁碳合金，它的碳含量小于等于 1.5%。碳以铁碳化合物的形式存在，因为它能够增加钢的硬度和强度。其他元素，例如硅、硫、磷和锰也或多或少影响钢的力学性能。如今生产的多数钢材为普通碳钢。碳钢的分类依据是碳含量，因为碳含量是碳钢机械性能的主要影响因素，同时碳钢中的硅含量不足 0.5%，锰含量不足 1.5%。根据碳含量（从 0.06% 到 1.5%），将碳钢划分成如下类型。

(1) 超低碳钢　　　　碳含量 0.06%～0.15%
(2) 低碳钢　　　　　碳含量 0.15%～0.45%
(3) 中碳钢　　　　　碳含量 0.45%～0.8%
(4) 高碳钢　　　　　碳含量 0.8%～1.5%

1.5.2　文章七　非金属材料

塑料

现在使用的塑料有许多种。塑料必须按照回收方式进行分类，因为每一种塑料的熔点不同，机械性能也不同。塑料行业已经定制了一整套识别体系对塑料进行分类。这个体系将塑料分为 7 组，并使用数字代码标识在容器的底部。下面说明这 7 个代码体系。

这是一种回收利用得最多的塑料，因为按照加利福尼亚"瓶子法案"，只有这种塑料具有回收价值。回收规程和回收中心都要求人们取下瓶盖，压平瓶体。

多数街头回收方案都会接受细口瓶。找到街头的回收网点，或者联系街头回收服务供应商以确定是否可回收 2 类塑料，是否需要事先按颜色将这些瓶罐进行整理。

回收中心很少接受 3 类塑料。尽量使用其他的塑料。
回收中心很少接受 4 类塑料。尽量使用其他的塑料。
回收中心很少接受 5 类塑料。尽量使用其他的塑料。

许多商店和礼品店都回收小块的聚苯乙烯泡沫塑料和其他包装材料。杯子、装肉类用的托盘和其他一些装食品的包装盒不易回收。如果有很多，可拨打回收热线，叫他们来收取。

之所以称其为"其他"，就是因为这类塑料与 1～6 类是不同的。这类容器可能由多种不同类型的塑料聚合物制成。回收中心也很少收取 7 类塑料。应尽量使用其他的塑料。

低密度和高密度聚乙烯胺，低密度和高密度聚乙烯，是在 20 世纪四五十年代发展起来的，特别是挤压成型低密度聚乙烯被广泛用于制造薄膜和保护材料（例如包装外壳）。

聚氯乙烯是建筑行业中使用的主要塑料材料，它有效地替代了许多传统材料，如铁、铸铁、铜、铅和陶瓷。例如，未增塑聚氯乙烯用于窗框和外盖板，因为它具有强度、硬度大，保温性好，防雨水等特点。由于 PVC 材料耐腐蚀，抗洪水冲击，所以 PVC 是铺设地下管道的标准材料，输水管道常用蓝色，煤气管道常用黄色。虽然 PVC 材料不适合制作大尺寸管件，但是用 PVC 材料制成的内衬可以对大尺寸管件起到保护作用（例如用混凝土作为内衬）。PVC 对温度变化比较敏感，温度稍微上升一点就会变软，所以人们正在积极寻找能用于地热系统的新型替代材料。

聚酰胺又名尼龙。尼龙有好多种（例如尼龙 6、尼龙 11），但是它们属于同一类工程塑料，尼龙因其强度、硬度高，经久耐用而广受赞誉。尼龙常用于制作小型齿轮、轴承、轴衬、链轮、接线盒和滑轮。在设计时要特别注意尼龙吸湿性较强，这会影响尼龙的机械性能和尺寸稳定性。玻璃纤维可以对尼龙起到增强作用，降低尼龙的吸湿性，于是就有了一种强度极高，特别抗冲击的材料。尼龙纤维是另一个应用大类，这种纤维的强度特别大。尼龙的密度约为 $1100kg/m^3$。

对于许多塑料，ABS(丙烯腈丁二烯苯乙烯)具有强度、硬度较高，经久耐用等特性，所以人们又把它列为一类工程塑料。在许多方面 ABS 的表现比尼龙更出色，同样也更便宜。然而，他们对酸碱等化学作用比较敏感。它们常用于制成电视机、电话机、汽车仪表盘、梳子的手柄、行李箱、头盔以及冰箱的内胆。

陶瓷刹车片

在驾车过程中，车辆的性能主要看刹车的表现。简而言之，就是司机每次想要刹车时，车辆一定要能刹得住。然而北美的一些用户并不仅仅满足于刹车的制动性。实际上，刹车的噪声，振动和声振粗糙度(统称为 NVH)，以及除尘能力等特点，都是他们所关心的。

如今先进的陶瓷刹车片技术，如图 1.17 所示，已经从 20 世纪 80 年代早期只在工业范围内使用，逐渐向无石棉摩擦材料方向发展。当时，因为许多健康法规的出台，许多发达国家都公布了一系列禁止使用石棉的计划。阿基波罗、日清纺(NBK)和住友等公司都致力于发展无石棉摩擦产品，首先专注于开发具有较低金属噪声的钢纤维刹车片技术。

图 1.17 陶瓷刹车片

在 20 世纪 80 年代，阿基波罗将该行业原先开发的陶瓷刹车片进行批量生产。同年，该公司就签了许多合同，为著名的本田雅阁和丰田凯美瑞轿车提供配件，这些轿车中的许多都销往北美。自然，一年后同行业竞争对手也生产出了类似产品，这是日新月异的逆向工程技术被许多制造商所使用的结果，他们认识到阿基波罗公司技术突破的价值。因此，阿基玻罗公司是陶瓷摩擦技术的先驱，如图 1.18 所示。

图 1.18 陶瓷摩擦技术的先驱——阿基波罗公司，能够进行刹车系统噪声测试和全车振动测试

经过 25 年不断的推陈出新，阿基波罗公司使得他们的陶瓷刹车片技术优于传统半金属刹车片和无石棉刹车片。在各种路况条件下，阿基波罗公司的先进摩擦技术能够明显提高 NVH 性能。(见表 1.1)

表 1.1 陶瓷刹车片与半金属刹车片：性能比较

项目二 机 器 人

2.1 项目引入

一般机器人都会产生机械运动，引起作用力和位移。例如，工业机器人(如图 2.1 所示)使用零件或工具完成生产任务，这些生产任务有材料加工、焊接、喷漆或装配；工厂和仓库内搬运材料的自动导航车辆。遥控机器人的机械手给了宇航员很大的帮助，可以实现远

程航天飞机维护。

图 2.1　机器人装配生产线

机器人可实现 24 小时无间断的高效、高精度操作。这个汽车装配生产线上的机器人用来焊接车身部件。通用汽车公司在焊接、装配和喷漆方面使用了 16000 个机器人。

行驶机器人用于勘探活火山。机器人的机械特征有多自由度运动、多形状、多角度空间操作、高强度、高硬度机械结构、重载提升能力、运动速度和承载加速等。机器人的工作方式包括不断重复的高精度定位、高速运动和无振动。微机器人如图 2.2 所示。太空机器人如图 2.3 所示。

图 2.2　微机器人

图 2.3　太空机器人

2.2　项目内容

机器人是由传感器、执行机构和计算机器件(一个微处理器)这几个部分组成。执行机构通常是一些伺服电机，这样关节就可以灵活运动，如图 2.4 所示。过去，由于劳动强度大和工作环境恶劣，大型机器人都使用液压机构。到了 20 世纪 90 年代，许多大型生产商都使用电驱动执行机构的工业机器人，这也成为一种趋势。

图 2.4　机器人的执行机构

2.3　任务一　机器人的机械构件

2.3.1　文章一　螺钉

螺钉或螺栓的外部有螺纹，螺母或螺纹孔的内部也有螺纹。螺纹使得螺钉可以沿着螺母螺旋前进。如图 2.5 所示，一般是在圆柱体的外表面或者内表面切割出螺旋线，起到紧固、承载和螺旋提升的作用。注意没有螺纹的地方叫做光杆，有螺纹的地方叫做螺栓长度。人们还可以看到螺帽下方的垫圈端面、倒角和螺纹起点。如图中所示，一些与螺纹有关的几何名称定义如下。

螺距 p 是相邻两螺牙在中径线上对应两点间的轴向距离。导程 L 表示螺母旋转一圈轴向移动的距离。旋转升角 λ，也称为导程角，可以是右旋(如图 2.5 所示)，也可以是左旋。未经说明的情况下，人们可以认为所有螺旋线都是右旋。

图 2.5　紧固型螺栓和螺母示意图

单头螺钉由一根螺旋线切割而成，在一圆柱体表面形成螺旋形凹槽。因为是单头螺纹，所以导程和螺距相等。如果在第一条螺旋线槽之间再切割出第二条螺旋线(试想用两根丝线并排绕在一支铅笔上)，双头螺钉就制成了。对于多头螺钉，$L = np$，其中 L=导程，n=螺旋线的头数，p=螺距。于是人们发现这样一个关系：相同螺距情况下，多头螺钉能够更快的旋入螺母，而单头螺钉则较慢。大多数螺栓和螺钉都是单头螺纹，但蜗轮和蜗杆有时采用多头螺纹。一些车用承载螺钉偶尔也会用五头螺纹。

如前所述，承载螺钉有时被称为线性执行机构或传动螺钉，它广泛用于将旋转运动转换为直线运动的机构中，承受载荷并传递动力。螺钉的使用包括虎钳、压榨机、千分尺、千斤顶(图 2.6)、车床丝杠和其他一些设备。在通常结构中，螺母原地打转，螺钉轴向运动。但在有些设计中，两者的运动方式正好相反。这样受力可能较大，但运动速度一般较慢，功率较小。在前述的情况中，承载螺钉就是基于这一原则操作的。

图 2.6　蜗轮-蜗杆千斤顶

2.3.2　文章二　齿轮

斜齿轮是由圆柱形毛坯制成，齿廓为渐开线齿廓。这类齿轮传动时齿轮轴或平行或交错。图 2.7(a)所示是平行轴斜齿轮。斜齿轮的轮齿有的向右倾斜，有的向左倾斜。如图中所示，人们用"右旋"(R.H.) 和"左旋"(L.H.)这两个名称来辨识这两类斜齿轮。注意辨别斜齿轮右旋和左旋的原则也同样适用于辨别右旋螺钉和左旋螺钉。

图 2.7　斜齿轮：
(a) 一对平行轴互为逆旋的斜齿轮啮合(最常用)；(b) 一对交错轴同向旋转的斜齿轮啮合

人字齿轮就是半个为右旋斜齿轮，半个为左旋斜齿轮(图 2.8)。在用到非平行轴和非相交轴时，人们就可以使用如图 2.7(b)所示的斜齿轮啮合方式。这类齿轮的啮合属于点接触，而不是常规斜齿轮的线接触。这将大大减低它们的承载能力。然而，交错斜齿轮经常用于传递较小的载荷，比如配电器和汽车计速器。当齿轮轴要求平行时，可以只考虑斜齿轮。

图 2.8　典型人字齿轮副

如图 2.9 所示为平行轴斜齿轮副轴向力、径向力和左右手的关系。注意轴向力的方向可以对主动轮用右手或左手定律加以判断。也就是说，对于右倾齿主动轮，如果将右手的 4 个手指沿着齿轮旋转的方向，那么拇指所指方向就是轴向力的方向。如图中所示，从动轮的轴向力方向与主动轮的轴向力方向相反。

图 2.9　3 组平行轴斜齿轮副的旋向和轴向力方向

2.3.3　文章三　挠性传动部件

与支承力相比，摩擦力是带传动、离合器和制动器中非常有用和必要的作用力。摩擦力通常产生于相互作用的垫片、连杆或传动带的平面或圆柱面上。它们构成许多组合，用于刹车和离合器，带(链)传动中带(链)和轮的结合也是这样。由连杆和传动带构成的机器人如图 2.10 所示。

图 2.10　由连杆和传动带构成的机器人

V 型带通常将动力从电机传递到从动机构，这是一种常用的传动方式。V 型带也用于家庭设备、汽车和工业设备中。一般 V 型带的转速大约为每分钟 4000 转。人们生产两种系列的 V 型带：标准 V 型带，如图 2.11 所示，以及重载 V 型带。V 型带的传动效率和平带差不多。

图 2.11　标准 V 型带横截面(所有尺寸都是以英寸为单位)

　　平带轮和槽轮也可以使用 V 型带。V 型带与带轮凹槽间的"楔作用"能够大大地提高带的牵引力。这些带轮的作用是改变 V 型带驱动机构的输入输出比。对于 V 型带的使用数量，一个槽轮上可以安装 12 个以上的 V 型带，从而使其成为一个复合传动机构。在 V 型带驱动机构中，所有 V 型带的收缩率应该相等，以保证载荷的均匀分布。复合 V 型带(图 2.12)用于满足高载荷传动的需要。

图 2.12　复合 V 型带传动机构

　　传动链的种类繁多，但滚子链使用最为广泛。在多种应用中，人们常见的是自行车上的滚子链传动。滚子链通常用硬质钢和链钢，或者铸铁制成。如图 2.1.3 所示为滚子链各部分的几何尺寸。滚子绕轴套旋转，而轴套与内链板过盈配合。销轴与外链板也是过盈配合安装以免两者发生相对转动。美国国家标准学会已经对滚子链的尺寸进行了标准化。

图 2.13　一段滚子链：(a) 单排；(b) 双排

　　滚子链可以制成单排(图 2.13(a))、双排(图 2.13(b))、三排和四排。显然，多排链可以增加链传动系统的承载能力。

2.4　任务二　电机与机器人运动控制系统

2.4.1　文章四　机电一体化系统中控制系统的作用

　　机电一体化系统是由执行某些运动的机械部件和实现智能化电子部件(许多情况下是嵌入式计算机系统)构成。在机电系统的机械部件中，动力起着主要作用。相比之下，机电系统中电子部件的主要任务是处理信息。一些传感器将机械运动转换成电信号，这些信号或是重要信息或是以数字形式表示的完整信号(如果需要，可通过一个 AD 转换器实现)。功率放大器将信号转换成所需的功率大小。大多数情况下，由电机等提供原动力，但也可以采用其他动力源，比如液体和气动等。一个带有控制功能的机械运动系统一般都由机械构件和控制器构成。机械构件就是一个或一个以上能产生所需运动的执行机构，控制器就是对执行机构进行前馈控制和基于传感器的反馈控制。

图 2.14　机电一体化系统

运动控制模式的分类

　　运动控制系统可分为开环系统或闭环系统。开环系统不需要测量输出变量以产生修正信号；相反地，闭环需要一个或一个以上的反馈传感器，用以测量误差，以及处理输出变量中的误差。

闭环运动控制系统

　　如图 2.15 所示为闭环运动控制系统，它有一个或一个以上的反馈回路，连续不断地对比输入命令与系统响应之间的变化，或者安装有多个设定装置以修正电机中的误差，比如负载速度、负载位置、电机转矩。反馈传感器产生电信号以修正与预设输入命令相异的偏差。闭环控制系统又称为伺服系统。在伺服系统中的每一个电机都有其配套反馈传感器、专用译码器、变压器，或者转速表，因为闭环系统中随处可见电机和负载。速度、位置和转矩的变化总是由负载的变化引起的，但是周围环境温度和湿度的变化也会对负载情况产生影响。

图 2.15　基本闭环运动控制系统结构框图

如图 2.16 所示为速度控制回路结构框图，该控制回路一般包含有能够检测出电机速度变化的转速表。传感器产成的误差信号与电机相对于预设值的正负转速偏差成比例。这些信号被送入运动控制器，运动控制器就能够为放大器计算出正确信号，使得无论负载如何变化都能将电机的转速保持在预设范围内。

图 2.16　速度控制系统结构框图

如图 2.17 所示为位置控制系统结构框图，该控制回路一般包含有解码器或者变压器，它们都能直接或间接地测量负载位置。这些传感器产生的误差信号被送入运动控制器，运动控制器随即为放大器生成正确信号。放大器的输出控制电机的加速或减速以调整负载的位置。大多数位置控制闭环系统也包含速度控制回路。

图 2.17　位置控制系统结构框图

开环运动控制系统

如图 2.18 所示，典型的开环运动控制系统包括一个带有可编程分度器或脉冲发生器的步进电机和一个电机驱动器。这类系统不需要反馈传感器，因为负载的位置和速度都可以由预设值和输入数字脉冲方向来控制，此脉冲方向是由控制器产生并由电机驱动器执行的。由于反馈传感器(正如在闭环伺服系统中的那类传感器)不能对负载位置进行连续不断地采样，负载的定位精度较低和位置误差(通常称为步进误差)积累过多，所以开环系统专门用于负载不变、负载运动简单和低速度定位精度的场合。

图 2.18　开环运动控制系统结构框图

2.4.2　文章五　伺服机构

永磁直流伺服电机是最常见的伺服电机，它是在传统电机的基础上发展而来的。这些伺服电机一般分为有电刷式和无电刷式两种。电刷式永磁直流伺服电机由绕线转子和轻型低惯量杯碟型电枢绕组组成。带有碟型电枢绕组的永磁直流伺服电机视图如图 2.19 所示。带有杯型电枢绕组的永磁直流伺服电机剖视图如图 2.20 所示。无电刷式伺服电机由永磁转子和绕线定子构成。无刷直流电机剖视图如图 2.21 所示。

图 2.19　带有碟型电枢绕组的永磁直流伺服电机爆炸视图

图 2.20　带有杯型电枢绕组的永磁直流伺服电机剖视图

图 2.21　无刷直流电机剖视图

一些运动控制系统使用双向线性伺服电机，它们可以沿轨道或轨迹运动。它们广泛应用于旋转电机与负载机械耦合产生误差的情况下，这类负载会引起很大的定位误差。线性电机需要在一个闭环环境中工作，同时必须为电机所连接的数据线和电力线提供前后运动所需要的空间。曲线伺服电机构成的线性执行机构如图 2.22 所示。

图 2.22　线性伺服电机构成的线性执行机构

步进电机一般用于运动控制精度要求不高的系统中，在这类应用中步进电机对负载的定位精度要求不高。通过使用闭环控制回路可以提供步进电机的位置精度。

在要求得到高效、高启动转矩和令人满意的速度转矩特征曲线时，永磁直流电机是非常可靠的运动控制驱动电机。在拥有传统转盘机、分路器、复式励磁电刷式直流电机的许多特征的同时，永磁直流伺服电机还引入了强瓷和稀土磁铁，而且这类电机能够很容易的用微处理控制器驱动，以上这些优势都使得永磁直流伺服电机不断地被普及。低马力永磁直流伺服电机剖视图如图 2.23 所示。

图 2.23　低马力永磁直流伺服电机剖视图

随着陶瓷和稀土磁铁磁场强度的增加，在同等额定电流情况下，现在的直流电机比以前采用铝镍钴合金磁铁的电机更小巧、更轻便。而且，集成电路和微处理器提高了数字式运动控制器和电机驱动器或放大器的可靠性，降低了成本，同时还可以给这些设备安装更加小巧轻便的外壳，这样减少了整个运动控制系统的尺寸，减轻了重量，并且集成度也更高。

用于指示转子位置的磁感应传感器如图 2.24 所示。

图 2.24　用于指示转子位置的磁感应传感器
① 无刷电机定子绕组；② 永磁电机转子；③ 三相换向电场；④ 磁感应传感器；⑤ 电路板

2.5　任务三　工业机器人

工业机器人是特殊的生产资料，于是，机器人的应用非常广泛。这些应用可以分为 3 类：材料加工、材料搬运和装配。

在材料加工方面，机器人使用工具对原材料进行加工处理。例如，如果给机器人安装上钻刀，它就会在原材料上钻出几个孔。

材料搬运包括在工厂中装卸和运输工件。有了机器人，这些操作变得既可靠又可不断重复，同时可以提高产品质量和减少废品率。

装配是机器人又一项重要的应用。自动装配系统整合了自动检测、机器人自动化和机械搬运设备，起到减少劳动力成本、提高产量和消除人工搬运的出错率的作用。图 2.25 为机器人自动装配。

图 2.25　机器人自动装配

2.5.1　文章六　工业机器人的好处

图 2.26　工业机器人的好处

自从工业革命时期出现了工厂，许多专用机器在创造文明财富过程中扮演了重要的角色。最普通的机器就是低收入、超负荷劳动的民众——男人、女人和孩子。早期的工作环境相当危险，但是薪酬优厚而且无人提出要提高生产效率。

水动力和蒸汽动力，以及后来的燃气动力和电力，替代并扩展了人力，使生产更高效、产品更便宜。创造出来的复杂的机器承担了工厂许多方面的工作。自动织布机就非常著名，时至今日许多专门机器还承担着各类工作任务。

图 2.27　自动织布机

你平时可能不会去关心，但是确实有一种复杂的机器，它的用途就是将线材弯成纸夹。可能在同一个工厂中，还有机器是做钉子的。其他的机器在执行其他的任务。这些机器对于工厂来说是非常重要的，它们大多以自动化的方式存在。

当机器人能够被程序控制的时候，工厂自动化开始向机器人方向发展。但依然有许多机器人不能完成的任务。以制钉机为例，人们给它输入一组控制指令，它就用各种尺寸的线材制造钉子，这些钉子有各种各样的钉尖和钉头。它就是自动机或者机器人吗？如果控制器是机械杠杆和旋钮，或者是电路，会有什么不同？

早期工厂中，工位就在机器旁边，即使工作不辛苦，这样也很危险。以前的机器是由一大堆不断旋转和移动的零件装配而成，即使手脚或者身体的其他部位被卷入，机器也不会停工。时至今日，在一些工厂和食品加工厂，人们使用机器时也面临着种种危险。机器设计得应该尽可能安全些，但是由于存在着一定的限制，有些设计需要兼顾，比如金属变薄冲压，既要安全又要生产出有用的产品。

当机器逐渐进化为机器人，它们就使得工厂中许多方面的工作变得更安全。机器人喷涂、点焊，或者装配机器都可以在一个空场地上完成，不需要人们的帮助。当机器人承担又脏又危险的工作时，监控人员可以安全地站在机器人的运动范围之外(图 2.28)。

图 2.28　焊接机器人

最常见的工业机器人大多数都是机械臂(图 2.29)。针对不同的工作任务(图 2.30)可以给机器人安装不同的工具，机器人在程序的控制下执行各类复杂操作。一个安装有一系列不同工具的机械臂，可以完成许多工作任务。这些就是人们今天所认为的"智能"机器，于是人们的梦想开始实现。

图 2.29　安装焊枪的机械臂

图 2.30　安装割枪的机械臂

机器人使得一些探险任务不仅安全而且成为可能。因为大多数人都不能直接靠近活火山口，不能在核事故中直接执行清理核废料的任务，不能在火星表面连续待上几个月，也不能钻进倒塌大楼的废墟中搜寻幸存者。

2.5.2　文章七　机器人的抓紧器

图 2.31 是机器人的抓紧器。有多种抓紧机构可供人们选择，它们包括连杆机构、齿轮和齿条机构、凸轮机构、螺纹机构和带轮机构等。下文所提及的是一些采用气/液压缸的抓紧器，它们也可以用其他机构来替代。

图 2.31　机器人的抓紧器

两指型抓紧器图 2.32(a)是非平行两指抓紧器。当气缸运动时，抓紧器的两指就会合拢或分离。图 2.32(b)是平行指抓紧器。图 2.32(c)是握力增强型抓紧器。

图 2.32　两指抓紧器

(a) 非平行型；(b) 平行型；(c) 平行增强型抓紧器

在图 2.33 所示的两指抓紧器中，气缸向外运动时抓紧器可以由内向外抓紧工件。

图 2.33　内张型两指抓紧器

电磁型抓紧器

显然，电磁型抓紧器只用于金属材料的抓取。一般使用电磁铁和永磁铁。电磁铁需要有电源和控制器。当需要剩磁反向时，可以翻转磁铁的磁极。有一个机构可以将永磁铁拆分成若干部分。拆分后的这些部分对那些不能有电火花存在的工厂环境是有好处的。

电磁型抓紧器的优点如下。

- 可适应不同零件尺寸；
- 能抓紧带孔金属零件；
- 捡拾时间较短；
- 只需一个抓紧面；
- 能抓起堆场的上层板料。

电磁型抓紧器的缺点如下。

- 在工件中会留有剩磁；
- 存在侧滑危险。

项目三　电　　梯

3.1　项目引入

一般来说，控制系统是由一组电子设备和仪器构成，它们能够有效地确保加工处理过程的稳定性、精度和平滑性。这就需要各种形式和各类规格的工具，从发电厂到半导体器件。随着新技术不断涌现，高自动化控制系统可以实现许多复杂的控制任务，它是以 PLC，也可能是主机等形式出现。除了使用信号控制现场设备(比如操作面板、电机、传感器、开关、电子阀)以外，还能让它们实现网络连接，这样不仅可以提高生产规模和实现协同作业，而且通过分散控制系统使生产更加灵活。控制系统中每一个部件无论大小都起着重要的作用。例如，图 3.1 所示的 PLC 系统中如果没有传感器，它将不知道如何处理。必要时，主控计算机将及时协调工厂车间中某一工位的生产活动。

图 3.1　使用 PLC 控制一个或多个输出设备

3.2 项目内容

如今许多工程系统包括电梯系统都是由可编程控制器(PLCs)来控制的。人们认为 PLC 是一种专用计算机,因为它具有与普通计算机相类似的基本结构,比如中央处理器(CPU)。PLC 中有一个存储器和一系列输入输出端子。PLC 编程所使用的软件是基于 PLC 专用语言设计的,这种语言称为梯形图。梯形图是一种简便的编程语言,因为它是在布尔逻辑函数的基础上发展而来的。于是修改系统的操作就变得更加简单、低廉。

PLC 在许多方面优于其他控制系统。PLC 以灵活多样、成本低廉、操作迅速、稳定无误、编程简便和安全可靠而著称,而且使用 PLC 更新和纠正差错也比较容易。PLC 的一大应用就是对电梯的控制。

3.3 任务一 电梯中的 PLC

3.3.1 文章一 什么是 PLC

PLC 是由一个安装有应用程序的中央处理器(CPU)和一些输入输出接口单元组成,这些接口单元可以直接与现场输入输出设备相连接。PLC 的结构框图如图 3.2 所示。由于程序控制着 PLC,所以只要接收到输入设备的输入信号,PLC 就会做出适当的反应。这些反应通常包括将输出信号传送给某些输出设备。

图 3.2 PLC 结构框图

中央处理器

中央处理器(CPU)是协调 PLC 系统运行的微处理器。它可以运行程序,处理输入输出信号以及与外部设备进行通信。

存储器

PLC 中有多种存储单元。它们用于存放操作系统和用户存储器。操作系统是协调 PLC 运行的系统软件。用户存储器用来存放梯形图、定时器和计数器值。根据用户的需要,可以选用不同类型的存储器。

1. 只读存储器(ROM)

只读存储器是不能修改的存储器,它只能被程序修改一次。所以 PLC 不适合使用该类存储器。与其他类型存储器相比,只读存储器很少被选用。

2. 随机存储器(RAM)

随机存储器通常用于存储用户程序和数据。关机后随机存储器中的数据将会丢失。但是,这一问题可以通过加装备用电池的方法解决。

3. 可擦写可编程只读存储器(EPROM)

可擦写可编程只读存储器可以像只读存储器那样永久地保存数据。它不需要后备电池。但是当它暴露在紫外线下时,它保存的数据就会被擦除。

4. 电可擦写可编程只读存储器(EEPROM)

电可擦写可编程只读存储器兼备随机存储器的灵活性和可擦写可编程只读存储器的数

据永久性。它存储的内容可以用电的方法擦除和再编程,但是擦除和再编程的次数有限。

扫描时间

读取输入信号、运行程序和更新输出信号的过程称为扫描。扫描通常是指连续的和一连串的读取输入状态、计算控制逻辑值和更新输出信号的过程。扫描时间的技术指标是指控制器对现场输入信号反应的快慢,以及正确解决逻辑控制的快慢。

影响扫描时间的因素

一个扫描周期所需要的时间从 0.1 毫秒到几百毫秒不等,这依赖于 CPU 的处理速度和用户程序的长度。PLC 的程序如图 3.3 所示。用户的远程输入输出子系统会增加扫描时间,因为要远距离传送更新数据给子系统。对控制程序的监控也增加了额外的扫描时间,因为控制器的 CPU 必须要发送线圈状态,以及要与电子管或者其他类型显示设备进行通信。

图 3.3 PLC 的程序

3.3.2 文章二 PLC 的组成

在自动系统中,PLC 通常被看作是整个控制系统的核心。在控制应用程序(存储在 PLC 存储器中)的管理下,借助现场输入设备的反馈信号,PLC 连续不断地监控系统的运行状态。然后,PLC 根据程序的逻辑判断决定处理步骤,再交由现场输出设备执行。

PLC 也可以用于控制简单重复的工作任务,或者通过网络通信与其他主控制器或主机协调作业,完成一连串简单任务,最终完成对综合复杂处理任务的控制。

输入设备

自动系统的智能化体现在 PLC 对各类现场输入设备自动和手动发出信号的辨识能力上。

按钮、键盘和转换开关都是手动输入设备,是人机交互的基本形式。而为了探测到工件的位置、监控机构的运动、检测液压压力或液面的高低等,PLC 必须通过自动感应设备采集数据,比如接近开关、限位开关、光电传感器和液面传感器等。PLC 中输入信号的类型一般是开/闭一类的逻辑信号或模拟信号。这些输入信号通过各类 PLC 输入模块与 PLC 进行连接。PLC 的输入设备如图 3.4 所示。

图 3.4 PLC 的输入设备

输出设备

倘若没有现场输出设备接口,自动系统将是不完整的,PLC 系统实际上也是处于瘫痪状态。PLC 所要控制的设备通常有电机、电磁阀、继电器和蜂鸣器等。通过电机和电磁阀的作用,PLC 能够控制简单的抓放系统,也能控制复杂的伺服定位系统。这类输出设备都是自动系统的机构,所以它们直接影响系统的操作。

但是,其他的输出设备,比如指示灯、蜂鸣器和警报器,仅仅起到提示作用。借助 PLC 的大规模输出模块,输出设备的信号也可以像输入设备信号一样与 PLC 进行交接。PLC 的输出设备如图 3.5 所示。

图 3.5 PLC 的输出设备

3.3.3 文章三 用于电梯的 PLC 举例

本项目的任务是设计安装一部由 PLC 控制的 4 层电梯系统。由梯的内部景观如图 3.6

所示。本设计不是遵循"先到先得"的运行规则，因为这种方法在现实中很少见。由于在现实情况中既要考虑能耗又要考虑反应速度，所以决定采用折中处理的方案，也就是把所有的请求归为或者向上或者向下的单向运动，然后在单向运动的过程中逐一响应。这样就能实现如下的运行规则：如果电梯正在上升，那么优先考虑所有的"上升"请求，电梯一直向上运动直至顶层。然后电梯再下降，于是优先执行"下降"请求。具体描述将在"软件设计"章节中给出。

图 3.6 电梯内部图

硬件设计的主要任务是设计连接 PLC 和电梯以及电梯控制面板的接口电路，控制面板上带有上升和下降请求按钮，如图 3.7 所示。PLC 处于运行状态时，按下按钮产生各类请求信号，同时向 PLC 连续不断地发送信号。每一个按钮都与一个 LED 指示灯相连，以指示请求的位置。

图 3.7 电梯控制面板总体布局

图 3.8 所示为电梯控制系统结构框图，图中可以看到 PLC 和带有控制面板的电梯系统之间的接口电路。

图 3.8 电梯控制系统结构框图

本项目所需要的 12 个输入和 8 个输出的名称和功能在表 3.1 中列出。

控制模式

控制模式分为两种：简易控制模式，或智能控制模式，简易控制模式现在不太普及，因为这种控制模式不实用。简易控制模式经常用于在建筑物内运送材料和设备，每一层都要连续不断地逐一停留。而智能控制模式对用户的请求作出反应，然后进行智能处理。这类控制模式是现代电梯最常用的模式。

3.4 任务二 用于电梯的传感器

传感器是一种仪器，它会对周围物理环境(温度、位移、外力等)作出反应，产生适当比例的输出信号(电的、机械的、磁性的等)。术语中转换器是传感器的同义词。但是理论上，传感器指的是对周围物理环境作出反应的仪器。而转换器指的是将一种能量形式转换成另一种能量形式的仪器。当传感器以一种能量方式感知输入而以另一种能量方式输出时，传感器就变成了转换器。例如，热电偶会对温度变化(热能)作出反应，输出一定比例的电动势(电能)。所以，热电偶可以称为传感器，也可以称为转换器。

3.4.1 文章四 传感器的分类

线性传感器和旋转传感器

线性传感器和旋转传感器是典型机电系统中两种最基本的测量装置。一般来说，位置传感器经过一定的位移时产生相应比例的电输出信号。现今有许多接触式传感器，比如应变仪、拉杆式位移传感器、角位移传感器和转速计等。拉杆式位移传感器和角位移传感器如图 3.9 所示。拉杆式位移传感器工作原理如图 3.10 所示。非接触器传感器包括编码器、霍耳效应式传感器、电容式传感器、电感式传感器和干涉仪式传感器。也可以按测量的有效距离进行分类。

高灵敏度传感器通常适用于有效距离较小(一般从 0.1 毫米到 5 毫米)的场合,例如霍耳效应式传感器、光纤电感式传感器、电容式传感器和应变仪。而差动变压器灵敏度较好,有效距离较广。干涉仪式传感器的灵敏度非常高(可以达到微米级),测量范围十分广(一般可达一米)。但是,干涉仪式传感器体积较大、价格昂贵、安装校正时间较长。

图 3.9　拉杆式位移传感器和角位移传感器

图 3.10　拉杆式位移传感器工作原理

图 3.11　干涉仪

图 3.12　常用微动开关

图 3.13　光电电路符号和常用光电发生器/接收器结构图

图 3.14　增量式编码器示意图

图 3.15　八位格雷编码绝对编码器碟

图 3.16　(a)当电位器的轴旋转时,电刷从电阻材料的一端移动到另一端。
(b)常用电位器内部情况,电刷与电阻片相接触。

图 3.17　使用偏磁和霍尔开关探测黑色金属轮齿

加速传感器

加速度的测量对于易受振动和抖动影响的系统比较重要。虽然加速度可以从线性或旋转传感器的以往数据中获得,但是加速度计的输出信号与加速度的大小成正比,人们更倾向使用加速度计。悬重式振弦加速度计如图 3.18 所示。

图 3.19　悬重式振弦加速度计

力、转矩和压力传感器

在众多类型的力/转矩传感器中,应变仪式传感器和压电式传感器是最常用的两种传感器。这两种传感器都可以用于测量单轴或多轴的力或者转矩。应变仪式传感器采用一些机械机构,承受负载时会发生弹性形变。这类传感器都受到自身频率的限制。而压电式传感器特别适合测量动态负载,频率范围较广。压电式传感器具有高硬度、在大测量范围内有较高灵敏度,以及较为小巧等特点。相对于液压传感器、应变传感器等,压电式传感器对交变负载的反应更加敏捷。根据检测环境的变化,有针对性地选择所需的传感技术。

图 3.19　使用应变仪测量普通应变的实验装置

图 3.20　各种负载感应片

图 3.21　金属薄片电阻式应变仪的结构
(a) 单一元件；(b) 双元件；(c) 三元件

3.4.2 文章五 电梯传感器举例

BERO 是西门子公司的一个品牌,用于标识该公司的"非接触式"传感器系列。西门子 BERO 传感器工作时不需要机械接触或者机械磨损。例如,在下述的应用中,BERO 传感器用于检测电梯的停留位置正确与否。

BERO 传感器有感应式、电容式、超声波式和光电式共 4 种。感应式接近传感器利用电磁场探测金属物体的位置。电容式接近传感器利用静电场探测金属物体的位置。超声波式接近传感器利用声波探测金属物体的位置。在接收到的光强度发生变化时,光电传感器会作出反应。一些光电传感器甚至可以探测到特定的颜色。

图 3.22 安装有电磁线圈的传感器应用探测导电金属的位置。它遇到非金属时不起任何作用

图 3.23 电梯舱经过传感器底部时,用电磁方法扫描其位置

西门子 BERO 感应式接近传感器采用涡流电流衰减振荡原理进行探测。这类传感器由 4 个元件组成:线圈、振荡器、触发电路和一个输出端,如图 3.24 所示。振荡器是一种感应电容调节电路,能够产生无线电频率。振荡器产生电磁场,线圈将该电磁场从传感器表面向外发送。振荡器中的电路从电磁场中接收大量反馈,进而控制振荡器继续工作。

图 3.24 西门子 BERO 感应式接近传感器

当被测金属物体进入电磁场时,该金属物体中会产生涡电流。这就引起了传感器的电负载,进而降低了电磁场强度。当被测物体靠近传感器时,涡电流增加,振荡器的电负载同时增加,进一步降低了电磁场强度。触发电路监控振荡器的振幅,振幅达到预设值时就将传感器由正常状态(开或关)切换到输出状态。当被测物体远离传感器时,振荡器的振幅增加。达到预设值时,触发器又将传感器从输出状态切换回正常状态(开或关)。西门子 BERO 的工作过程如图 3.25 所示。

图 3.25 西门子 BERO 的工作过程

3.5 任务三 液压与气动电梯

在机电一体化系统中,能源的基本类型包括电力、气压和液压。每一种能源和每一类电机都有它自己的特性、优点和局限性。使用交流电机还是使用直流电机依赖于系统的设计需要和用途。这些电机将电能转换为机械能,从而为电梯提供能量。大多数新型机器人和电梯都使用电力驱动。气动执行机构用于高速、无伺服机器人,并且经常用于大功率工具比如抓紧器。液压执行机构已用于许多重型起重系统,一般这些系统精度要求不高。

3.5.1 文章六 液压和气动系统

液压和气动执行机构通常可以是液压或气动旋转马达,也可以是线性活塞式液压缸或气缸,或者控制阀。它们都非常适合于在大位移的情况下产生大推力。气动执行机构利用空气产生压力,能够满足低中型推力、冲击力小和高速的应用需求。液压执行机构使用的

是不可压缩液压油。它们能在大位移的情况下产生大推力，而且成本低廉。液压执行机构的缺点是它们比较复杂，需要较多的维护。气动机器人臂如图 3.27 所示。

图 3.27　气动机器人臂

所有液压系统都遵循帕斯卡定律，该定律是以发现者布雷斯·帕斯卡的名字命名的。该定律描述的是在封闭容器(比如罐子或管子)中，流体在外部压力作用下，容器中各点处的压强相等。

在实际液压系统中，帕斯卡定律定义的是从系统中得到的基本结论。在此基础上，泵就能够推动液体在系统中运动。泵的进油口与液体源相连接，通常被称为油箱或储油罐。大气压作用在储油罐液体的表面，使得液体流入泵。泵一旦运行起来，它就将液体从油箱中压出，充满出油管，保持其适当的压力。

液压油的流动由泵排出，由阀控制。大多数液压系统中液压阀有 3 种控制功能：①控制液体压力；②控制液体流量；③控制液体流动方向。

泵

泵可以将电能或机械能转换为液压能。它们构成液压系统的液流原动力，而从泵输出的液体压力则是由流体阻力所决定的。外啮合齿轮泵如图 3.28 所示。旋转式叶片泵如图 3.29 所示。轴向斜盘式柱塞泵如图 3.30 所示。

图 3.28　外啮合齿轮泵

图 3.29　旋转式叶片泵

图 3.30　轴向斜盘式柱塞泵

液压旋转马达

在压力作用下，液压旋转马达将液压能转换为机械能。因此，这些执行机构属于液压容积马达，它们显著的特点是产生运动的方式与泵非常相似。但是，液压旋转马达的工作原理正好与泵相反。液压旋转执行机构如图 3.31 所示。

图 3.31　液压旋转执行机构

控制阀

控制阀是液压回路中的一些部件，它们的任务是调节传向执行机构的液压能。控制阀可以关闭或导通油路，可以根据需要改变液压油的流向，因此它们可以调节液压传动的两个基本物理量：压力和流量。控制阀按照其实现的功能又可以细分为：方向控制阀、开关阀、压力控制阀、流量控制阀。

方向控制阀控制液压油的流通和流向，它的控制是通过内部相应活动部件的运动来实现的，并从外部激活。方向控制阀也称为分配器，其活动元件的类型各不相同，因此内部结构也各有其特色，它可以按照连接外部液压管件的数量和切换位置的数量进行分类。

开关阀是只允许流体单向流动的阀。因为它们可以阻止流体反向流动，所以它们又被称为止回阀或单向阀。开关阀一般放置在液压泵和执行机构之间，所以当液压泵停止运转时，液压回路中的液压油不会流回储油罐，依然在管道内。这样就可以防止再次填充无油管道而浪费能量，保证执行机构在负载作用下不动作。

压力控制阀可以保证无论上游端口的压力如何变化，液压控制阀下游端口有恒定的压力。压力控制阀可以手动调节，可以用监控信号调节，或用电逻辑指令调节。在用电逻辑指令调节中当压力控制阀内部的传感器检测到所需控制的压力时，闭合电路中的压力控制阀开始发挥作用。有许多控制阀的符号，如图3.32所示。

图3.32 控制阀的符号

液压动力系统

如图3.33所示为液压动力系统。在图中示例中，机动部件由执行机构—双作用液压缸构成，双作用液压缸的前后两个腔连接了一个两位四通换向阀，该换向阀构成了液压调节界面。

阀的切换指令来自于控制部件。控制指令与移动方案相一致，根据液压缸所需的循环操作编制控制器中的控制指令，液压缸的传感器为控制器提供反馈信号，图中所示的传感器是限位开关。

图3.33 液压动力系统

3.5.2 文章七 液压电梯举例

常用电梯有两类：液压式和牵引式。液压电梯的客舱安装在液压千斤顶的顶部，类似于维修站里的车用千斤顶。如图3.34所示，液压千斤顶一般安装在地板下方，由液压泵和储油罐驱动，它们都安装在靠近电梯轴的一个隔间内。液压电梯通常在独门独户的居民家中使用。

图3.34 液压电梯

必要时，液压电梯的千斤顶要求安装在地板下方，因此一般安装在建筑物地基以下。千斤顶外安装有保护罩，保护罩可以防止水的渗入，因为洪水泛滥将造成液压油污染，同时可能损害液压缸，影响千斤顶的密封性。盐水因为具有腐蚀性，严重威胁着电梯的安全。如图3.34所示，液压电梯的液压泵和储油罐也易受到水的损坏，但是它们可以非常方便地安装在建筑物地基以上高出千斤顶两层的位置上。

有些普通电梯装置也会因为易受洪水损坏而需要保护起来。最显而易见的例子就是电梯舱。但是，在大多数电梯控制系统中，电梯舱会因为停电自动下降到最底层。在电梯轴上安装一个或多个带浮控开关的安全互锁系统，可以防止电梯舱下降到洪水中，这样就使得整个电梯系统较为安全，如图3.35所示。一些电气设备，比如接线盒、电路板和控制面板，应安装在建筑物地基上方，如图3.34所示。其他电梯部件，比如电梯门和底坑开关必须安装在建筑物最底层，或者在其下方。必要时，有时可以将电梯各部件替换为防水型系列。

图3.35 浮控机构控制电梯舱下降

第二类就是牵引式电梯。这类是最常见的电梯系统。如图3.36所示，牵引系统主要有缆索构成，缆索连接在电梯舱顶部，由一台安装在电梯轴上方阁楼内的电机带动。

图3.36 牵引式电梯

项目四 MP4 播放器

4.1 项目引入

图 4.1 所示为两个型号的 iPod Video 播放器,分别是 80GB 版和 30GB 版,后者外壳更薄。它们的内部结构几乎是一样的,如图 4.2 所示。所以苹果公司只是采用了图片所指出的不同后盖而已。

图 4.1　iPod Video 侧视图

图 4.2　iPod Video 的内部芯片

新型的苹果 iPod Video 播放器采用 Broadcom 公司的 BCM2722 多媒体/视频处理器。苹果公司选择了 Broadcom 多媒体/视频处理器,拓展了前一代 iPod 播放器的功能,使得 iPod 播放器具有了播放视频的功能,而 BCM2722 的潜在特性预示着 iPod 家族有进一步扩展的可能,包括 iPod 将来可能增加的抓图功能。

4.2 项目内容

当数字计算机的所有电路都包含在集成电路中时,就称为微型计算机。即使微型计算机自带存储器和输入/输出电路,仍然需要增添同类型的外部电路,特别是存储器,因此微处理器和微型计算机之间存在着很大的区别。为了使专业集成电路满足应用软件或市场的需求,人们为集成电路增加了存储器、输入/输出接口、信号调节器、计时器和计数器等功能,一种称为微控制单元(MCU)的微型计算机应运而生,它已经可以满足工控市场的需求。

4.3 任务一　MCU 简介

4.3.1 文章一　模数转换器(ADC)

如图 4.3 所示,从模数转换器中发出的数字数据用编码表示,在计算机网络的控制下,对数据进行转换、修改和重定义,但是当数字数据以一系列数字编码的形式再一次在计算机网络中出现时,由定时网络控制其不断循环往复。这些数字编码传递到数模转换器后,被转换回模拟信号。这里所讨论的电路可以从数模转换器谈起。

图 4.3　计算机网络调控数字数据

图 4.3 中的输入端是一个 ADC,模数转换器。图 4.4 所示的是早期 ADC 中的一种:计数式模数转换器。它由一个二进制计数器构成,该计数器用于计数中央时钟发出的脉冲。二进制计数器的两个输出端口分别连接两个单元:一个数模转换器和一个锁存器。这两个单元都带有多根输入/输出数据线,这些数据线涵盖了模数转换器所需要的数据位数。

图 4.4　8 位计数式模数转换器

注意回路中有数模转换器，这就是先讨论数模转换器的原因。将二进制编码输入数模转换器，这时会产生一个模拟电压信号并进入比较器的一个输入端口。比较器的另一个输入端口处也有一个模拟输入信号，它将会被转换成数字信号输出。当来自于数模转换器的电压低于模拟输入信号时，那么比较器输出一个高电压(数字1)。当来自于数模转换器的电压等于或者高于模拟输入信号时，比较器输出一个低电压(数字0)。当比较器的输出电压由高电压变成低电压时，它就启动了锁存器，将锁存来自计数器数据线的二进制值。于是，锁存器输出端的二进制编码就与输入端的模拟电压相等。

模拟转换成数字的工作方式也是如此。计数器归零后，数模转换器的输出为零。如果模拟输入电压 V_{in} 是正电压，那么比较器的输出为1。随着计数器对时钟计数量的不断增加，数模转换器的输出也逐步增加，每次增加一个小幅电压。如果数模转换器输出的是一个小于输入电压 V_{in} 的正电压，那么计数器连续计数并且增加输出电压值直到大于输入电压 V_{in} 为止，这样就触发了比较器，它的输出值为 0，将输出到模数转换器的二进制代码锁存，并将计数器归零。计数器的归零随即造成了比较器的输出值为 1，于是模数转换器又为下一次转换做好了准备。计数式模数转换器的一大缺点就是转换时间较长。转换时间可以长到 $2^n - 1$ 个时钟周期，上标 n 是模数转换器输出端的二进制位数。

例题：求计数式模数转换器的最大转换时间

当时钟频率为1MHz时，8位、12位和16位模数转换器的最大转换时间各是多少？

解：由于一个时钟周期内的最大转换时间为 $2^n - 1$，而且因为 1MHz 频率的时钟周期为 $1\mu s$，所以：

……

4.3.2 文章二 微控制单元(MCU)简介

前面已经提及了模拟信号的概念，信号的调节以及将信号由模拟的转换成数字的。对数字信号进行修改、计算、处理、类型变换或者信道改变的处理，都是为了完成预定的任务，而这些预定值是由前期完成的应用程序所确定的。整个系统都是为了完成一个任务而设计的，数字处理器是整个系统中一个非常重要的部分。

图 4.5 所示的是中央处理单元示意图。主要部件有程序计数器、指令寄存器、指令解码器、数据地址寄存器、算术逻辑单元(ALU)、时序控制电路，以及永久性存储器和临时性存储器。正如前文所述，数字编码也被称为指令，按照一定的顺序构成程序，随机送入中央处理器，指挥中央处理器执行具体操作。指令的地址存放在一个被称为程序计数器的指令地址寄存器中。程序被存储在存储器中，地址一个挨一个地有序排列着，于是存有地址的程序计数器随着程序指令的一个个增加而不断地累加，所以程序计数器又称为地址寄存器。随着操作任务的不断进行，程序计数器将指明程序中要执行的下一条指令的地址。

图 4.5 通用型中央处理器

通常可以通过提高处理器的时钟频率提高数据处理的吞吐量。但是时钟频率的增加将直接影响到能量的损耗，这对于一些移动设备来说是不可接受的。人们采用另外一种方法来提高时钟频率，也就是修改处理器的结构以增加每一个循环周期内的计算量。

许多因素都会影响到中央处理器执行指令的效率，包括：①数据进出处理器的循环次

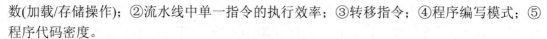

数(加载/存储操作);②流水线中单一指令的执行效率;③转移指令;④程序编写模式;⑤程序代码密度。

可以通过以下几个步骤提高中央处理器的数据计算吞吐量。

减少加载/存储操作的循环次数。 30%以上的加载/存储指令采用精简指令集机构,因为执行加载/存储指令需要一个或一个以上循环周期。减少加载/存储指令的循环次数可以有效地提高处理器的吞吐量。

流水线重复操作。 有些算法,比如多媒体算法,总是重复操作一些数据流,多达成千上万次。例如在 MPEG-4 编码的过程中,一些算法所包含的许多操作必须对图像的每一个像素重复进行。对多个数据同时进行这类操作(单指令多数据流)会导致处理数据流操作周期的直线下降。

最大化流水线资源利用率。 一些算数操作只需要一个周期,而有的需要几个周期。例如执行一个除法操作需要 32 个周期。如果在发送新指令之前,处理器必须要等待一个多循环操作执行完毕,那么流水线上的其他资源将闲置。

提高代码密度。 由于存储器非常廉价,所以人们不需要顾虑代码密度问题。但是由于处理器对指令缓冲存储器有相当大的依赖性,所以代码密度会直接影响到处理器的性能。如果代码较简短,在缓冲存储器中就可以存储更多的指令,减小缓冲存储器丢失数据的可能性,降低从外部存储器取指令的操作周期。减少系统总线上的数据通信也可以显著减少能耗。

4.3.3 文章三 用于 MP4 播放器的 MCU 举例

爱特梅尔公司已经开发出了高性能 32 位精简指令集处理芯片,该芯片的指令序列大大增加了循环周期内的计算吞吐量,同时也实现了超低能耗。AVR32 芯片,如图 4.6 所示,最小化加载/存储以及转移操作的出错率,最大化流水线吞吐量,实现了在比传统处理器的时钟频率和能耗更低的前提下执行复杂的算法。

图 4.6 AVR32 架构

对于目标算法,AVR32 每个指令周期的吞吐量要比 ARM11 高出 35%。AVR32 执行每秒钟 30 帧的四分之一型视频图形阵列(320×240 像素)MP4 解码操作,其只需要 100MHz 频率,而 ARM11 架构则需要 150~175MHz 的频率,如图 4.7 所示。

图 4.7 ARM 处理芯片 MPEG-4 解码

最小化加载/存储操作所消耗的周期。 AVR32 架构支持一个字节(8 位)、半个字(16 位)\一个字(32 位)和双字(64 位)长度的加载/存储指令。这些指令由多种指针运算构成,可有效地存取表,数据结构和随机数据。用于加载比特位和半字的指令都具有随意信号或数据值零延拓。

多流水线乱序执行。 一般来说,当多条指令进入流水线时,处理器将同时执行这些指令。如果有一条特别复杂的指令需要多个时钟周期,那么直到指令执行完毕流水线才会前进。可用的计算资源在该指令执行时处于闲置状态。AVR32 的流水线具有大规模逻辑电路,允许在一个周期内执行更多的处理任务。AVR32 具有 3 条流水线(加载/存储单元、乘法器和算术逻辑单元),允许不按序执行独立数据的算术运算,如图 4.8 所示。

图 4.8 多流水线支持技术

AVR32 另一种节省周期的特点就是数据在流水线各阶段之间进行前送。如果有一些指令正在等待计算结果,这些已经执行完的指令在进入写回阶段之前将快速前送至流水线起始处。例如,当加法指令完成 ALU1 这一流水线阶段时,其计算结果将被前送至 MUL1、ALU1 和数据地址阶段,这样处理使得计算结果可以被用于加法操作之后的一个周期,而不是等待 3 个周期再将结果送到写回阶段。

AVR32 中的单指令多数据流架构能使数字信号处理算法的吞吐量翻两番,该算法需要数据流重复操作(例如 MPEG 解码的运动评估)。

指令序列支持高级操作系统。中央处理器的大多数结构在操作系统使用之前就已经被开发出来,这些操作系统如今已经随处可见。中央处理器芯片在调用操作系统或外部应用软件时容易浪费周期。AVR32 利用节省周期指令对 Linux 操作系统的使用提供强有力的支持。节省周期指令包括程序调用指令和系统调用指令,前者用于从转移表中调用带有 8 位指针的子程序,提供了更为简捷的代码,后者则用于调用操作系统程序。AVR32 最大的特点是它提供了先进的存储器管理单元和安全模式,可以保证高级操作系统的正常运行,比如 Linux。

……

4.4 任务二 半导体材料

4.4.1 文章四 半导体的概念

导体是一种元素,它的电子可以自由运动;而绝缘体也是一种元素,但它的电子被牢牢地限制在一定范围内。如果学过通过回顾可以知道,原子核由质子和中子组成。原子核带正电。电子云围绕着原子核高速旋转,该电子云所带的电量足以使得原子呈中性。

每个电子具有能够表征运动快慢的能力等级,这些能力等级几乎都是以自然数的形式表示的。电子的能力等级可能为 1 或 2,不可能为 1.25。能力等级是离散的,被称为量子。

每个轨道层都与特定的能力等级相对应。只有电子具有与给定层相等的能力等级,才能停留在该层上。如果可以用锤子敲击电子或者用灯光照它,给电子增加一个能量 e,那么它将不再停留在当前层上,而是阶跃到高一级的能量层上(图 4.9)。

图 4.9 硅原子

每个层只能容纳有限个电子。越是靠近原子核的层,越容易被占满。这里主要研究外层,因为它们通常是有空缺的。如果给一个原子增加能量,电子就会从外层阶跃到更高能量层。同样,当电子失去能量时,电子便回落到它的常规能级上。

原子外层"当量"就是价电子,而该层的能力等级就是价电子带,再往外是导电带。当电子处于导电带时,它受到的原子约束非常弱,能很容易地进入相邻原子的导电带中。电子从价电子阶跃到导电带所需要的能量值由能带间隙决定(图 4.10)。

图 4.10 价电子和导电带

导体的能带间隙非常窄，所以在室温下的能量就可以将一束导体电子推入导电带。绝缘体的能带间隙则非常宽。它需要较大的能量才能将电子从价电子带推入对电子约束松散的导电带。半导体的能带间隙适中，通常都是绝缘体。

4.4.2 文章五 半导体材料的应用

硅(Si，元素编号 14)是一种半导体。在室温情况下，硅呈现微弱的导电性。在普通处理环境下可获得的能量即可将一些硅的价电子推入导电带。不需要很大的能量，可能非常小就足够使电流发生明显变化。

硅的温度越低，导电性越差，因为这时电子失去能量返回价电子带。一个简单的电器元件——热敏电阻，就是利用这种特点，随着温度的变化改变它的阻抗。

硅半导体的导电性可以用适量杂质或添加剂与其合成的方法加以调节。硅晶体如图 4.11 所示。

图 4.11 硅晶体

由于只有外层与相邻的原子相互作用，所以对原子进行简化，只绘制外层的 4 个电子。硅可以与相邻的 4 个原子构成共价键，也就是说它们在价电子层上共用电子对。价电子层上有 4 个电子，但还有 4 个空穴。正是这几个价电子层中的空穴被来自相邻原子的电子填充，这样就在原子间建立起了牢固的键连接，使得电子稳定在价电子层上。

如果在硅中加入些磷(P，元素编号 15)，由于磷的价电子层有 5 个电子，依然可以和硅形成共价键。图 4.12 所示的就是上述情况，只是较难辨别。5 个电子中的 4 个与硅形成了共价键，还有一个自由电子，这个电子可以自由地进入导电带，使得这个合金具有较多自由电子。

图 4.12 N 型半导体(硅和磷)

N 型半导体是带自由电子的半导体。注意材料依然是电中性的，正如铜一样具有电中性。只有当产生电压的时候，这些自由电子才能自由地运动。

如果在硅中加入些硼(B，元素编号 5)，如图 4.13 所示，虽然硼的价电子层只有 3 个电子，但依然可以和硅形成共价键。在这种情况下，许多共价键位置没有被硼电子占用。这些空穴可以被其他自由电子占用，这种合金就是 P 型半导体。材料的电性还是中性的。有趣的是，这些空穴可以像自由电子那样运动。正因如此，人们称这些空穴为电荷载流子。在大多数情况下，人们认为这些空穴带正电荷。

图 4.13 P 型半导体(硅和硼)

晶体管的工作方式类似于可变电阻器，或者用水打比方，它就类似于水龙头。最基本的晶体管是双极结型晶体管，简称 BJT。晶体管有两种类型：NPN 型和 PNP 型。注意晶体管不是数字式的，而是模拟转换器。

顾名思义，NPN 型晶体管由 3 层材料组成，两层 N 型半导体材料中间夹着一层 P 型半导体材料(图 4.14)，这就类似于将两个二极管背对背连接在一起(图 4.15)。晶体管的图形符号甚至也可以反映出双二极管形状。使用显示耗尽区的方块图，快速浏览一下晶体管的工作过程，如图 4.16 所示。图 4.16(a)表示原 N-P-N 配置结构。注意耗尽区在 P 节的两侧。

图 4.14 NPN 型晶体管

图 4.15 NPN 型晶体管的图形符号(双二极管)

图 4.16 NPN 型晶体管的工作过程

在晶体管的各部分名称中，晶体管中间是基极，用字母 B 表示。一端为发射极，用字母 E 表示；另一端为集电极，用字母 C 表示。如果将发射极和集电极用电路连接起来，那么不会有电流通过晶体管，因为耗尽区将发射极和集电极相互隔绝开。

如果在基极和发射极两端加上一个低电压，假设为 0.5V(图 4.16(b))，就其本身而言，这两个部分就是一个二极管，而且正向偏压。发射极和基极之间绝缘层的绝缘性可以降低到足以导通的程度。

现在，如果在发射极和集电极两端加上一个较高的电压，假设为 9V(图 4.16(c))，发射极和基极构成的二极管不会受到直接影响，因为它们两端的电压还是 0.5V。当集电极处的电子逸出以后，它就带正电荷，而发射极处聚集了大量来自电池的负电荷。

但是，基极与集电极之间依然有绝缘层，但并不是这个原因使电流无法流动。基极层很薄，基极与集电极之间的电势差很大，于是绝大多数电子在经过发射极后激增，然后跨过能带间隙进入集电极。只要发射极和基极处 PN 结两端电压足以让此绝缘层变薄，那么电流就会从发射极流向集电极。如果去除基极电压，那么发射极流向集电极的电流将截止。如果增加基极电压，使得发射极与基极间的绝缘层变薄，就会有更多的电子通过绝缘层进入集电极，发射极和集电极间的电流就会增加。

晶体管 transistor 是 transfer 和 resistor 两个单词的组合。晶体管基极处的电压控制着其他两极电流的通断。事实上，晶体管是电压控制可变绝缘体。由于晶体管是低端产品，所以不推荐大家使用，除非想要设计简单电路。对于大部分电子转换应用，使用 MOSFET 设备。如果想放大信号，最好还是去购买商家设计好的集成电路放大器。

……

4.5 任务三 MP4 播放器电路

4.5.1 文章六 直流电路简介

欧姆定律

电路中用得最多的电学定律就是欧姆定律。之所以用欧姆定律这个名称是为了纪念乔治·西蒙·欧姆，他在 19 世纪用公式建立起了电压、电流和电阻值之间的关系。欧姆定律："一段电路中的电流与电路两端的电压成正比，与该处电路的电阻值成反比。"欧姆定律用等式形式表示为：

$I = \dfrac{E}{R}$　　　其中：I 表示电流，单位是安培

$E = I \times R$　　　E 表示电压，单位是伏特

$R = \dfrac{E}{I}$　　　R 表示电阻值，单位是欧姆

图 4.19(a)所示的是简单有效地记忆欧姆定律的方法。盖住圆圈中的某个字母，并读取

由剩下的几个字母构成的方程式。如果电流未知，但电压和电阻值已知，可以借助图 4.19(b) 找到求解电流 I 的基本方程式。其结果为：

$$I = \frac{E}{R}$$

同样，如果知道电流和电阻值，电压就可以用图 4.19(c)所示的方程式计算：

$$E = I \times R$$

图 4.19(d)所示为电流和电阻的取值不适合以安培和欧姆为单位的，可以取其他单位。

图 4.19 欧姆定律圈

(a) 基图；(b) 求电流；(c) 求电压；(d) 单位为 mA，kΩ 和 μA，MΩ 的特殊情况

电阻网络

电阻网络是一种罕见的电路，该电路中只有电阻这一类元件。通常可以在电路中将一些电阻进行不同形式的配置。可以采用以下方法计算这些电路的整体电阻值。

首先，之所以要计算电阻网络的电阻值，是因为如果知道电路的电阻值和工作电压，这两者通常是已知的，就可以使用公式 $I = \dfrac{V}{R}$ 计算出电路所消耗的电流大小。知道了所需电流的大小之后，就能确定选用何种电源和所需的热能耗。

电路的功率用瓦特表示，其计算方程式为：$P = I^2 \times R$。该方程式有另一种形式，可以用欧姆定律 $I \times R$ 替代 V，得：

$$P = I \times V$$

电流的微小变化可能引起能耗的剧烈变化。电阻值的计算取决于电阻器的连接方式。

如图 4.20 所示，当设备串联时，这就意味着它们首尾相连。电阻的串联使得电阻合起来成了一个大电阻。

图 4.20 串联电阻

如图 4.21 所示，当设备并联时，它们并排连接。因为电流在电路中的流动不止一个路径，所以电路中的并联电阻要比单个电阻阻值小。对于两个电阻并联，其阻值为：

$$R = \frac{R_1 \times R_2}{R_1 + R_2}$$

如果有两个以上的电阻并联，总电阻为：

$$R = \frac{1}{\dfrac{1}{R_1} + \dfrac{1}{R_2} + \cdots + \dfrac{1}{R_N}}$$

图 4.21 并联电阻

印制电路板

如果想使电路真正发挥作用，就需要将电路原理图中的线路和元件转换成真实的电子线路和电子部件。人们平时所接触到的绝大多数电路都安装在印制电路板(PCB)上，或只是简易电路板。图 4.22 所示的是电路原理图所对应的电路板。

大多数印制电路板采用摄影技术制造。在专用的纤维板一面或者双面上覆盖上一层铜，覆盖完铜后再罩上一层光阻材料，然后将电路图投影到这层光阻材料上。随后大多数光阻

材料保护罩被洗去，只留下电路图留下的轨迹线。接下来用强酸溶解去除将光阻材料去除后留下的铜层。完成以上工艺以后，再在板上钻出安装电子器件用的孔，这样印制电路板就制作完成了。

板上的这些轨迹线就是导线。这些导线是扁平的，但跟人们平时所使用的导线的作用是一样的。焊点区是圆的或椭圆的区域，电子器件可以在该区域处插入电路板，并焊接到位。焊接过程稍后讨论。

价格低廉的电路板只有单面有铜材料，或者双面都有，但是孔中没有。昂贵一点的电路板孔是镀铜的，铜直接电镀到板孔中。镀铜后，孔就与焊接区相连，这样更易于焊接板上的电子器件。镀铜孔也更结实，焊接区也不易于从板上翘起。铜用胶水粘在纤维板上，但在焊接过程中过多的热量可能熔化胶水，造成焊接区和轨迹线从板上脱落。

图 4.22 印制电路板

如果板子双面都有铜，镀铜孔就会将电路板的上下两面焊接区牢固地连接起来。有一些镀铜孔不用于安装电子器件，而是用于连接上下两面的电路，这些镀铜孔称为通路孔。

有些电路板具有两层以上的铜层。这些多层电路板就像是粘合或者压制在一起的几个双层电路板。在这些情况下，通路孔对于建立层与层之间的连接是至关重要的。

当用计算机辅助软件设计了一块专用电路板时，也可以采用化学光阻材料或黏贴式光阻焊接片和轨迹线的方法，手工制作电路板。我个人并不推荐使用这些方法加工电路板，因为这些方法很难达到高质量要求，而且化学制剂不干净，对人体有害。

4.5.2 文章七 集成电路(IC)

集成电路是一组电子器件的集成，比如晶体管、二极管和电阻，这组电子器件被集成在一小块半导体片上，并且这些电子器件间可以相互通电连接。

半导体由碟形硅晶片制造而成。晶片(直径为 75～150mm，不到 1mm 厚)是由单晶硅锭切割而成。使用最为广泛的单晶生长方法是提拉法(图 4.23)。将一定量的掺杂剂加入到熔融多晶硅中得到所需要的半导体混合物。要避免混入其他有害物质，因为有害物质会影响硅的电性。单晶硅锭，长 1m，直径为 50～150 毫米，可以采用提拉法工艺制造。随后将硅锭制成圆柱形，再切割成硅晶片，最后进行抛光。

图 4.23 提拉法

光刻法的工艺过程是将描绘各类电子器件的几何图形通过光掩模板转换到硅晶片上。

光掩模板是一种屏蔽单元，计算机辅助设计技术在其设计和制造中起了主要作用。光刻法能确保光掩模板位置精度和尺寸精度。二氧化硅可以起到阻碍(或屏蔽)半导体混合物的作用。掺杂剂原子能够进入到没有二氧化硅的晶片内。光刻法是选择性去除二氧化硅的工艺。二氧化硅覆盖有耐酸层，但不包括需要扩散窗口的地方。去除二氧化硅采用腐蚀法。耐酸层通常是光敏有机材料，被称为光刻胶，光刻胶在紫外线的作用下聚合。如果紫外线穿过包含有所要几何图案的光掩模板，耐酸层就会聚合，几何图形就出现了。然后，可以用有机溶剂去除掉没有聚合的区域。电子束蚀刻(EBL)用于避免衍射，实现高精度线宽。

……

项目五　机械设计及制造

5.1　项目引入

　　制造就是生产零件并把它们安装在一起。如果你可以生产零件并把它们安装在一起制成产品，你就是在制造。制造产业对社会和经济都非常重要。经济是一个生产和销售产品和服务的系统。现在有许多人从事制造业。这些人生产产品，同时用他们挣来的钱购买产品。人们所购买的产品越多，被生产出来的产品也就越多。这样人们就有了更多的工作机会。从另外一个方面来看，生产制造对经济也很重要。材料在变成有用的产品后，它就升值了。那也就是增值，即通过加工制造增加了其价值。产流水线如图 5.1 所示。

图 5.1　生产流水线

5.2　项目内容

　　多年来，随着其他领域技术的迅猛发展，制造技术也有了很大的进步。现代生产技术是由机械、电子信息和现代管理技术构成，这些技术应用于产品存续期间的所有阶段，目的是为了实现 T(高效)、Q(高质量)、C(低成本)和 S(优质服务)。下文并非列举出了所有生产制造中的新技术，而只是列举出一些具有代表性的实例。

　　FMS 表示柔性制造系统。顾名思义，柔性制造系统能够适应产品型号变化或加工顺序改变的要求。柔性制造系统包括 3 个主要部分：① 计算机控制系统；② 材料自动装卸系统；③ 数控机床。人们需要考虑解决单一型号产品的高速生产线和多型号零件数控机床的低生产率相冲突的问题。如图 5.2 所示是柔性制造系统在制造过程中的相对位置。

图 5.2　柔性制造系统在制造过程中的相对位置

5.3　任务一　基础知识

5.3.1　文章一　计算机集成制造系统

　　CIMS 是计算机集成制造系统的缩写。如果柔性制造系统代表的是车间级水平，那么 CIMS 代表的是企业级水平。虽然计算机集成制造系统包含了许多先进制造技术，比如机械人技术、计算机数字控制技术(CNC)、计算机辅助设计技术(CAD)、计算机辅助加工技术(CAM)、计算机辅助工程技术(CAE)、和准时制生产技术(JIT)，但是它远胜于这些技术。

　　计算机集成制造系统是解决企业诸多问题的新途径，这些问题包括保证企业整体质量、稳步提升企业水平、客户满意度、各部门产品制造和设计信息的计算机数据库集成、部门间通信障碍的消除，以及企业资源的集成。

5.3.2 文章二 什么是机械设计

机械设计指的是设计方法、机械零部件的选用，以及这些零件的安装配置，从而实现预定功能。毫无疑问，机械零件必须具有很好的互换性、装配稳定性及运行安全可靠性。工程师不仅需要考虑在给定时间内所设计的机械零件的动作，还要考虑它们互相之间的连接。

为了说明机械零件设计必须与机械设计相结合，这里以拖拉机减速箱为例加以说明。假如要实现减速功能，你决定使用单级蜗轮蜗杆减速装置。如图 5.3 所示，你选定了一个蜗轮、一根蜗杆、一根轴、4 个轴承和能够将各个零件固定到位的轴承座。这时应该意识到你已经为以上设计绘制了一张草图。

图 5.3 减速器

首先，你选择了蜗轮蜗杆而不是直齿轮、斜齿轮，或者锥齿轮。事实上，其他类型的减速设备比如带传动、链传动等也可使用。蜗杆和蜗轮的安装、支承蜗杆和蜗轮的轴承的放置位置，以及轴承座的结构都是设计时需要考虑的。如果没有先行解决这类问题，那么整个设计过程将无法继续进行。当构思完成整体设计后，减速器中各个独立部件的设计才可以继续进行。设计过程的模型如图 5.4 所示。

图 5.4 设计过程的模型

5.3.3 文章三 公差与配合

质量与精度是机械零件制造过程中主要考虑的因素。零件的互换性要求只有精度一致才能安装匹配。设计尺寸和加工尺寸应该合理选用相同的配合制。然而，制造具有较高形状精度和尺寸精度要求的零件既没有可能也没有必要。大多数尺寸都具有精度等级以及尺寸偏差容许范围的表示方式，尺寸偏差指的是零件保持其工作性能前提下的误差允许值。

尺寸通常包括标称尺寸、基本尺寸、设计尺寸和实际尺寸等。

标称尺寸通常指零件无误差时的整体尺寸。

基本尺寸是用来决定极限尺寸和偏差的一个基准尺寸(起始尺寸)。

设计尺寸是设计时使用公差等级制定的尺寸范围。

实际尺寸是零件的制造尺寸，它可能大于或小于标称尺寸。

零件尺寸标注如图 5.5 所示。

图 5.5 零件尺寸标注

(a) 基本尺寸；(b) 实际尺寸；(c) 设计尺寸

公差是零件尺寸所允许的总变动量，或者最大极限尺寸减去最小极限尺寸所得尺寸值的总量范围。

单向公差是由基本尺寸向一侧变化的公差值。

双向公差是由基本尺寸向两侧变化的公差值。

公差的标注如图 5.6 所示。

图 5.6 公差的标注
(a) 单向公差；(b) 双向公差

配合公差是零件配合时允许的间隙或过盈的变动量(例如孔和轴的配合)。配合公差分为配件的间隙配合公差(配合公差为正)和过盈配合公差(配合公差为负)。

配合是总体的松紧程度，是在设计配件时权衡余量和公差的结果。配件或组件的配合方式有间隙配合、过盈配合和过渡配合。

间隙配合是孔和轴连接时总是留有间隙的配合制。孔的下偏差大于等于轴的上偏差。

过渡配合是孔和轴连接时间隙和过盈都有可能发生的配合制(取决于孔和轴的实际尺寸)。孔和轴的公差带部分或完全发生干涉。

过盈配合是孔和轴连接时总是会发生干涉的配合制。孔的上偏差小于等于轴的下偏差。

间隙配合，过渡配合和过盈配合的对比图如图 5.7 所示。

图 5.7 间隙配合，过渡配合和过盈配合对比图
(a) 间隙配合；(b) 过渡配合；(c) 过盈配合

5.4 任务二 材料成形工艺

机械加工工艺用于获得金属材料的机械性能。金属加工可以减少内空隙或空洞的出现，提高金属密度。金属中的杂质可以随着晶粒一起，在金属加工过程中断裂，随即扩散到金属中去。这样就降低了杂质的危害性，提高了机械强度。

机械加工通常分为热加工和冷加工两种方式。其区别就在于在施加作用力之前所需加热量的多少。

5.4.1 文章四 车削

车削是通过使用切削刀具一层层去除金属材料来加工各类圆柱形工件的工艺，它是人们熟知的并应用较为广泛的材料去除工艺(图 5.8(a))。工件材料定轴旋转，切削刀具纵向进给。切削刀具比加工材料更硬、更耐磨。车床的种类有很多，还有一些是自动加工车床。车床往往由电机带动，通过轮系传递加工材料所需的转矩，以及为刀具提供进给运动。

大量机械加工使用的金属切削原理都是相同的。其中最常见的是使用不同加工刀具的铣削加工和钻削加工。通过改变刀具的形状以及刀具与工件之间的相对运动形式，许多形状各异的工件就可以被生产出来(图 5.8(b)和(c))。

图 5.8 车削

5.4.2 文章五 锻造

锻造是加热金属坯料后再给其施加压力从而加工成所需形状的加工工艺。这是最古老的金属加工工艺，它一直可以追溯到青铜器时代。虽然有时也使用冷锻，但通常都使用热锻。

锻造工艺通常分为以下4种。

自由锻是传统的锻造工艺，其变形的方向可以不受限制，或者由乡村铁匠在开式模具中进行，或者由现代化车间中的手动锻锤或液压机完成，如图 5.9 所示。

图 5.9　自由锻

模锻是利用闭式压力模具在锻锤的作用下使毛坯变形而获得锻件的锻造方法。工件成形压力是连续不断地作用在坯料上的。坯料被加热到适当温度,并放置在下模凹槽中。上模向下闭合,于是金属坯料在压力作用下充满整个凹槽。多余坯料从分模面处挤出并向四周扩散,随后修剪工序会将这些挤出部分去除掉。模锻如图 5.10 所示。

图 5.10　模锻

与模锻相类似的是压锻,压锻也是对闭式压力模具施压,不同的是压锻采用的连续挤压力是由液压产生的。

与模锻或压锻的压延工艺不同,机锻是将坯料镦粗后得到所需的形状。

5.4.3　文章六　轧制

轧制是将金属坯料放在一对旋转轧辊的间隙(各种形状)中,压缩它并使其横截面面积减小、长度增加的加工方法。

轧制通常采用热轧,除非指明要用冷轧。金属坯料在摩擦力的作用下通过轧辊,使其在压力的作用下最终成形。金属坯料能被放进轧辊的厚度取决于轧辊表面的粗糙度。粗糙轧辊比光滑轧辊有更高的减薄率。但是,这样坯料表面被压印出粗糙印迹。

轧制广泛应用于生产平板、薄板、结构钢梁等。图 5.11 所示就是平板或薄板的轧制。铁锭通过铸造而成,通常在加热后经过一些工序减薄。由于工件的宽度不变,厚度变薄后其长度就增加。在最后的热轧工艺结束后,将工件进行冷却以提高工件的表面质量和尺寸精度,并增加其强度。在轧制工艺中,轧辊横截面的形状应与所需工件的横截面形状相同。

图 5.11　轧制

5.4.4　文章七　铸造

在公元前 4000 年至公元前 3000 年期间出现了铸造技术,人们使用石质模子和金属模子铸造铜。各种铸造工艺在漫长的历史进程中都得到了发展,每种都有其特点和针对性,以满足具体工程和服务的需要。

传统金属铸造工艺采用砂模,这种方式已经延续了一千年。简言之,砂铸工艺由以下几个部分组成:①在砂中开设形腔以得到预定形状的铸件;②开设浇注系统;③将熔融的金属注入形腔;④将金属冷却至凝固状态;⑤去除砂模;⑥取出铸件(图 5.12)。

图 5.12　砂模结构示意图

由于许多铸件内部带有孔穴或通道,比如汽车发动内腔或阀体内芯,所以要使用铸芯。在铸件形成内表面之前,将铸芯放置在模腔内,并在落砂和进一步处理的过程中,将铸芯从已经完成的铸件中取出。跟铸模一样,铸芯必须具有一定的强度,能够抵御高温并方便拆卸;因此,铸芯由砂聚合物制成。

熔模铸工艺,也称为蜡模铸造工艺,早在公元前 4000 年至公元前 3000 年人们就已经开始使用。模型由蜡或塑料(比如聚苯乙烯)通过模塑或快速成型技术制作而成。图 5.13 所示为熔模铸工艺的操作步骤。模型是由熔化的蜡或塑料注入金属模具中形成的。然后将模型浸入耐热材料浆中，比如高纯度二氧化硅，以及含水、硅酸乙酯和酸的粘结剂。等第一层涂层干了以后，模型又被反复涂抹以增加其厚度。

图 5.13　熔模铸工艺示意图(蜡模铸造工艺)

5.5　任务三　计算机集成制造系统的组成部分

5.5.1　文章八　计算机数字控制

什么是计算机数字控制，或者说 CNC？简言之，计算机数字控制就是由计算机和计算机程序自动控制的机床。换句话说，也就是由计算机而不是人直接控制机床。数控机床在计算机的引导下沿轴线运动，这是在计算机读取程序并指引一些电机执行相应操作的条件下完成的。电机旋转移动工作台并加工机械零件。

在计算机数字控制出现之前，机床操作是由手动或机械控制的。如今，传统机床已经被大量数控机床代替。本质上机床依然是它原有的功能，但是机床的控制由手动变成了电动。数控机床能重复生产相同零件，几乎没有误差。它们昼夜不停地工作，连续几周可以不停歇。数控机床与传统机床相比有明显的优势，传统机床做任何加工都需要大量的人力。而数控机床，如图 5.15 所示，具有较高的生产率。数控机床的售价、安装维护费用都比较高。然而，如果能够合理使用数控机床，它的生产率优势可以弥补其高成本的缺陷。

图 5.15　数控机床

数控机床原理

如图 5.16 所示是典型数控机床的基本操作单元。数控机床的功能单元和其所包括的部件表述如下。

- 数据输入：数控信息从计算机存储器中读取，并存储到计算机存储器中。
- 数据处理：程序读入数控机床控制单元以待处理。
- 数据输出：这些信息被转换成伺服电机控制指令(特殊脉冲指令)(图 5.17)。然后，伺服电机驱动工作台(工件安装的部位)精确定位，通过步进电机、丝杆和其他类似装置实现直线或旋转运动。
- 控制回路的类型：数控机床采用两种控制回路，即开式回路和闭式回路。在开式回路系统中(图 5.17(a))，控制信号可以传送给伺服电机，但工作台的运动精度和位置精度无法校核。闭式回路系统(图 5.17(b))中安装有多种转换器、传感器和计数器，它们能够精确测量工作台的位置。通过反馈控制，工作台的位置与控制信号能够作比较，从而不断地修正工作台的位置直至达到正确的坐标位置为止。
- 定位测量：可以分为直接测量和间接测量(图 5.18)两种方式。各类传感器大多是基于磁和光电原理。在直接测量系统中，传感器读取直线运动的工作台或滑轨上的刻度值(图 5.18(a))。在间接测量系统中，回转式译码器或解算器测量工作台或滑轨的位置(图 5.18(b))。

图 5.16　数控机床定位控制的主要部件

图 5.17 控制系统类型
(a) 开环控制系统；(b) 闭环控制系统

图 5.18 定位测量方式
(a) 直接方式；(b) 间接方式

常用数控机床

数控车床

如图 5.19 所示为数控车床，它是在车间中随处可见的生产设备。数控车床有许多优于传统车床的地方。传统车床切削圆弧线时需要专用工具，而数控车床则不需要。数控车床也擅长车螺纹。

图 5.19 数控车床

数控铣床

如图 5.20 所示为数控铣床，它可以执行传统铣床同样的操作，但是数控铣床采用的是自动运行而不是手动。

图 5.20 数控铣床

数控磨床

数控磨床如图 5.21 所示。平面磨床和圆柱磨床可能是最新的前沿数控系统。磨削加工对高精度的要求意味着运动控制技术必须要跟上高精度的步伐。如今，定位系统可以达到百万分之五十英寸，这在精密磨削中很常见。

图 5.21 数控磨床

数控加工中心

数控加工中心是一种先进的、由计算机控制的机床，它能在工件的不同表面和不同方向上执行多种多样的加工任务，不需要重新拆卸或装夹。数控加工中心一般被认为是高精度、多用途机床，它们已经成为加工车间和单件小批量生产的主力军。数控加工中心是非常灵巧的机器，能轻易胜任多种多样的工件加工任务。

如图 5.22 和图 5.23 所示，立式加工中心(VMC)和卧式加工中心是现在车间中常见的两类数控机床，它们的运行具有很好的可视性。

图 5.22 立式加工中心(VMC)
1—基座；2—托架；3—工作台；4—伺服电机；5—全动立柱；6—机床控制单元；7—刀库；
8—换刀机械臂(图 5.24)；9—刀架；10—控制面板；11—动力单元

图 5.23 卧式加工中心(HMC)

图 5.24 换刀机械臂

5.5.2 文章九 计算机辅助设计(CAD)

计算机辅助设计是指使用安装有高级图形软硬件的计算机能够精确的制图或生成技术说明的系统。如果该系统设计的零件用于加工制造，那么设计师只需要绘制和建立零件的三维模型,而不需要建立其物理模型。

计算机辅助设计系统大致可以分为两类:二维计算机辅助设计和三维计算机辅助设计。二维计算机辅助设计系统实质上是经过美化的电子图板,可以代替纸、铅笔和丁字尺。三维计算机辅助设计也可称为几何建模。三维 CAD 有 3 种建模方式:线框建模、曲面建模和实体建模。图 5.25 所示就是线框建模的实例。该图形的作用就是指明其合理的模型。实体模型如图 5.26 所示。曲面模型如图 5.27 所示。

图 5.25　线框模型

图 5.26　实体模型

图 5.27　曲面模型

线框模型是简单三维模型,它用各类线条元素来表示物体,并能精确地表示边缘、角和曲面分离体。但是这种建模方式无法分清物体的内外部关系。而曲面模型则可以精确地定义模型的外部情况。曲面模型通过各部分线段将各类型曲面连接到一起。实体模型应用拓扑学,物体的容积和质量都给出了定义。曲面模型类似于实体模型,但是曲面模型内部是空的。

每一种计算机辅助设计系统都有一套绘图要素和图元供设计时调用。

5.5.3　文章十　计算机辅助制造

计算机辅助制造(CAM)主要包括 4 个组成部分:数控技术、工艺规程制定、机器人学和工厂管理。

计算机辅助制造中的数控技术

数控技术是计算机辅助制造中的重要组成部分,该技术是由计算机将几何模型或零件直接转换成数控程序。现在,自动化程度还只局限于有着高度几何对称和其他并不复杂的零件。但是在不久的将来,有些公司不再需要使用图纸,只需通过数据库将零件信息直接从设计部门发送到加工部门即可。随着图纸的消失,许多问题随即出现,因为计算机模型都是使用设计部门和加工部门共用的公共集成数据库。

工艺规程制定

工艺规程制定包括详细制定从开始到结束的生产流程。工艺规程制定系统与计算机辅助制造相关的地方就在于:该系统能从几何模型数据库中直接产生工艺规程,不需要人为辅助。

工业机器人

许多先进技术将机器人集成到制造系统中,比如在线安装、焊接和喷涂。

工厂管理

工厂管理使用交互工厂数据收集系统,时时接收来自工作现场的信息。同时,使用该数据计算生产优先权,并动态决定下一步的工作任务,以确保大批量生产计划的顺利完成。该系统也可以直接进行调整以满足某一具体要求,不需要计算机程序专家的帮助。

……

项目六　现代新技术

6.1　项目引入

将来，机电一体化系统的蓬勃发展将得益于其各个组成部分的发展。通过提供"促成技术"，许多传统学科的进步对机电一体化系统的发展起到推波助澜的作用。例如，微处理器的发明对机械系统的修正和新型机电一体化系统的设计有着深远的影响。人们期待着廉价微处理器和微控制器的不断改进、传感器和执行机构的不断发展，而这些都是在不断运用微机电系统、自适应控制技术、实时编程方式、有线和无线网络连接技术、成熟的计算机辅助先进系统建模工程技术、虚拟样机和测试技术的情况下得以实现的。

6.2　项目内容

微机电系统是一种促成技术，它使得用于机电一体化系统的传感器和执行机构更为廉价。许多微机电设备已经运用到汽车领域，包括安全气囊弹出时用的机构和传感器，以及多用途压力传感器。将带有CMOS信号调理电路的微机电系统集成到同一块硅晶片上，也是一个促成技术发展的实例，这也使得机电产品有了进一步的发展，比如汽车技术。

6.3　任务一　微机电技术

6.3.1　文章一　微机电系统简介

在美国，这种技术被称为微机电系统(MEMS)；欧洲则称为微系统技术(MST)。每一次对微机电系统具体定义的询问都会收到大量回复，这些回复大部分都将"微型"看作是微机电系统的主要特点。但是这些回复的明显分歧仅仅反映出该技术应用的多样性，而不是缺乏共性。微机电系统就像工具箱、物理产品和方法论，并集这些功能于一身。

(1) 它是装有设计和创造微型系统的技术和工艺的文件夹。

图6.1　微型机器人

(2) 它通常是实现最终应用目标而专门定制的物理产品——人们很少能从邻近电子商店内买到通用微机电产品。

(3) 美国微系统技术办公室报告称："微机电系统是一种制造方法"。这些"制品"在微观上表现出传感和执行功能，对局部物理量进行计算和交换，但在宏观上对整体产生影响。

与传统设备相比，新型执行机构反应更快、尺寸更小、效果更佳，以及功重比更高。例如，电磁式电机的尺寸通常至少要大于1厘米，因为如果再小就无法提供足够的转矩和功率。图6.2所示是一个即将要装配的最小电磁式电机。一个直径为1.9毫米的微电机一般只能提供7.5微牛米大小的转矩和每分钟100000转的转速。选用此类电机制作减速47%的微型变速箱，可以将传递的转矩提高到 300 微牛米。但是使用该变速箱将大大降低电机的机械效率。而且，当电磁式电机尺寸减小时，绕线圈的厚度也随之减小，这样就导致电阻和焦耳热量显著增大。

图 6.2　1.9 毫米电磁式微电机

图 6.3　音圈电动机示意图

6.3.2　文章二　纳米喷墨打印机微机电系统

纳米颗粒的直径一般在 1 纳米到 100 纳米之间，由一系列金属、半导体，或绝缘体原子构成。由于尺寸微小，纳米粒子表现出的熔点低于普通粒状材料，只有 1000 摄氏度。低熔点是由纳米粒子相对较高的表面积与体积比率造成的，这使得相邻粒子容易形成键连接。纳米粒子可以制成胶体，用作墨水一样打印。

喷墨打印机打印素材是通过从喷嘴中喷出极小墨滴实现的，每次喷出一滴，同时在底板上横向移动大约 1 毫米。每一个墨滴在压力脉冲控制下，从与喷嘴相连的墨腔中喷出，沿墨滴轨迹喷射到底板上，有时也采用可变形压晶体控制方式(图 6.4)。墨滴在底板上留下的图案构成了打印机的输出。喷墨打印采用颜色叠加的打印方法，它比除墨打印方式更节约、更高效。它由数据驱动，不需要蒙版，减少了平版印刷的回程时间。喷墨打印不受底板构造和形态的限制，比平版印刷和半导体电路板批量印刷更适应多层大幅面素材的打印。以后打印头的制造技术将能够制造形体尺寸在 20 微米以下的打印头。总之，喷墨打印是一种具有许多优点的打印技术。伴随着新型纳米粒子被用作原材料，纳米工艺为电路系统或微机电系统提供了切实可行的桌面打印系统。

图 6.4　压电式随机型喷墨打印系统

在打印头处，压电晶体在电信号的驱动下伸长，使墨腔中黑水表面凹陷，在墨腔内产生一个压力脉冲，将单个墨滴从喷嘴中喷出。喷嘴中产生的毛细管作用使墨水经由墨口重新注满墨腔。层叠的墨滴留在底板上打印出图案。

原子力显微镜下的纳米银喷墨打印墨滴显微图，如图 6.5 所示，该墨滴被烧结在载物玻璃片上。

图 6.5　原子力显微镜下的纳米银喷墨打印墨滴显微图

(a) 轴测图，垂直放大 80 倍；(b) 俯视图；(c) 横截面轮廓图

6.4　任务二　未来机器人

6.4.1　文章三　蚁群机器人

电影里的机器人都是依据人们自己的想象制成的。每个机器都安装有灵活多样的操作工具(机械臂、机械手和机械手指)，能够穿越各种地形，同时也安装了独立的复杂控制系统(大脑)。

工业机器人几乎与此相反。它们是执行单一任务的专用机器，一般固定不动，但是它

们也不仅仅只是复述当前指令的脚本阅读器。

蚁群机器人与机器人有几分相似，但本质上各异。蚁群机器人的设计灵感来自于蚂蚁和蜜蜂的复杂群体行为。单个蚂蚁并不复杂。构造蚁脑要比构造人脑容易得多。蚂蚁的群体行为要比单个蚂蚁复杂。这非常像大脑的行为远比人们所预期的单个神经元复杂得多。

以上的思考使人们想要去发明蚁群机器人。它们中每个都是廉价的小型机器人，而且是简易程控单元。它们彼此之间可以进行通信，人们可以将一群机器人同时投入使用。即使一小部分机器人损坏了或者丢失了，蚁群依然可以完成它们的任务。这些机器人都很廉价，所以人们可以大量使用，而且正是因为它们的大量使用，它们中的个体也就变得无足轻重了。

这些机器人的结构特点是集群，使得它非常适合执行探查任务。人们立刻想到用蚁群机器人去探索太空，但是在地球上的探查任务也很重要，比如将蚁群投放到灾害地区搜寻生还者。蚁群也可以用于战时，侦查城市局势和报告侦查情况。飞行机器人群，又是一个引起人们极大兴趣的课题，它们对于侦查同样非常有用。

6.4.2　文章二　代理机器人

随着互联网在全球的普及，人们的许多活动不再局限于现实领域，而是包括了可以徜徉和操作的电子世界领域。对于有些在线任务人们并不喜欢亲自去做，因为这些任务都比较艰难、乏味，要么就是更适合自动操作。同时完成这些任务需要具有一定的智能水平。

电子机器人拥有许多和实体机器人相同的特性，这些特性也正是人们所需要的。它们能够在互联网中畅游。它们能够感知网络状态，把握网络运行最佳状态，并且能够根据不完整的或者不明确的计划制订执行方案。

这种虚拟机器人被称为代理机器人。代理机器人倾向于团队工作，可与具有不同功能的其他代理机器人相互交流。代理机器人没有实体，所以不用担心其硬件出错和费用问题。代理机器人是抽象的，是纯信息化的。

只要建立机器人的计算机模型，人们就可以在仿真环境下创建仿真机器人。在将设计转换成实体形式之前，进行这样的计算机仿真将使实验更便捷、更快速。但是它们依然是仿真机器人，最终都要在真实世界中得以实现。代理机器人所处的环境是一个信息世界。

6.5　任务三　光机电一体化系统

6.5.1　文章五　光机电一体化系统简介

纵观历史，电子技术的变革加速了机械与电子的融合，随后光学技术的发展又促成了光学部件与电子器件的一体化。这一趋势使得大量传统系统由低自主性和低性能向高自主性和高性能演化。

图 6.8 所示为当前所使用的新型改进系统的实例。直到现在，工人们还是借助显微镜用肉眼检测印刷电路板，但是同样的检测用光学检测技术就可以实现。芯片安装设备起初大多数是机械式的，现在由集成安装设备来代替，它包括零件定位测算仪、视觉传感器和伺服控制单元。坐标测量仪(CMM)刚问世时是接触式的，紧接着是非接触式数字电磁式的，再后来是光电式的。近几年来，人们对坐标测量仪进行刻苦研发，希望借助传感器集成技

术研制出精确、可靠和多用途的产品。如图 6.9 所示，洗衣机也是由机械操作控制演变成具有光学传感器反馈功能及智能控制功能的产品。

图6.8 插图演化说明

(a) 印制电路板检测；(b) 芯片或表面贴装器件的安装；(c)坐标测量仪

图6.9 具有光电传感器反馈功能的现代洗衣机

机械/工艺/系统的相关技术的不断发展，增强了它们的性能，同时也创造了新的价值和功能。机电一体化技术集成了机械、电子和计算机技术，它在这一变革中起到了重要的作用。然而，为了使它们进一步演变成为精确智能和自主的系统，人们不得不将光学和光学工程技术融入到机电一体化系统中去，完善其已有的功能，并创造新的更多的功能。因此，光机电系统就是一个光学器件、机械零件、电子元件和计算机系统的集成系统。

光学部件或器件在光机电系统中的主要功能和作用被划分为多个技术领域，如图 6.10 所示。

图6.10 光学技术的基本作用

(a) 照明；(b) 感应；(c) 执行；(d) 数据存储；(e) 数据传送；(f) 数据显示；
(g) 计算；(h) 材料性能变化

6.5.2　文章六　光机电系统实例

在许多控制系统和仪表、检测和测试仪器、光学产品、生产设备、耗电产品和工业电子产品中，还有在微机电系统、自动化工程领域、生物工程技术领域及其他一些工程领域中都可以找到光机电一体化的实例。以下是一些这些应用的实例。

照相机是典型的光机电操控设备。例如，傻瓜相机装有光圈控制器和焦距调节装置，其中焦距调节装置带有亮度计，其用于独立判断周围环境的亮度。由于有了上述系统结构，人们可以创造新的功能以提升现在相机的性能。如图 6.11 所示，照相机的主要部件有镜头、光圈、快门、胶卷或如电荷耦合器件或互补型金属氧化物半导体一样的电子成像单元。经过对物体进行一系列镜头的变焦和聚焦后，图像就聚焦并曝光到胶卷或者电子成像单元上。改变有关成像平面内透镜的位置就可以改变图像的放大倍数和焦点。通过透镜的光束被光敏传感器感知，同时光束受到光圈或快门速度的充分调控。现在，光敏传感器或互补型金属氧化物半导体类传感器已经用于可控变焦镜的自动对焦操作。

图6.11 照相机

自动对焦单反相机使用可替换镜头，是多功能的集成光机电产品。如图 6.12 所示是现代 35 毫米自动相机的电路设计图，其机身内部装有微控制器，另一个微控制器位于透镜座内。当镜头与机身安装到位后，两个微处理器就可以进行通信。

图6.12 自动相机电路子系统

在摄影师按动快门键(处于初始位置)的瞬间，机身中的微控制器根据计算测距仪得到的测量结果，计算出快门速度和光圈参数，并将计算结果显示在取景器和外部液晶显示面板上。

当根据当前的采光情况调整快门速度和光圈时，机身内的微控制器就会判断投射图像是否正确地聚焦到照相胶片上。在视野范围内，物体反射出的光线通过照相机镜头后，光线就落在两个48位线性阵列光敏传感器上。当图像在照相胶片上聚焦到位时，传感器阵列将可测出信号间距值。但是，如果图像模糊，测得的间距值将偏离期望值，其偏差值转换为一个出错信号。出错信号传递给镜头微控制器，以便产生一个控制信号驱动直流电机调整机身上的镜头焦距。

项目七 机电行业应聘

7.1 任务一 招聘广告

西门子产品生命周期管理软件(上海)有限公司

西门子产品生命周期管理软件(上海)有限公司是西门子自动机与驱动器(A&D)公司的一个分公司，坐落于上海浦东经济技术开发区，是产品生命周期管理软件和服务供应商中的领导者，注册安装点数为550万个，全球客户51000家。由于在华东地区的业务增长迅速，我公司正寻求高素质并有意向来我公司的人才，上海地区招聘岗位如下：

1. 助理秘书(2人)

岗位职责：
- 行政管理
- 安排营业执照申请
- 管理办公室账户和日常秘书任务等。

任职资格：
- 优秀大学本科毕业生，工商管理专业
- 擅长英语口语和英文写作，会计上海话和普通话
- 掌握基本的计算机知识和技能，例如Word、Excel、Outlook(e-mail)、汉字输入
- 性格开朗，工作态度积极，勤奋肯干，自觉自愿
- 30岁以下并且形象良好者优先
- 2年以上独立管理办公室的相关工作经验

待遇：
给予正式录用者每小时12美元的工作报酬，车贴，住宿，利润分红，外加医疗/牙科/人身保险。

请应聘者在10日内将简历(中英文)通过邮件发送到我公司，并附上证书复印件，近期照片，现在收入水平和薪酬要求，以及详细联系方式。请在信封的左下角注明要应聘的岗位。

2. 可编程控制器工程师(5人)

岗位职责：
- 接受客户咨询，制订培训计划

- 正确理解和分析客户需求
- 管理项目实施
- 项目总结和文档编制
- 销售支持

任职资格：
- 大专以上学历，主修机械/电气/电子工程或相关专业
- 工作积极勤奋
- 英语口语流利、文笔流畅，能与外商进行对话
- 熟悉 WINCC、PCS7、SIMATIC S7-400 系统
- 3 年以上工程机构工作经验
- 具有专业英语能力者优先
- 录用后将给予培训

其他：
- 本岗位需要经常出差

待遇：
- 薪酬福利优厚
- 为录用者提供优越的发展前景
- 出国培训机会

请将完整简历(中英文)，包括照片、学历证书复印件、以前用人单位的推荐信和联系电话号码，寄至：上海浦东经济技术开发区，88 号邮政信箱，人事经理收。

7.2　任务二　求职信

1. 助理秘书

敬爱的先生/女士：

　　看到今天报纸上贵公司的招聘广告，特来信应聘助理秘书岗位。本人认为完全胜任贵公司所提出的具体任职要求。

　　本人今年 26 岁。高中毕业后在上海的一所名牌大学学习了 3 年工商课程。大学毕业后，在一家律师事务所工作了 3 年，一直任职至今。本人过去 3 年的薪酬是每月 1500 元，我希望将来也不会低于这个薪酬。

　　本人能够胜任助理秘书岗位的具体理由如下：

　　本人头脑灵活，适应能力强，为人热情；打字速度快；文笔清晰，简明，幽默；能说流利的上海话和普通话。

　　附上本人的简历，希望能有机会与您面谈。感谢您考虑本人的请求。

敬礼

李红

2. 可编程控制器工程师

敬爱的先生/女士：

　　阅读了贵公司 5 月 17 日在《二十一世纪人力资源报》上刊登的招聘启事后，我觉得我

可以胜任该职位。

我今年毕业于上海电子信息职业技术学院，主修机电一体化工程。

我能胜任可编程控制器工程师职位的具体理由如下：
- 适应能力强，工作积极勤奋；
- 具有电子设备维修和数控机床维护实践经验；
- 上海话和普通话流利；
- 熟悉机电一体化工程专业英语。

希望您能够接受我的申请，我必将努力工作不辜负您对我的信赖。附上两份学位证书复印件和一份简历供您审阅。

提前谢谢您能够考虑我的申请和对我的恩惠。

敬礼

李明

7.3 任务二 简历

简 历

姓名：李明　　　　　　　　　　出生年月：1987年2月1日
出生地：上海，徐汇　　　　　　性别：男
身高：175cm　　　　　　　　　体重：67kg
健康状况：良好　　　　　　　　婚姻状况：单身
电话：021-57132333　　　　　　E-mail：Li@126.com
现住址：上海市南京西路567弄8号楼1201室
应聘职位：可编程控制器工程师

教育背景：

2008—2011　上海电子信息职业技术学院，机械工程系，机电一体化专业毕业(2011)

主修课程：大学物理，模拟电子基础，C语言编程基础，微机原理及应用，数字电子基础，高等数学，工程制图，工程力学，电路原理，PLC原理及应用，液压控制技术，测量技术，数控编程原理及应用，计算机辅助设计/计算机辅助制造等

英语证书：

全国大学英语考试四级，2009

计算机能力：

全国计算机等级考试二级，2009
精通C语言编程
熟练运用Office、AutoCAD和MasterCAM

课外活动能力：

在首届校园文化艺术节期间成功组织了英语演讲比赛，并受到相关领导的好评
学实部部长
《校园生活》周刊编辑

技能证书与专长：
电子装配高级工
导游资格证书
六级电工
每分钟打字 50 个

获奖情况：
2009、2010 年学院奖学金
2010 年优秀学生会干部称号

工作经验：
设备维修与装配工
在社区服务中心维修电子设备
2010 暑假在上海电气集团实习期间维护自动生产线

证明材料：
如有需要立即提供

7.4　任务四　面试

A：我可以进来吗？
B：请进。
A：先生，您好。我是李明。我是前来面试的。
B：很高兴认识您。我叫汤姆。请坐。
A：谢谢，我是来应聘可编程控制器工程师职位的。
B：我们已经收到了你寄来的求职信。我想和你交流一下你的任职资格情况。别紧张，我们随便谈谈，好吗？
A：好的。很高兴您给我这次面试机会。
A：你为什么要想进入我们公司呢？
B：我对叮编程控制器工程很感兴趣，而且非常喜欢解决各类工程问题。我认为能够为贵公司工作是一件非常令人激动和极具挑战性的事情。同样重要的是，到贵公司任职可以开阔眼界，到达我人生的一个新巅峰。我知道贵公司在业界享有盛誉。
A：你以前有在其他公司应聘过这类岗位吗？
B：有的，前几天我到 ABC 公司应聘过，以免贵公司拒绝录用我，不过我还是更喜欢为贵公司工作。
A：你觉得你是一个什么样性格的人？
B：我认为我是一个主动性强、有责任心的人。个性随和，与人为善。我不喜欢盛气凌人、发号施令，而是喜欢与他人同舟共济，共创业绩。
A：你觉得最能令你高兴的事是什么？
B：我以事业为重。如果事业有成，大有前途，我会非常高兴。
A：你对未来有什么计划？
B：只有贵公司需要我将长期为贵公司工作。如果我觉得我在工作中不断进步，我将一直为贵公司服务直至退休。
A：你对工作抱有什么样的态度？
B：总的来说，我对工作总是怀有积极的态度。只争朝夕，分秒必争。即使时间很紧张，我也会努力完成任务，绝不放弃。
A：你对薪酬有什么要求？
B：由于这是我的第一份工作，我也没有太多的工作经验，所以我对薪酬没有过多的要求。先生，您可以根据我的表现定夺。
A：怎么联系你？
B：这是我的电话号码。您可以随时联系我。
A：我们将在一周内告知你面试结果。感谢你的到来。
B：谢谢。我将期待您的回复。

参 考 文 献

[1] Robert H. Bishop. Mechatronics An Introduction. New York: CRC, 2006.
[2] Godfrey C. Onwubolu. Mechatronics Principles and Applications. Oxford: Elsvier Butterworth-Heinemanm, 2005.
[3] Andrzej M. Pawlak. Sensors and Actuators in Mechatronics Design and Applications. New York: CRC, 2007.
[4] Neil Sclater, Nicholas P. Chironis. Mechanisms and Mechanical Devices Source-book. New York: McGraw-Hill, 2000.
[5] Hyungsuck Cho. Opto-Mechatronic Systems Handbook Techniques and Applications. New York: CRC, 2003.
[6] 刘晓莉. 机电一体化及数控专业英语[M]. 北京：人民邮电出版社，2008.
[7] 张延. 机电类专业英语[M]. 北京：机械工业出版社，2009.
[8] 翟天利. 科技英语阅读与翻译实用教程[M]. 北京：新时代出版社，2004.
[9] 戴文进. 科技英语翻译理论与技巧[M]. 上海：上海外国语大学出版社，2003.

北京大学出版社高职高专汽车系列规划教材

序号	书号	书名	编著者	定价	出版日期
1	978-7-301-13661-4	汽车电控技术	祁翠琴	39.00	2013.8 第5次印刷
2	978-7-301-13658-4	汽车发动机电控系统原理与维修	张吉国	25.00	2012.4 第2次印刷
3	978-7-301-14139-7	汽车空调原理及维修	林钢	26.00	2013.8 第3次印刷
4	978-7-301-15378-9	汽车底盘构造与维修	刘东亚	34.00	2009.7
5	978-7-301-15578-3	汽车文化	刘锐	28.00	2013.2 第4次印刷
6	978-7-301-15742-8	汽车使用	刘彦成	26.00	2009.9
7	978-7-301-16919-3	汽车检测与诊断技术	娄云	35.00	2011.7 第2次印刷
8	978-7-301-17079-3	汽车营销实务	夏志华	25.00	2012.8 第3次印刷
9	978-7-301-13660-7	汽车构造(上册)——发动机构造	罗灯明	30.00	2012.4 第2次印刷
10	978-7-301-17711-2	汽车专业英语图解教程	侯锁军	22.00	2013.2 第3次印刷
11	978-7-301-17821-8	汽车机械基础项目化教学标准教程	傅华娟	40.00	2010.10
12	978-7-301-17532-3	汽车构造(下册)——底盘构造	罗灯明	29.00	2012.9 第2次印刷
13	978-7-301-17694-8	汽车电工电子技术	郑广军	33.00	2011.1
14	978-7-301-18477-6	汽车维修管理实务	毛峰	23.00	2011.3
15	978-7-301-17894-2	汽车养护技术	隋礼辉	24.00	2011.3
16	978-7-301-18850-7	汽车电器设备原理与维修实务	明光星	38.00	2011.5
17	978-7-301-18494-3	汽车发动机电控技术	张俊	46.00	2013.8 第2次印刷
18	978-7-301-19147-7	电控发动机原理与维修实务	杨洪庆	27.00	2011.7
19	978-7-301-19027-2	汽车故障诊断技术	明光星	25.00	2011.6
20	978-7-301-19334-1	汽车电气系统检修	宋作军	25.00	2011.8
21	978-7-301-19350-1	汽车营销服务礼仪	夏志华	30.00	2013.8 第3次印刷
22	978-7-301-19504-8	汽车机械基础	张本升	34.00	2011.10
23	978-7-301-19652-6	汽车机械基础教程(第2版)	吴笑伟	28.00	2012.8 第2次印刷
24	978-7-301-18948-1	汽车底盘电控原理与维修实务	刘映凯	26.00	2012.1
25	978-7-301-19646-5	汽车构造	刘智婷	42.00	2012.1
26	978-7-301-20011-7	汽车电器实训	高照亮	38.00	2012.1
27	978-7-301-20753-6	二手车鉴定与评估	李玉柱	28.00	2012.6
28	978-7-301-21989-8	汽车发动机构造与维修(第2版)	蔡兴旺	40.00	2013.1
29	978-7-301-22363-5	汽车车载网络技术与检修	闫炳强	30.00	2013.6
30	978-7-301-22746-6	汽车装饰与美容	金守玲	34.00	2013.7

相关教学资源如电子课件、电子教材、习题答案等可以登录 www.pup6.com 下载或在线阅读。

扑六知识网(www.pup6.com)有海量的相关教学资源和电子教材供阅读及下载(包括北京大学出版社第六事业部的相关资源)，同时欢迎您将教学课件、视频、教案、素材、习题、试卷、辅导材料、课改成果、设计作品、论文等教学资源上传到 pup6.com，与全国高校师生分享您的教学成就与经验，并可自由设定价格，知识也能创造财富。具体情况请登录网站查询。

如您需要免费纸质样书用于教学，欢迎登陆第六事业部门户网(www.pup6.com)填表申请，并欢迎在线登记选题以到北京大学出版社来出版您的大作，也可下载相关表格填写后发到我们的邮箱，我们将及时与您取得联系并做好全方位的服务。

扑六知识网将打造成全国最大的教育资源共享平台，欢迎您的加入——让知识有价值，让教学无界限，让学习更轻松。联系方式：010-62750667，yongjian3000@163.com，linzhangbo@126.com，欢迎来电来信。